THE SERMON ON THE MOUNT

THE CHURCH'S
FIRST STATEMENT OF THE GOSPEL

DAVID P. SCAER

CPH.
SAINT LOUIS

Copyright © 2000 David P. Scaer

Published by Concordia Publishing House
3558 S. Jefferson Avenue, St. Louis, MO 63118-3968

Manufactured in the United States of America

Library of Congress Cataloging-in-Publication Data

Scaer, David P., 1936–
    The Sermon on the Mount: The Church's First Statement of the Gospel / David P. Scaer.
        p.   cm.
    Includes bibliographical references
    ISBN 0–570–05254–8
    1. Sermon on the Mount—Commentaries I. Title.
BT380.2 S29 2000
226.9'07—dc21
                      00–009997

1 2 3 4 5 6 7 8 9 10   09 08 07 06 05 04 03 02 01 00

CONTENTS

PART 2:

LIFE WITHIN THE COMMUNITY OF THE FOLLOWERS OF JESUS

PART 3:
OTHER MATTERS OF CHURCH CONCERN

PART 4:
THE SERMON AS TEACHING AUTHORITY IN THE CHURCH

PREFACE

No other section of the Scriptures has received as much attention as the ✓
Sermon on the Mount. In monographs on pericopes to full length commentaries on the gospel, commentators have explored the wealth of materials in these three chapters of Matthew. From the first available post-apostolic writings to the present, the Sermon on the Mount has preoccupied
Christians. If no other books had been written except commentaries on the
Sermon on the Mount, the lament of Ecclesiastes (12:12), "of making
many books there is no end," would have been satisfied.

If Matthew is the first of the gospels, then its influence may be detected in other parts of the New Testament, especially Luke who provided a
shortened and in most cases simpler version in his Sermon on the Plain
and assigned some sayings to other parts of his gospel. The Sermon on the
Mount is a magnet which sooner or later attracts not only biblical scholars
but theologians and religious leaders who see their expertise in other areas
besides the New Testament. It becomes the required scaffolding on which
theologians set forth their own programs and it often finds its way into
devotional studies. What commentators find in the Sermon on the Mount
generally reflects their own views. In light of what they have written elsewhere, their views on the Sermon are predictable. Explanations of the
Sermon on the Mount only reinforce what they said elsewhere. This
writer begs no exception for himself in seeing the Gospel as the Sermon's
chief content and purpose. My argument is the Sermon on the Mount is ✓
Gospel. I do not separate Law passages from Gospel ones and then determine a majority by calculating the columns. Such an approach would only
indicate a failure to understand that the Gospel fulfills and assumes the
Law and draws its structure into itself. If the Law were not intricately
involved in the shape of the Gospel, the Gospel could not be the fulfilling
of the Law and it would have no meaning for the hearer, who by nature
can understand the Law but to whom the Gospel without the Law is alien.
Many of the Sermon's condemnations, like the house which collapses during the flood (7:27), do not belong to what is commonly called the Law,
but should be eschatologically understood as divine judgment against

9

unbelief, a prevalent theme throughout Matthew. Condemnation of sin, resolved in the Gospel, must be distinguished from the condemnation of unbelief for which no relief exists.

While no section of the Bible is immune from controversies emanating from a variety of different and contradictory interpretations (after all, this is the nature of biblical studies), many interpretations of the separate pericopes can be boiled down to a few serious options. Debates over the meaning of "the word was God" in John 1:1 take place today as if the triumph of Athanasius over Arius at Nicea in 325 A.D. had never taken place.[1] Biblical scholars have not really gone much further than the Reformation debate between Lutherans and the Reformed in their failure to agree on the meaning of the word "is" in "This is my body."[2] Today biblical studies cross denominational lines, but differences of interpretations on certain sections of the Bible still tend to fall into predictable categories. Old debates about interpretations keep surfacing in contemporary, scholarly discussions.[3] Newer critical methods do not prevent traditional differences of interpretation over the biblical texts from surfacing like bad pennies.

In the same vein, interpretations of the Sermon on the Mount are not infinite, but they may seem so to anyone who attempts to locate all of them. No serious student of the Sermon on the Mount can escape frustration over the seemingly endless commentaries written to explain it, but nevertheless few offer interpretations which the reader will find surprising or really new. Somehow in reading commentaries on the Sermon, one senses he has gone down these roads before, a critical hurdle which this book also must face.

Even a first-time reader of the Sermon on the Mount approaches it with a sense of familiarity, since even some of its most obscure sayings have a firm place in the modern language. For example, "don't cast your pearls before swine" is used as a kind of friendly gibe that one's words should not be wasted on some people. No one using this phrase would seriously think of tossing real pearls to pigs and few would be acquainted with the options scholars offer. "Blessed are the peacemakers" adorns the walls of the United Nations headquarters in New York City and other governmental buildings. How many people reading them know that they are taken from the Sermon on the Mount? How many recognize that the original context has little to do with international relations? The expectation that people in general should be familiar with the Sermon on the Mount flows from understanding that the teachings of Jesus are hardly more than common

sense proverbs, a heritage of eighteenth-century Rationalism which held
that the Bible contained truths which were accessible to everyone. This
common-sense approach to the Sermon on the Mount has allowed or even
encouraged some to make use of its sayings for purposes which Jesus and
the compiler of these sayings would have hardly recognized. Such random
application of the sayings of the Sermon on the Mount finds unrequested
support in current scholarly opinion that posits a common source for some
of the materials in Matthew's and Luke's versions of the Sermon in the
hypothetical "Q" document.[4] "Q" never really existed as a written document, but it is regarded as the source of similar or nearly identical material in Matthew and Luke but absent from Mark.

In spite of the multiple variety of approaches to the Sermon on the
Mount, nearly all commentators see the Sermon on the Mount as essentially Law and not Gospel, though some do recognize forgiveness as a central theme. Most are agreed that the Sermon on the Mount with its
instructions tell us little about salvation by grace. Commentators, whether
they are scholarly or popular writers, Neo-Evangelical, Lutheran,
Reformed or Roman Catholic, may widely disagree in interpreting the
Sermon on the Mount, but most agree that the Sermon on the Mount is a
collection of regulations. Ironically viewing the Sermon on the Mount as
Law allows non-Christians to make use of it. Differences of interpretation
consist in how they define the Law, the possibility of keeping it and to
whom it applies. Nearly all its interpreters have in one way or another
found in them principles for living and only differed in whether or how
these principles are carried out.[5] So for example, following the Reformer,
Lutherans are likely to see the Sermon on the Mount as Law incapable of
being fulfilled and Roman Catholics are likely to see it as Law which can
be fulfilled, at least partially, by all Christians. Those with ascetic discipline
can and do reach higher levels of spirituality for which they are posthu-
mously recognized by beatification and canonization as saints.[6] Arminian
spirituality, which characterized early Methodism, as it was articulated by
John Wesley, and is still typical of the holiness and Pentecostal bodies, sees
complete sanctification as attainable. These perfectionist interpretations
hold that the Sermon's imperatives are moral demands which can be fulfilled to overcome sin. Others directed the Sermon on the Mount to the
ordering of society. Leo Tolstoy applied it to a commune in Russia and
failed. During its heyday, early twentieth-century liberal Protestantism
found in it a program for improving society. About the same time New
Testament scholars suggested that its severe ethics were applicable only

during the life of Jesus or a restricted time period in the early church, when the end of the world was thought to be imminent. They saw the Sermon on the Mount's demands as an interim ethic whose severe require-ments have long since expired. Lutherans skirted the Sermon's harsh demands by applying its mandates to the inner spiritual life. After all, no one was expected to amputate offending hands and extract wandering eyes. For them the Sermon's chief purpose was alerting sinners to the enormity of sin and the impossibility of fulfilling God's law. In the Sermon on the Mount Jesus appeared as a sterner Moses. True and lasting salvation was not to be found in the Sermon but elsewhere. Here they parted with Roman Catholics and some Protestants for whom the Sermon plays a pos-itive role in obtaining salvation. For Lutherans the Sermon's role in salva-tion was negative, giving sinners impossible moral goals which could only be resolved in the Gospel (found elsewhere).

If a unique contribution is to be found of this volume, it is presaged in its subtitle: *The Church's First Statement of the Gospel.* The Sermon on the Mount is Gospel in several senses of this word. It is Gospel because its message not only originates with Jesus, but because it is about him. Jesus is the speaker of the Sermon and its subject. Preaching the gospel of the kingdom means that he preached about himself. Matthew claims that Jesus is the speaker of these discourses whose authority is both self-derived and given to him by the Father (7:29; 21:23–27; 28:18). These are not simply human opinions but the words of the God who has appeared in Jesus. Putting into practice the words of Jesus assures salvation to the believer. Failure to do so brings eternal ruin (5:24–27). The Sermon on the Mount, as well as the other four discourses, are also the words of Jesus' disciples who are the first to hear and understand them (13:51) and then as apostles required to preserve and teach them (28:20). The Sermon on the Mount became the church's statement of its faith. Through its teaching or *didache*, she brings believers into her fellowship through Baptism (28:19).

The Sermon on the Mount and with it the entire gospel of Matthew is a record of the preaching of Jesus who is described as going "about all Galilee, teaching in their synagogues and *preaching the gospel of the king-dom*" (Matt 4:23; also 9:35.) Like John the Baptist, Jesus vigorously preached the Law in condemning man's enmity to God and fundamental immorality, but his preaching was chiefly characterized as Gospel, that is, how God through him would bring salvation (1:21) and accomplish atone-ment (20:28). Since the Gospel is about Jesus, it also about the God whom Jesus reveals (11:27). In preaching about himself, Jesus preaches about

God, because not only is he the Father's Son, he is God (1:23). What can be said about God in the Sermon on the Mount is first said about Jesus.[7] Hence theology is really Christology and Christology is what the Gospel is all about.[8] It is Matthew's first window into who God is and what he is really like and what Christians will be like in forgiving others.

Perhaps most telling in the argument that the Sermon on the Mount is primarily Gospel in distinction from the Law is Jesus' own description of his ministry which not only includes miracles, especially the resurrection of the dead, but "the poor have good news preached to them" (11:5). To be true to the Greek, it is better to say "the poor have *the Gospel preached* to them." The ultimate sign of the messianic kingdom, with which even John the Baptist must content himself, is that the poor hear the Gospel and are not offended, i.e., they believe in Jesus. Those poor who hear the Gospel and believe are described in the First Beatitude, "Blessed are the poor in spirit" (5:3). In hearing the Sermon on the Mount, they hear the Gospel intended for them and do not take offense in Jesus.

At the conclusion of the Sermon on the Mount, Matthew did not intend to leave his readers in the impossible position of facing a condemnation which could be resolved only later in this gospel, *or worse in the writings of Paul*! Quite to the contrary! In the Sermon Jesus reassures weak believers of the Father's love for them. Sadly finding solutions for the Sermon's hard sayings in other places is not uncommon. Ironically the most critical scholars of the New Testament come to a similar conclusion in seeing Jesus as a preacher of the Law and Paul as the formulator of the Gospel. For them Jesus was a wisdom teacher or a revolutionary[9]—have your pick—but Paul was the theologian who shaped Christianity by defining the Gospel. If Jesus is both the revealer and revelation of God, Paul cannot be given an honor which belongs in the first sense exclusively to Jesus. This issue is addressed in this commentary in seeing the Sermon on the Mount as Gospel.

In the Sermon on the Mount believers are given a taste of a forgiven life with God which Matthew will unfold in the remainder of his gospel. At its conclusion, the reader will recognize the Sermon on the Mount, especially its First Beatitude, "Blessed are the poor in spirit, for theirs is the kingdom of the heavens," as sweet Gospel, something which Luther also saw. In that Beatitude the believer sees himself not simply as an isolated individual struggling between God and Satan or even as a member of the community of the poor who make no claims for themselves from others or God, but he will see himself as one with the speaker of the Sermon on the Mount whose impoverishment was expressed throughout his life[10] and particularly in death by crucifixion. That gruesome death provides a fuller meaning of the words "the poor in spirit." The Sermon on the Mount introduces themes that Matthew develops throughout his Gospel, in turn providing the context in which the Sermon is to be fully understood.

Apart from the question of the Sermon's message as Gospel, Matthew has arranged his gospel so that the phrase, "preaching the gospel of the kingdom," introduces the Sermon on the Mount and so describes it (4:23–25). This introduction includes the itinerary of Jesus' ministry in "Galilee and the Decapolis and Jerusalem and Judea and from beyond the Jordan," suggesting that while Jesus addressed the crowds in one particular sermon, which later became known as the Sermon on the Mount, the materials in this first discourse, as his other discourses, were preached wherever he went. What Jesus preached in the Sermon on the Mount was in no way limited to one place or the first year of his ministry. Matthew frames the ministry of Jesus within his birth and the resurrection, but he gives no hint to its length in terms of months or years. Because of its introduction and content, the Sermon on the Mount could just as well be titled "The Preaching of the Gospel" or simply "The Gospel." About four hundred years after this first discourse was delivered and written down did it become known only as "The Sermon on the Mount." Based on Matthew's own words and its content "The Gospel" would be an even more appropriate title.

Unlike Mark,[11] Matthew does not call what he wrote a "Gospel." Later "Gospel" was applied to Matthew, Luke and John. Matthew seems to have begun his task of writing a catechesis of the teachings of Jesus to provide a conclusion to the Old Testament[12] and not to initiate a "New Testament," which was Luke's contribution. He nevertheless clearly understood that the words of Jesus he recorded, which included the Sermon on the Mount, were qualitatively superior to the words of the Old Testament prophets (13:17). Not only was Jesus the content of their prophecies, but he was God. As Matthew approached the conclusion of his document, he appears to have thought of it as a gospel, as the term was later applied to a book about Jesus, and so he anticipated Mark's attachment of this word to his document.[13] In speaking of the preaching of the Gospel throughout the world (24:14), Matthew is thinking of how evangelization would take place through what he wrote. A public reading of his document, as this would have taken place in the weekly celebration of the Eucharist, was preaching *the Gospel*, not only as a proclamation of the good news of salvation but also as an officially sanctioned book. Matthew's sense of the importance of his own gospel was taken over by the post-apostolic church which recognized it as *the* gospel whose most influential section was the Sermon on the Mount. The Evangelist's awareness that his document was really Gospel is evident in the anointing of Jesus: "Truly, I say to you, wherever *this gospel* is preached in the whole world, what she has done will be told in memory of her" (26:13). He is not thinking of an oral report of the woman's actions but of his document which will be read not in one place but throughout the world.[14]

The Sermon on the Mount: The Church's First Statement of the Gospel looks backward to my *James the Apostle of Faith*, whose goal and purpose were also suggested in the subtitle, *A Primary Christological Epistle for the Persecuted Church*. Like the Sermon on the Mount, the Epistle of James should not be understood as Law, especially as a disjointed collection of wisdom sayings of varying value, as Luther held, but a letter of encouragement to those earliest persecuted Christians who may have erroneously assumed that their allegiance to the resurrected Jesus made them immune to suffering. James seems to have constructed his epistle as a mosaic of those materials which were later organized into the Sermon on the Mount. Had Matthew's version of the Sermon on the Mount been available, James would have felt himself compelled to follow its words and form more closely, at least in the sense that the fathers of the second and third centuries did. The Seventh and Eighth Beatitudes, with their promises to those who are persecuted for the sake of righteousness and Jesus (5:10–11), may well have included the smaller audience that James addressed.

Both James and the entire Gospel of Matthew, especially the Sermon on the Mount, seem at odds with Paul's doctrine of justification. Some scholars see James and Matthew as protests to Paul's teaching of justification by grace through faith without works. This raises the question if anyone recognized these opposing soteriologies with their glaring contradictions when these writings were formally canonized. Opposing soteriologies in the sixteenth century led to splitting the church with Rome using the Sermon on the Mount to its advantage and Lutherans using Paul's writings to theirs. It would be presumptuous for anyone to resolve this division, but the subtitle, *The Church's First Statement of the Gospel*, is an attempt to move the Sermon on the Mount on to the side of the Gospel and partially to address soteriology.

"First" in the subtitle *The Church's First Statement of the Gospel* needs explanation. The Sermon's pre-eminent place in Matthew and the New Testament canon gives it the honor as the first statement of the Gospel. It is the first of five discourses in which the earlier ones anticipate later ones and later ones build on the earlier ones. These discourses were the catechesis or what Matthew calls the *didache* through which candidates were led to Baptism in which God was fully revealed as Father-Son-Holy Spirit (28:19) and then to participate in Jesus' atoning death through his Supper (26:19). In the Sermon on the Mount the candidate first heard the Gospel, first learned about God and how the community of the followers of Jesus was ordered. In several senses Matthew was not the first. He is not responsible for the process of catechesis through which catechumens were prepared for Baptism. Peter as first among the apostles (10:1–2) fittingly was also the first catechist (Acts 2:14–43). Matthew, the preserver and conservator of the words of Jesus, is still editorially responsible for the internal arrangement of the Sermon on the Mount and its place within his gospel, especially how it is related to the other four discourses. He does not exercise his editorial skill arbitrarily, as is evident in that he preserved the more difficult sayings of Jesus which another editor with a keen eye to his readers' sensibilities would have reframed or simply excluded, as Luke arguably does. Matthew is his teacher's trusted scribe (13:52) and lets the difficult sayings stand. In regard to its content, Matthew also is not the first. Before anything was written, the church lived from the oral words Jesus entrusted to his disciples (28:16–20). Through the Spirit's intervention they were preserved and only later were they encased in scrolls and codices by the apostles and their assistants (10:20). Warnings against false prophets (7:15; 24:11, 24) presupposes that alongside of the tradition of the apostles, unofficial traditions flourished. In them the teachings of Jesus and the events connected with his life were bowdlerized by the church's adversaries and those who were indifferent.[15] Matthew's concern with an explanation other than the resurrection for the empty tomb suggests that he was aware that his readers may have been aware of this false tradition which he intended to address in his gospel.

At the start, we said that commentaries on the Sermon on the Mount inevitably confirm the theological agenda of their writers. Hence conclusions are predictable and tell us as much about the writers as they do about the Sermon. This writer anticipates this judgment. As a Lutheran, he can be expected to find the Gospel as the Bible's ultimate purpose; however, in this book he breaks with his tradition in finding the Gospel and not the

Law as the chief content and purpose of the Sermon on the Mount. *The Sermon on the Mount: The Church's First Statement of the Gospel* is hopefully only a beginning in anticipating other volumes on Matthew and the New Testament as catechesis. The Sermon on the Mount has the distinction of being the first.

NOTES

1 John A. T. Robinson, whose contributions in New Testament studies are invaluable, cannot identify the Word with God, *The Priority of John* (ed. J. F. Coakley; London: SCM Press, 1985), 393–97.

2 For the record, a cursory survey of contemporary commentators comes to conclusions on the Lord's Supper which are closer to Calvin than Luther, which means that this controversy is not finished.

3 For example the debate over whether *morphe* in Philippians 2:5 refers to the human nature of Jesus, as the Lutherans contended, or his divine essence, as the Reformed held, is the subject of intensely scholarly essays collected in *Where Christology Began* (ed. Ralph P. Martin and Brian J. Dodd; Louisville: Westminster/John Knox Press, 1998).

4 So, for example, Bart D. Ehrman, *Jesus, The Apocalyptic Prophet of the New Millennium* (New York: Oxford University Press, 1999), 81–83; 153.

5 Charles R. Swindoll, *Simple Faith* (Minneapolis: Grason, 1991). As the title indicates, this explanation of the Sermon on the Mount sees that its meaning is easily accessible and able to be fulfilled.

6 See the *Catechism of the Catholic Church* (Mahwah, N.J.: Paulist Press, 1994), 488. This document has a helpful interpretation of the Beatitudes as descriptions of Christ, but something is lost in its holding that the Virgin Mary and the saints have procured these blessings in ways believers in general have not. They are also placed along the Ten Commandments as ways to heaven, which can only be judged to be an unfortunate mixture of the Gospel with the Law (426–49). See also William Barclay, *The Old Law and the New Law: The Ten Commandments and the Sermon on the Mount*, rev. ed. (Edinburgh: St. Andrew Press, 1991).

7 The title of an article by Mogens Muller, "The Theological Interpretation of the Figure of Jesus in the Gospel of Matthew: Some Principal Features in Matthean Christology," *New Testament Studies* 45 (1999): 157–73, is self-explanatory. In his final section, "Christology as Theology," he writes: "For if 'theology' is defined as a clarification of what we mean when speak of God, then Matthew is theology. What takes place in this gospel is that all that is said about Jesus is in fact said about God and his will to save sinners" (172).

8 One can hardly improve on this statement from the *Catechism of the Catholic Church*: "The Beatitudes depict the countenance of Jesus Christ and portray his charity" (427).

9 See for example John Dominic Crossan, *The Historical Jesus: The Life of a Mediterranean Jewish Peasant* (San Francisco: Harper, 1991). This book demonstrates that Jesus was both a teacher of wisdom and a political revolutionary. A list of the alleged authentic teachings of Jesus are found on pages xiii–xvi. See also Ehrman, *Jesus, The Apocalyptic Prophet of the New Millennium*.

10 Matthew 8:20: "And Jesus said to him, 'Foxes have holes, and birds of the air have nests; but the Son of man has nowhere to lay his head.'"

11 "The beginning of the Gospel of Jesus Christ" (Mark 1:1). C. E. B. Cranfield lists this as a reference to this Gospel's title as one of ten possibilities; *The Gospel According to Mark*, *The Cambridge Greek Testament Commentary* (London: Cambridge University Press, 1959; reprint and revised ed., 1972; reprint ed. 1974), 34. Martin Hengel goes further than Cranfield and states "Gospel" is part of the title in *Studies in the Gospel of Mark* (Philadelphia: Fortress Press, 1985), 72–74. John Wenham follows Hengel and explains how the term "Gospel" was attached to the four documents which are identified in this way; see *Redating Matthew, Mark & Luke* (Downers Grove, Ill.: InterVarsity Press, 1992), 133–35. Along with Hengel in supporting the view that Mark identified what he had written as a Gospel, Wenham lists J. A. T. Robinson, W. Marxsen, and M. D. Goulder (235).

12 So Mogens Muller remarks that Matthew's genealogy is a "rewritten Bible" (165).

13 Hengel suggests that this happened by 100 A.D., if not before (76).

14 Challenging the generally accepted view that the gospels were intended only for specific audiences is Richard Bauckham, who offers the thesis that the evangelists expected that their gospels would be widely circulated. "For Whom Were the Gospels Written?", *The Gospel for All Christians* (ed. Richard Bauckham; Grand Rapids: Eerdmans, 1998), 9–48.

15 Though disciples are designated as the guarantors of Jesus' teaching and are given the prominent place in hearing his discourses, the crowds are in hearing range and listen intently, even when they do not fully understand. Matthew uses the words 'crowd' or 'crowds' approximately forty times and often in connection with the discourses, including the Sermon on the Mount (4:25; 5:1; 7:28). A significant part of the total population of Galilee heard him preach. Consider that five thousand who are miraculously fed first listened to his preaching. An early date for Matthew, perhaps around 40 A.D., would allow for some of its recipients to be among those who heard Jesus preach and witnessed his miracles (4:24–25), but did not fully accept him (12:23). Their knowledge of Jesus would have formed a tradition independent of the oral teachings authorized by the church leaders in Jerusalem. These people would have been chiefly Jews who after the resurrection over a longer period of time became more and more convinced of the claims Jesus had made for himself and which the church was now making for him and wanted to be included in the church. If an official 'tradition' of Jesus was put in place by the apostles, an unofficial 'tradition' existed among the people who had heard Jesus directly or indirectly from those who did. They would have been aware of the different twist Jewish authorities were giving to the church's teaching, as it is evident in conflicting explanations of the empty tomb (28:11–15). Working with a later date would still allow that this kind of tradition still was in place, even if none of the crowds who had seen and heard Jesus were still alive.

INTRODUCTION

1

THE CHURCH'S FIRST
STATEMENT OF THE GOSPEL

THE PLACE OF HONOR

Putting Matthew's gospel in the first and honored place in the New Testament was an outgrowth of two processes. First, the gospel that begins with a genealogy serves as a connecting link between the testaments. The second process, involving many persons over many years, was the church's organizing of the canon. The end result being Matthew's gospel was placed first in the New Testament. The Sermon on the Mount, as an introduction to Jesus' teaching and the Gospel as a whole, occupies a prominent position.[1]

Apart from questions of authorship and origin, the Sermon on the Mount, as the first discourse of Jesus, was given the honor of introducing the reader to the entire New Testament in general and to the person of Jesus in particular. It was a matter of first impressions.[2] The effect was that the Sermon had to serve not only as an introduction to Christianity, but at the same time had to reach back and reaffirm the Hebrew Bible as authoritative for the church. Jesus' words "I say to you" (5:18) were balanced with "Think not that I have come to abolish the law and the prophets" (5:17). The Sermon not only became the introduction to New Testament Christianity, but the connecting link between the Old and New Testaments. It was given the pivotal position in the canonical Scriptures.

This crucial role within the canon was evidenced in the early post-apostolic church: the Sermon on the Mount is the most frequently cited portion of the New Testament.[3] Thus from the beginning of the church, the task of offering an explanation of the faith went most often to the Sermon on the Mount. Here were found the Beatitudes and the Lord's Prayer. Was its prominent place in the canon responsible for its great influence? Or was it the reverse? Did the force and beauty of its message not only account for its influence in the early church but also contribute to its being given the place of honor in the canon? Both positions have their implications.

Most scholars see the gospel of Matthew as dependent on Mark and the "Q," the abbreviation for the German word *Quelle* (source), and a special document called "M," available to Matthew and not the other evangelists. A small but persistent group of scholars sees Matthew as the first gospel and Mark as a compilation of material common to Matthew and Luke. This study of Matthew's Sermon does not depend on defending one view over another. It does, however, look at parallel materials in defining meaning in Matthew's gospel. Little of Matthew's Sermon is found in Mark, which has no lengthy sermon. Many of Luke's parallels to Matthew's text are found outside of Luke's Sermon on the Plain. The *Didache*, a catechetical document regarded as Scripture by some in the early church, contains remarkable parallels to the Sermon. Until recent times it was considered dependent on Matthew, but some scholars date it anywhere from the middle to the end of the first century. Even those favoring an earlier date for the *Didache* hold that both Matthew and the *Didache* are dependent on the same sources.[4]

Regardless of when Matthew and the *Didache* are dated, it can be assumed that the material incorporated in the Sermon was known to the church in the 50s. The Epistle of James provides a point of comparison, since so much of its material reverberates with the sounds and echoes the themes of Matthew's Sermon. Though much of the substance found in the Sermon can be found in other documents already by the end of the first century,[5] Matthew's version assumed a place of influence in the church that it would never relinquish.

If the Sermon's influence came from its being placed in the most prominent position in the canon, then it could be assumed that the general shape of our canon with Matthew as the first gospel happened at a very early stage, perhaps even before the end of the first century. Another possibility accounting for the Sermon's great influence is both its message and its style. It has a literary attractiveness all its own. When going to other parts of the New Testament or even other parts of Matthew after reading the Sermon on the Mount, one knows, almost instinctively, that he has come down from a plateau. Luke's version is pale by comparison and the *Didache* approximates the words of the Sermon but not its grandeur. Though the Epistle of James may be earlier, it seems to be an adjustment and application of an earlier message. Matthew's version of the Sermon proved itself to be the most enduring.

Perhaps there is no *one* explanation for the Sermon's popularity, but several factors complement each other. The forcefulness of its message was only reinforced by its being placed first by Matthew in his gospel and subsequently first by formers of the canon in the New Testament. Though the evangelist is responsible for preserving the Sermon for the church, he is not its originator or the composer of its words. Its message, if not the actual words at least in the specific content, was being used in the immediate post-resurrection church. This view is reinforced by seeing James and the *Didache* as earlier than the final composition of Matthew. When the church for which Matthew intended his gospel first heard his written version of the Sermon on the Mount read aloud, they were not hearing something new and strange. Matthew handed on the Sermon's contents and its parts very much in the form in which his church already knew it. Yet he is responsible for its arrangement, just as he is for other parts of his gospel.[6]

The Sermon's place in Matthew can be understood by Matthew's fivefold arrangement of his gospel, which is arguably patterned after the five books of the Pentateuch, the books of Moses in the Hebrew Bible.[7] One implication of such an arrangement is that the evangelist wants his writing to be understood as God's new revelation in the same sense that Genesis through Deuteronomy was the old written revelation. Within this scheme the Sermon on the Mount parallels Genesis, which is not only the first book of the Pentateuch but the most important, as it tells of God's creation of the world and the call of the patriarchs, and thus establishes the foundation for Israel as God's people. The Sermon on the Mount lays down the foundation of the new religion without repudiating the older one.[8]

There is no reason to suggest that the Sermon's logia first came into prominence either in Matthew's gospel or after the initial phases of canon collection had begun. Its teachings were influential perhaps even before the church began its Gentile mission. One of the indications of this is the Epistle of James, which one English don in the 19th century called a mosaic of the Sermon on the Mount.[9] Throughout James there are allusions to the Sermon without direct quotations. This suggests that James had at his disposal the oral traditions later incorporated in Matthew's version.

The relationship of Matthew's Sermon on the Mount and Luke's Sermon on the Plain is problematic and not capable of an easy resolution. Luke's shorter version is assumed by some to be the earlier text on which Matthew was dependent.[10] Yet Matthew's version is more characteristically Jewish in its vocabulary and style, pointing to the originality of its tradition. What this means is that the words that Matthew would later use in his version of the Sermon circulated independently, even though Luke had penned his own version. There is much to suggest that Matthew is older than Luke and for this reason comes closer to preserving the oldest form of the Sermon.[11] While we can say with more certainty that James is earlier than Matthew, we will not insist on giving an overall answer to the question of the relationship of Matthew and Luke. Where there are obvious similarities, we will not resist the temptation of letting one version of the Sermon interpret the other.

Another indication showing the place of the Sermon in its original form is perhaps the reference in Acts 2:42 to the early Christians remaining in the teaching (*didache*) of the apostles. *Didache* may have been used as a reference to the entire gospel of Matthew with a special focus on the Sermon on the Mount. Jesus had a *didache*, a teaching, recognizably different from the scribes (Matthew 7:29).

Regardless of whether Matthew or Luke was the first-written gospel, it was Matthew's *written* Sermon that prevailed as the "authorized version." The *Didache* offers this introduction to the Lord's Prayer: "Neither pray ye *as the hypocrites*, but as the Lord commanded in his Gospel, *thus pray ye: Our Father, which are in heaven....*" The *underlined* parallels with Matthew reflect the upper case Greek letters found in the manuscript. If the *Didache*'s "gospel" in the phrase "as the Lord commanded in his Gospel" is a reference to a written document, it seems to be an allusion to Matthew.[12] If the reference in the *Didache* is to oral tradition, then it would indicate that it had already assumed a more or less permanent form at that time.

Even before the Sermon took its final written form in Matthew, it had already reached a position in prominence of being the deposit of what the church believed.[13] This is shown by the parallels in James, the *Didache*, Second Clement, and Ignatius. It was, in effect, *the church's first statement of the Gospel*. Matthew's version of the Sermon on the Mount continued to maintain this central position throughout church history. Augustine, Thomas Aquinas, Martin Luther, John Calvin, C. H. Dodd, and Martin Dibelius have all used it as the scaffolding to set forth their understanding of the religion of Jesus. In contrast, some view the Sermon as essentially an expression of contemporary Judaism.[14] The widely held view that the Sermon functioned as a statement of what the church believed was matched, however, by disagreement over its meaning. These disagreements often amounted to downright contradictions. A complete history of these interpretations still remains to be written.[15] Before these are briefly surveyed, a word must be said about the evangelist who not only received the Sermon from Jesus but who intended the Sermon as his own address to his church.

MATTHEW THE SCRIBE

The teachings of Jesus in Matthew's gospel are divided into five groups of sayings: the Sermon on the Mount (5:1–7:28); the commissioning of the apostles (10:1–42); the parables of the kingdom (13:1–53); the discourses on the church (18:1–35); and the discourses on the end times (25:1–46).[16] The last section is expanded by some to include Chapter 24. Though there are other explanations for Matthew's fivefold structure, it may approximate the five books of the Pentateuch.[17] Each begins differently and each ends with the evangelist's commentary, "And when Jesus had finished." For the Sermon on the Mount it is "these sayings" (8:28); for the commissioning of the apostles it is "instructing his twelve disciples" (11:1); for the parables it is "these parables" (13:53); for the discourses on the church it is the same as for the Sermon on the Mount: "these sayings" (19:1); and for the discourse on the end times, it is "all these sayings" (26:1). This last phrase concludes not only the fifth and final discourse but all of the discourses by joining them together. It also anticipates the gospel's conclusion with its command of Jesus to teach the Gentiles "all things" which Jesus has taught (28:19, 20). This conclusion in chapter 28, while pointing to all the sayings of Jesus in this gospel, directs the reader specifically to reexamine all five discourses as comprising the totality of Jesus' teaching. Matthew's conclusion is reminiscent of God's command to Joshua: "be strong and very courageous, being careful to do according to all the law which Moses my servant has commanded you" (Joshua 1:7). While the entire Pentateuch is in view, the Sinaitic legislation and its Deuteronomic expression are singled out. Jesus is painted in such Mosaic overtones throughout Matthew's gospel that these five discourses should be seen as constituting for the church the new Torah, interpreted here not as threatening demand, but written scroll.

The person of Moses thoroughly permeates Matthew's picture of Jesus. As the speaker of the Sermon on the Mount, he resembles Moses on Sinai in the sense that through him God is revealing himself. Seeing Jesus as Moses does not necessarily mean that the Sermon must be understood as Law and not Gospel which comes from a rigid dichotomy that views the Old Testament as Law and the New as Gospel. This approach led Marcion in the second century to reject the Old Testament and Matthew with its Sermon on the Mount. This view that the Sermon is chiefly Law has filtered down into opinions on the Sermon as diversified as those of Aquinas, Luther, Calvin, and Tolstoy, who agreed in seeing it as Law. When Moses is understood chiefly as a figure of redemption and not regulation and condemnation, it becomes possible to understand the Sermon as coming from the one who resembles Moses, as an agent of redemption and therefore also (and not in spite of this resemblance) as a proclaimer of the gospel.[18]

Debated issues are whether Matthew is the originator and organizer of these discourses or whether these discourses were handed down to him in the same forms in which they were recorded in his gospel. Some scholars have stressed the creative mind of the evangelist.[19] This can be done to such an extent that the person of Jesus as an influence on his disciples or on the first-generation church becomes minimal. Granting the historical assumption that we cannot be closer to the person of Jesus than the historical documents of the gospels themselves, the clear impression from the gospel of Matthew is that the flow of influence is from Jesus to the disciples. The disciples are the ones who in each of the five discourses hear the words of Jesus. The words Jesus speaks are essentially his and not the evangelist's.[20] Matthew is responsible for organizing the material into the Sermon on the Mount and its strategic location within his gospel.[21]

This lack of substantive creativity on the part of the evangelist seems to be the message of the final parable in Matthew 13 which might serve as one of the evangelist's several "signatures" in his work. After the disciples reply affirmatively to Jesus' question that they have understood all things, he speaks of the scribe who has been trained as a disciple for the kingdom of the heavens (51–52). It is not unlikely that this scribe is Matthew's own signature. In the ancient world the scribe was obligated to record accurately the words of his teacher. Though the four gospel writers later came to be known to the church as "evangelists," the earliest designation of the first gospel writer would have been "scribe." But the term "scribes" was used frequently with "Pharisees." The phrase "scribes and Pharisees" carried with it such negative connotations that it was understood in nearly all cases as synonymous with the enemies of Jesus. This is true of all the gospels with the exception of two references in Matthew. It may point to the irreparable split between the Christian church and the Jewish community.[22] For Luke the term has become so completely negative that in his parallel (11:49) he omits Matthew's "scribes," keeps "prophets," and substitutes "apostles" for "wise men" (23:34).[23] Because of these negative connotations, the word "scribe" as a designation for an evangelist likely fell into disuse. Matthew's gospel appears to reflect the earlier church situation when the disciples were still known as "wise men," those who have learned the mysteries of the kingdom of the heavens and not "apostles." The term "evangelist" for a gospel writer developed later and is not known in

Matthew. Matthew 23:34 would have been quite appropriate in the mouth of Jesus, who still understood the Twelve as his "disciples," not "apostles." Matthew 10:1–2, in referring to the Twelve first as disciples and then apostles, suggests that their being called disciples fell into disuse in the church that knew them as apostles. It is not impossible or for that matter improbable that the scribe of 13:52 is one of the twelve disciples. Paul's writings make explicit references to scribes or amanuenses (Rom 16:22).

By calling himself a scribe, the writer of the first gospel would have characteristically taken to himself a self-designation indicating a subservient role. A scribe is one who *receives* the revelation of God in Jesus and not one who originates it. At the end of the discourse on the parables (13:52–53), Matthew is the one who had understood what Jesus has said and records it.[24] In 23:34 he is authorized by Jesus in being sent (*apostellō*) as an apostle and who now shares in the persecution of his teacher. The scribe, in preserving the teacher's message, remains the disciple or learner (Matthew 23:10). His self-abasing posture and his position as the one who has received the revelation from Jesus characterize the self-portrait of the evangelist.[25]

The term "scribe" as used by Matthew first suggests one who understands himself as passing on the original written revelation. In Judaism, which was a religion of the book, the scribes played an important role in making the scrolls available for the worshiping communities (synagogues). With the removal of the Jews from the land during the Babylonian captivity and their diaspora in Egypt and Babylonia, the scribes occupied a crucial role in taking the place of the priests in interpreting the law. They were ecclesiastical lawyers, interpreters of the law. Since the great majority of the Jews never resumed residence in Palestine (where the synagogue replaced the temple as the center of regular worship), the scribes served as an important link in the continuation of the Jewish religion. Their work assured the purity of that religion.[26] The rabbis, not the scribes, were adapters of the religion as preachers. Matthew wants to be understood as a scribe, a preserver of Jesus' religion, not as an adapter and modifier. The evangelist wants further to be understood as an authorized interpreter of the words of Jesus, as would be the task of an apostle.

The identification of the tax collector called Matthew as the writer of the gospel (9:9) is a matter of scholarly debate. A date for the gospel between 80–100 A.D. renders this view impossible. As a self-reference it would indicate Matthew's self-effacing position. In this pericope "tax collector" is almost synonymous with "sinners" and is used elsewhere as the designation for one excommunicated from the community: "let him be to you as a Gentile and a tax collector" (18:17). Designating excommunicated persons as Gentiles would hardly fit in churches that were predominantly Gentile. Attaching the similarly derogatory reference of tax collector to the name of an apostle, if he indeed did not have this occupation, is also difficult to explain.

In the lists of apostles, only the first evangelist puts the designation of tax collector behind the name of Matthew (10:3). This designation is missing from Mark (3:18) and Luke (6:15), though both contain the call of Matthew. Simply to state that this apostle is being distinguished from the others by his former occupation seems less than an adequate explanation, since none of the other apostles are similarly designated. Its inclusion is made additionally unnecessary, as the reader has previously been informed of Matthew's status as tax collector (9:9–13). The other designations supplied in Matthew's list of disciples are by their family relationships (e.g., father and brother). Judas Iscariot is distinguished by his infamous deed of betrayal.

The inclusion of the call of Matthew from the tables of the tax collectors in all three synoptics is surprising because of that disciple's undistinguished career in comparison with Peter, James, and John. All synoptic evangelists put the tax collectors on the same level as the public sinners (Matthew 9:11; Luke 5:30; and Mark 2:16). Apart from his call and the lists of disciples Matthew is not mentioned in the other gospels. Aside from the traditional ascription of the authorship of the first gospel, there is no obvious reason why his call as a tax collector to the apostleship should have received the attention of three evangelists. This is putting aside for the moment the suggestion that his name later took the place of a certain Levi. Unlike Peter, John, or Judas, there is no record of dialog with Jesus and his being the recipient of any exceptional treatment. The self-portrait of Matthew as tax collector in this first gospel does not contradict but rather reinforces the self-deprecating attitude of the Christian scribe who is trained by Jesus for the kingdom and suffers with him in his persecution. Matthew's self-designation as tax collector, while referring to his former occupation, has a theological purpose in pointing to one who as an outcast did not deserve God's mercy but nevertheless received it (9:13).[26]

The disciple Matthew is also placed within the gospel as one who has not only heard the words of Jesus (13:51) but who has been authorized to bring them to the Gentiles. This gospel is very careful to say that only the Eleven go to the mountain in Galilee at the direction of Jesus (28:16).

Thus the later apostles, Paul, Barnabas, and James, the brother of Jesus, who are known figures at the time of the writing of the gospel, are excluded from the list, perhaps deliberately. This differs from Luke, where two non-apostles are introduced into the Easter narrative as recipients of a resurrection appearance of Jesus on the Emmaus Road even before he appears to the apostles (24:13–35). This appearing in Galilee to the Eleven is in fulfillment of the promise of the suffering Jesus (Matthew 26:32) and the commands of first the angel (28:7) and then of Jesus himself (28:10), conveyed through the women at the tomb. No record is given when the women tell the disciples about the command, but the command is transmitted and obeyed. Matthew's choice of the number "Eleven" and not twelve excludes Matthias and Paul, and focuses directly, exclusively, on the original disciples. Matthew's use of the term "Eleven," in whose number he places himself, may allude to apostles other than those originally chosen by Jesus. The Eleven are constituted by the original twelve disciples mentioned (less Judas) as the specific recipients of the five discourses and named individually at the beginning of the second discourse (10:1–4). At the time of the gospel's composition, they are no longer the twelve disciples of Jesus, i.e., his followers (10:1), but apostles (10:2), the ones whom Jesus has entrusted with his authority. Thus Matthew is not the only one to whom Jesus has entrusted his message to the Gentiles (28:16–20), but one regarded in the early church as an apostle. He is also one to whom the secrets of the kingdom have been made known (13:11) and who claims to have understood the message of Jesus in the parables (13:51).

Matthew 10 develops the apostolic self-awareness of their authority in regard to the message of Jesus. They are entrusted with the same message (10:7) proclaimed first by John the Baptist (3:2) and then by Jesus (4:7). This message was abbreviated simply by the phrase "the kingdom of the heavens is near." Ulrich Luz makes the point that proclamation for Matthew is "oriented on the earthly Jesus and has no other content than his words and deeds."[27] This message would attain its goal when the disciples, like Jesus, are brought to trial before governors and kings. There it serves as a converting confession to the Gentiles (10:18).[28] In these circumstances their ordinary remembering will be replaced by the Spirit of their Father, who is speaking through them. In the persecution that brings death, the apostles' dependency on and connection with the persecuted Jesus becomes evident. The disciples are made apostles in order to be vehicles of his message and to share in the persecution of Jesus (23:34). They appear before governors and kings (10:18) as he did (27:2). The apostles' words are simply not the starkly divine words of the Spirit, but of the Spirit who has become their common possession and whose work was seen first in the suffering of Jesus (4:1) and then of the apostles (10:17). He is the Spirit of the same Father to whom they and the Christian communities pray "Our Father" at the command of Jesus. The disciples, including Matthew, are pictured as those who have been given the words of Jesus (28:16–20), have understood them (13:52), and have heard the five major discourses. They are the vehicles of the Spirit's speaking (10:18), and have been designated as apostles to preach, understand, and preserve the words of Jesus (23:34). As the message of Jesus brings about his death by crucifixion and thus brings this message to reality, so the disciples who have become apostles to preach the same message can expect no less (Matthew 10:16–23).[29] If these can be taken together as self-references, the scribe of Matthew's gospel has been a hearer of Jesus and is one of the original Twelve or at least is closely associated with him (13:53). He also has gone through the church's first persecutions.

Matthew as evangelist should be regarded not only as the faithful scribe who preserves the words of Jesus, but the one who has received the Spirit for prophetic, creative utterance.[30] At the time of Matthew's composition the word "prophet" in the church meant a preacher or proclaimer of the word of Jesus (Acts 13:1).[31] Matthew 10 not only refers to the historical connection that the disciples have with Jesus (v. 1), but it is especially meaningful for the circumstances of Matthew's church, where the apostles were facing trial before courts and persecution in the synagogues.[32] The words of the apostles made under threat of the loss of life are the confessional statements of martyrs, designed to bring about the conversion of the governors and kings (vv. 17–18).

The reference to councils and governors might reflect "the story of Jesus: he was first delivered to a Jewish council and then taken to the governor,"[33] but governors and kings might also reflect the events of Paul's trial in Jerusalem and perhaps Rome (Acts 21–28) and thus suggest a post-70 dating for this gospel.[34] More importantly the apostles give their testimony under threat of persecution and of the loss of their lives. They become martyrs as Jesus had been (1 Timothy 6:13). The concept of persecution which permeates the gospel is known by both the evangelist and his hearers and will play a prominent role in the Sermon on the Mount as will be shown below.

A persecuted church will find the words of Matthew 23:34 particularly pertinent: "Therefore I send (*apostellō*) you prophets and wise men and scribes, some of whom you will kill and crucify, and some you will scourge in your synagogues and persecute from town to town." Rather than seeing these as different offices in the early church, it would be better to understand all these as references to the apostles in their roles first as preachers (prophets), then as those who understand the mysteries of the kingdom (wise men), and finally, as those who have been entrusted with preservation of the message (scribes).[35] The words of Jesus reflect, in the first instance, a local Palestinian persecution of the church by Saul (Acts 8:1) rather than a more global one brought on later by Rome.[36]

Matthew is not only a scribe who preserves the words of Jesus, but also the one who under persecution is the Spirit's vehicle. His oral preaching and written gospel bear the marks of persecution. The persecution theme in presenting the person of Jesus is evident from the birth narratives right through into his crucifixion. The Sermon on the Mount consists also of words for the church in its persecution. Through this persecution the church is attached to Jesus and thus it becomes the basis for an explicit and profound Christology.

Matthew's role as faithful scribe in preserving the words of Jesus does not militate against his being a creative writer in arranging the words of Jesus.[37] While on one hand he has restricted himself to the words of Jesus as they were known in his community, he did have the freedom of selection within these boundaries. He was responsible for the arrangement of the historical settings into which the five discourses including the Sermon were placed. Matthew's high Christology cannot be disconnected from the five discourses including the Sermon.[38] The type of materials chosen by Matthew can be measured against the selection made by Luke, who has some of the same material Matthew has, adapts it, or often omits it. Mark is of little service here as he includes only a few isolated allusions to the Sermon and makes no attempt to place them in a comparable discourse. Matthew's gospel reflects the persecution of the church as he knew it.

Within his gospel Matthew gives the words of Jesus placed in the Sermon on the Mount the most important position. There seems to be no suggestion that the evangelist is concerned with the chronological order in which the teachings of Jesus were given. The Sermon does not have to be understood as containing the first words that Jesus ever taught his disciples or even that these words belonged to the first part or year of his ministry. Quite to the contrary, the five-discourse arrangement of the gospel suggests that the evangelist has grouped the important words of Jesus into topical divisions. The other four discourses are even more specific and restricted in their scope than is the Sermon on the Mount. Each of these is characterized as more closely revolving around more narrowly defined themes. Matthew 10 establishes and describes the nature of the apostolic authority. Matthew 13 describes the progress of God's kingdom from its origin in Jesus, the sower (13:1), to its finale, the judgment, in the parable of the Good and the Bad Fish (13:49–50). Matthew 18 comes as close as anything that the evangelist has to do with church matters in handling such issues as the place of children in the congregation, maintaining order, and repentance. Matthew 25 (23 or 24–25) is clearly eschatological and contains the little apocalypse. The Sermon on the Mount not only is the first and longest of the five Matthean discourses, but is the most varied in the subject matter presented. It is not unreasonable to assume from the outset that the Sermon anticipates the rest of Matthew's gospel and hence could serve as a compendium of the early church's message. Though the Sermon prepared catechumens for Baptism, it continued to be used as a summary of the Christian message in post-baptismal instruction in the first generation of the church. Themes developed in the rest of the gospel, especially in the four discourses, are an explication of what was first introduced in the Sermon.

The Sermon does not provide an outline for the gospel, but is more characteristic of the teachings of Jesus than are any of the other four discourses. No other section of the New Testament is as comprehensive as the Sermon. Here is not a collection of the random sayings of Jesus that fell into the lap of the evangelist, but a carefully selected collection of those sayings arranged for use in church instruction. The post-apostolic use of the Sermon would support the plausibility of such a view. The final selection was made by the evangelist, though certain blocks of material came down in the same arrangements in which they are now in the Sermon. It hardly does justice to the Sermon to understand it apart from the totality of the gospel in which it is placed and the role it played in the early church.[39] The equally important question should be asked, "How did the early church receive the Sermon?"

THE SERMON AS CATECHETICAL INSTRUCTION

The *Didache* is a recognized catechetical document and the Sermon's resemblance to it suggests that it too was used in preparing catechumens for baptism. Whether the *Didache* used the same materials later incorporated in the Sermon or used the Sermon, both documents served the same purpose. Their catechetical purpose is suggested among other things by the prominent use of the word *didache*. What the Sermon puts in the conclusion (7:29), the *Didache* puts in the title. That the Sermon consisted of materials preached on many occasions may be suggested by 4:23: Jesus teaches in their synagogues. Until recently it was assumed that the *Didache* was dependent on Matthew's gospel. In this event the *Didache* may have been an attempt to update the Sermon on the Mount, the church's first *didache*, instruction in Christian doctrine. The *Didache* would have drawn its inspiration for both its title and content from the Sermon on the Mount. This view is both plausible and attractive, but not beyond challenge, especially if a pre-70 date for Matthew is unacceptable. The problem of relationship cannot be unraveled here, but both documents, the *Didache* and the Sermon, served catechetical purposes.[40]

The Sermon on the Mount is specifically called *didache* by the evangelist. "And when Jesus finished those sayings, the crowds were astonished at his *didache*" (7:28). This is reinforced by the introduction (5:2) and the conclusion (7:29), where Jesus is described as teaching (*edidasken, didaskon*). While the evangelist understands his entire gospel as teaching (28:20), the term applies initially to the Sermon. Acts 2:42 describes the first Christians devoting themselves to "the apostles' doctrine" (*hē didachē ton apostolon*), in language reminiscent of Matthew's conclusions to the Sermon and his gospel. If this is not a reference to the Sermon as a body of material within the context of Matthew's gospel, it may be a reference to formally organized material transmitted orally and used for catechesis, which later was taken up into Matthew's gospel. Thus the earliest type of instruction was not haphazard but structured.

Not above challenge is the suggestion that the Sermon as a catechesis favors looking upon it as Law and not Gospel. The codification of religious principles frequently suggests that they simply set forth ethical principles in an orderly form. A comparison with the *Didache*, for example, shows that the Sermon does not intend to regulate life in the same way. Rather the Sermon sets down the Christian life according to the higher principles of the Gospel. Not until Augustine in the fifth century was Matthew 5–7 called "The Sermon on the Mount." Whether this led to any confusion about how it should be interpreted is another question. Sermons are intended as much for the inquirers of the faith as well as for the faithful. The Sermon on the Mount is for those who have recently joined themselves to the community of faith; it was never intended as a sermon to awaken faith. When the Sermon is understood within the context of the community of faith, its christological content becomes clear. Outside of this context, it has frequently been interpreted as ethic and regulation. It might better have been called "The Teaching" or "The Catechism," as will be shown below.

The Sermon's use as a catechism can inform us about the order of the gospels, though resolving this question is not essential for our discussion. Luke does not understand itself as the earliest life of Jesus. Luke 1:1 points to the existence of another gospel or other gospels. If the reference is to one document, the balances lean in favor of its being Matthew with the mention of a document speaking about the things which have been fulfilled among us. If Acts and Luke come from the same hand, these seem to be a document circulating resembling our Matthew. More than any other gospel, Matthew explicitly sees the acts of Jesus as fulfilling the Old Testament Scriptures and understands itself as *didache*. The title of the *Didache, The Lord's Teaching to the Heathen through the Twelve Apostles* shows echoes of Acts 2:42, Matthew 7:28 and 28:19. Thus if Matthew's gospel is not in view in Acts and the *Didache*, an oral or written tradition strongly resembling it was most likely in circulation. Catechesis was a vital part of early church life and Matthew was the premier example of it. The Sermon is an early compendium of Christian doctrine used in preparing for Baptism or used with the baptized in preparing them for a fuller participation in the Christian community.

INTERPRETATIONS OF THE SERMON

A highly challenging task is to sort through the various and often opposing interpretations of the Sermon from the first century to the present. The survey here depends unabashedly on the works of others and only intends to lay down a skeleton of past opinions as a way of introduction. Martin Luther's interpretation of the Sermon is a study in itself and has been the subject of several scholarly investigations.[41] Harvey McArthur in his *Understanding the Sermon on the Mount* (1960) categorized the various approaches to the Sermon into twelve divisions, and Carl F. H. Henry in his *Christian Personal Ethics* into seven divisions.[42] W. Harold Row spent a lifetime collecting books on the Sermon, which were later the basis for Warren S. Kissinger's *The Sermon on the Mount: A History of Interpretation and Bibliography*. This extremely useful handbook outlines significant interpretations from the *Didache* (ca. 80–150) up to W. D. Davies (1966). Clarence Baumann in *The Sermon on the Mount: The Modern Quest for Its Meaning* (1985) presents in depth the views of nineteen persons from the end of the nineteenth century until now.[43] The Sermon has also not escaped study by Jewish interpreters. If Christian scholars since the end of the first century have been drawn inexorably by the lure of the Sermon, they have hardly agreed on its interpretation. It was almost as if the words of the Sermon provided an alluring scaffolding for theological programs which were determined long before the Sermon was studied for itself. In a way they all were testifying that if any words of Jesus expressed his most intimate thoughts and could be regarded as authentic, it would have to be the words of the Sermon on the Mount. Any serious interpreter of the Christian religion would sooner or later have to call upon the Sermon as a witness for the legitimacy of his own position. Among the historical great names who have commented on the Sermon on the Mount are: Justin Martyr, Irenaeus, Tertullian, Origen, Chrysostom, Augustine, Aquinas, Luther, Zwingli, Calvin, Wesley, and Kierkegaard. In addition it provided a foundational basis for Anabaptists and for later pacifists in general. Even the most theoretical exegete cannot avoid using the Sermon on the Mount to "do" his own preaching. As one's own interpretation is strongly, if not in some cases solely, shaped by religious tradition, a brief survey of these historical interpretations can serve as an introduction to the study at hand, since no study on the Sermon is new and independent of the others. More importantly these interpretations provide a perspective for critiquing one's own position.

In the early post-apostolic church, where the Sermon on the Mount was, as Kissinger points out, more frequently cited than any other three chapters in the entire Bible, it was generally understood as a guide and description of Christian life. This was true from the *Didache* (if it is dated after 100) to Chrysostom (ca. 400). The question of the apparent impossibility (or at least the extreme difficulty) of its ethical demands would only be raised later. With its reassertion of Old Testament authority together with the claim that Jesus makes for his own, it was used against Marcion and the Manicheans, who called for a radical rejection of the older written revelation.[44] The first commentary on the Sermon was prepared by St. Augustine, who is said to have first coined its title "The Sermon on the Mount." Following his predecessors, he understood the Sermon as applicable to all of Christian life. In his debates with Faustus, a leading Manichean, Augustine seems to have put the old and new revelations of the law on the same level, though this is a controverted issue among scholars. This caused a problem in that, in an earlier exposition of the Sermon, Augustine had asserted that the law of the older revelation was of lower status. Some note a tension seen in that he later taught that Christ fulfilled the older law in at least six ways. This position he developed against the Manicheans, who looked upon the Old Testament as inferior.[45] Augustine's encounter with antinomianism may have been responsible for the understanding that the Sermon was a statement of the Law, a position from which only a few have been able to extricate themselves.

The position of Thomas Aquinas, the great synthesizer of medieval theology, is today more familiar, since it was strongly opposed by the sixteenth century Reformers, including Luther and Calvin. Aquinas made a distinction between commandments or precepts, obligations which had to be carried out, and evangelical counsels, which were optional and brought one closer to Christ. The evangelical counsels found their expression in the monastic system and the special place of the clergy as possessing a higher moral quality. In a sense it was a qualitatively higher level of sanctification. This division between commandments and evangelical counsels remain characteristic of the Roman Catholic interpretations of the Sermon on the Mount and foundational for its ethics.[46]

While the sixteenth-century Reformers may have rightly complained about the double standard of medieval morality, one for the laity and another for priests, monks, and nuns, they were also in one sense in debt to Aquinas and others for pointing out the impossibility of the Sermon's demands, at least for the vast majority of Christians. Aquinas stood halfway between the early church, which did not question the possibility of practicing the Sermon on the Mount, and the sixteenth-century Reformers, who saw it as impossible Law. This position of Luther and Lutheran Orthodoxy on the Sermon on the Mount as impossible Law became the accepted Lutheran understanding.

For Luther the Sermon does not tell one how to become a Christian but how to live as one. The Sermon was Law driving the sinner to despair. The Reformer interpreting the Sermon could take refuge in his doctrine of the two kingdoms, which separated the life of the Christian into two spheres. He can thus serve as a soldier, judge, or lawyer, but within his heart maintain a loving and forgiving attitude to all men, including his adversaries. In Luther's position on the Sermon several factors may be noted. He was disturbed both by the double standard of medieval theology with its division between commandments and evangelical counsels, and by the Anabaptists who were using the Sermon on the Mount as a manifesto for their refusal to participate in society. In requiring the commandments for some, the medieval church had not gone far enough, and in extending the Sermon to society the Anabaptists had gone too far. The

Sermon was applicable to all, but in a spiritual sense, not as a program for society. Luther's doctrine of the two kingdoms provided a solution for him. Also motivating the Reformer was his theology of the Law and the Gospel, which was set within a canon that consisted not only of the synoptic gospels, but also of the epistles of Paul. The impossible Law of the Sermon on the Mount was resolved in the gospel, as it was preeminently presented by Paul, especially in Romans and Galatians. This view required that the Bible be seen as a unified whole, since the problems of the law presented in the Sermon had to be answered elsewhere in the New Testament. A certain antagonism was seen between Jesus and Paul, but it was the antagonism of the Law and the Gospel. Paul resolves the demands of the Sermon, as the gospel resolves the demands of the Law.[47]

The Anabaptists understood the Sermon in an absolutist sense, applicable to both private and public life. Taking oaths, waging war, holding government positions, and even owning property were not allowed.[48] Governmental matters were supervised by God, but left to those of this world. Where Luther's doctrine of the two kingdoms acknowledged God's working in both secular and spiritual spheres, the Anabaptists bordered on the older Manicheanism, as they treated the created order as so inferior as to make meaningful participation for the Christian in it impossible. It also isolated the Sermon from its place within the rest of the canon, where such participation was not condemned. The position of the Anabaptists resurfaced in the milder social experiments of Leo Tolstoy at the end of the nineteenth century.[49]

Throughout the nineteenth century the position known as Protestant Liberalism prevailed as the heritage of the Enlightenment. The miraculous in the Bible was minimalized and man's moral capabilities were stressed. In this kind of setting the Sermon on the Mount prevailed as ethical precepts which the Christian could and should fulfill. Adolf von Harnack, who stood at the apex of this ethically optimistic era, understood the Sermon as summarized by the loving of the neighbor.[50] This view was minimalistic, as it ignored some of the Sermon's harsher judgments.

Another view popular in the twentieth century was an understanding of the Sermon as an interim ethic in anticipation of the final return of Jesus. Since Jesus' return was imminent, a new radical ethic was imposed as a type of emergency procedure before the end. Of course, Jesus and the early church were wrong. The view was formulated by Albert Schweitzer.[51] Since the interim never really existed except in the minds of those who erroneously awaited the return of Jesus, the demands of the Sermon on the

Mount are hardly applicable now. Futuristic in a different sense is millenialism (dispensationalism) which sees the Sermon on the Mount as the law for the millenium. The dispensational position is on the surface highly improbable, simply because the Sermon speaks of human behavior not in a perfect, but imperfect world where things are being illegally taken away and physical harm is being imposed. This hardly fits the millenium as described by any of its advocates.[52]

Much research in the twentieth century has shifted away from the sole concern with the interpretation of the Sermon to the search for its origin. A leader of this approach was Martin Dibelius who, along with Rudolph Bultmann, inaugurated the method known as form criticism. Form critics argue that Matthew 5–7 represents a collection of random sayings with each group complete in itself.[53] Eduard Schweizer, a more recent interpreter of Matthew, and W. D. Davies, who devoted one volume to tracing the origins of the Sermon, have adopted the same approach in their interpretation of the Sermon.[54] Such approaches work under the hypothesis that "Q" is the source for both Matthew's and Luke's versions of the Sermon. Davies provides an extended study into the question of sources.[55]

More recent interpretations of the Sermon on the Mount have attempted to emphasize the *christological* element.[56] Such an approach, where it is consistently carried out, resolves the tension between the demand of the Sermon (the Law) and its fulfillment in Christ (the Gospel). *The message of the Sermon is not a demand, driving the Christian to an impossible moral perfection, but it comes to the Christian as a demand fulfilled already in Christ and which is now made possible for believers, since it has first reached its demands in Christ.* This is basically the approach taken in this present work, which also takes the Christology of the Sermon as the one pervasive theme. This is not, however, an isolated, dogmatic Christology, but one in which Jesus comes into a living relationship with his disciples. Thus ecclesiology in its highest expression is only an extension of Christology, what the church believes and confesses about Jesus. The Sermon describes what the church has *already* become in Christ (Christology) and the manifestation of perfection at the end time (eschatology). Graham Stanton put the matter in this way: "If Christology is Matthew's primary concern, discipleship (ecclesiology) is not far behind."[57]

If it is improbable that an exhaustive study of the interpretations of the Sermon on the Mount will ever be written, it is surely impossible that a final, once and for all interpretation of it will ever be written. Past interpretations of the Sermon have caught one of its many facets and later interpreters have built upon these insights, reshaping and refocusing them, sometimes even rejecting them.

The process of interpreting the Sermon on the Mount may have begun before the last books of the New Testament were written. As the Sermon appears in two different versions in Matthew and Luke, one of these writers was probably using the work of the other and by selection of materials each was making his own interpretation of an earlier tradition. For those who hold to the "Q" hypothesis, this work was going on at different earlier stages. The dependency of the Sermon on "Q" does not militate against seeing its original function as catechetical, since some scholars have argued that this document also had this kind of purpose.[58]

The early post-apostolic writings saw in the Sermon _the_ exposition of the teachings of Christ and hence Christianity. This view is approximated by Dibelius, who, while uncertain about the Sermon's origins with Jesus, is less uncertain as to its use as handbook of Christianity.[59] These early church writers by their random, homiletical use of the sayings of the Sermon probably came closer in understanding its message as fulfilled Gospel than later writers who set out to give full, detailed interpretations. St. Augustine, seeing the Old Testament Law's validity supported by Christ's fulfillment of it, provided a key for understanding the Sermon in the same sense. The message of the Sermon was perfectly realized in the one who preached it. Jesus, the Sermon's preacher, in his preaching becomes the living content of the Sermon. In Jesus the impossible Law becomes accomplished and fulfilled Gospel reality.

The evolution of the interpretation of the Sermon as description of the Christian life in the early church to law and regulations in the medieval church can only be sketched here. By the time of Aquinas the Sermon had become law not as written revelation of both Law and Gospel, but Law as _possible_ demand. All were capable of keeping the commandments and a select, committed few could aspire to be like Christ in following the evangelical counsels of the Sermon. Aquinas did understand the reality of the Sermon's demands. They were not simply pie-in-the-sky goals. The problem was his exempting most Christians from some of them and making other Christians capable of all of them. His evangelical counsels did keep the christological motif so essential for understanding the Sermon; however, Aquinas may be faulted for offering a Christology which was simply a form of medieval asceticism. Against this lowering of the Law's demands for some, the Reformers made their protest.

Luther saw the entire Sermon as cut from one cloth and equally applicable to all. Here his views were not unlike those of the early church. Its demands seen as harsher than the Old Testament were resolved in the Gospel found elsewhere in the New Testament. This implied a view of the canon which required that one writer wrote to complement the other. Since the Sermon's demands made life impossible in the secular world, they were applicable only in the spiritual realm, the kingdom of the right hand, where they drove the sinner to despair. In spite of Luther's generally harsh interpretation of the Sermon as Law, he still saw isolated sentences as Gospel proclamation. The Anabaptists also saw the Sermon as one cloth and, taking a diametrically opposed view to Luther, applied it as law to society as necessary and required demand. Carried to its logical extremes, as for example by Tolstoy, human society without government would become extinct. Beginning with Calvin, the Sermon on the Mount was seen as a statement in sanctification by the Reformed. Sanctification, without a prior Christology, deteriorates into mere ethical moralism. Protestant Liberalism in its reductionism of Christianity may have accidentally hit upon the major theme of the Sermon on the Mount as love, but a love not defined by Christ's death as atonement. The problem here was that without even embryonic doctrines of incarnation and atonement what was meant by love was inevitably left open to a fuzzy and unsupported definition of love. Love, left undefined by the cross, is indistinguishable from humanism. This view also fails to see the Sermon within the total framework of Matthew with a Christology that includes incarnation, atonement, and resurrection.

The eschatological understanding of the Sermon on the Mount, set forth by Schweitzer, has been picked up by interpreters after him, but hardly completely in the same sense. The perfection of the Sermon which is already present reality in Christ will become visible at the end times. The church in the Sermon on the Mount is caught between the dichotomy of a present imperfection which belongs to human existence and the manifestation of that perfection which already belongs to it now because it belongs to Christ.

Form criticism, uncertain about tracing the words of the Sermon back to Jesus or at least to one occasion in his life, did raise the question for what use the evangelist intended it for his church. This was hardly a new question, since it was raised by Chrysostom and Luther, who noted that even if the Sermon was addressed originally by Jesus to the disciples, it was also intended for those who read Matthew's gospel.[60] Though these scholars were not in each case able to trace any order in the collection, others saw order and hence deliberate purpose in the evangelist's selection of materials.

Although the Sermon on the Mount is a self-contained collection of the sayings of Jesus for which the evangelist is in some sense responsible, the Sermon finds its fuller meaning within the entire gospel of Matthew. Luther gave it a meaning within the wider context of the New Testament canon in which the Law-Gospel theme of the Pauline epistles was made to predominate. As an intermediate step between understanding the Sermon on the Mount as a self-contained unit and interpreting it in the light of a fuller canon, *the interpreter of the Sermon should ask the question of how the evangelist intended his version of the Sermon to be used, heard, and understood within the context of his entire gospel.*

The Sermon on the Mount in the gospel of Matthew comes to the reader as a summary statement, a theological handbook, a theology, stressing Christology, ecclesiology, and eschatology. These themes radiate out to all of Matthew's gospel and serve as a guide within the New Testament canon, for which it served as the seedbed of the teaching of Jesus.

NOTES

1 William R. Farmer speaks of the Sermon on the Mount as occupying "the pride of place" in Matthew's gospel. *Jesus and the Gospel* (Philadelphia: Fortress, 1982), 155.

2 Farmer, *Jesus and the Gospel*, 18, also takes note of Matthew's crucial position in the canon. "Matthew, at the beginning of our New Testament, is transitional. The Gospel points back to the prophets who stand at the heart of the Old Testament, and bridges the two with the prophetic story of Jesus proclaimed as publicly crucified."

3 Warren S. Kissinger, *The Sermon on the Mount: A History of Interpretation and Bibliography* (Metuchen, N.J.: Scarecrow, 1975), 6.

4 Clayton N. Jefford, *The Sayings of Jesus in the Teaching of the Twelve Apostles* (Leiden: E. J. Brill, 1989). Davies and Allison, who can place the final version of Matthew no earlier than before the beginning of the second century because of its trinitarian theology, are still inclined on the basis of the Lord's Prayer to see the *Didache* dependent on Matthew's Sermon on the Mount. W. D. Davies and Dale C. Allison, *A Critical and Exegetical Commentary on the Gospel According to Saint Matthew, The International Critical Commentary*, 3 vols (Edinburgh: T & T Clark, 1988–97), 1, 133 and 597–98.

5 See Edouard Massaux, *The Influence of the Gospel of Saint Matthew on Christian Literature before Saint Irenaeus*, 3 vols. (trans. Norman J. Belval and Suzanne Hecht; ed. Arthur J. Bellinzoni; Leuven: Peeters and Macon, Ga.: Mercer, 1990), 1:7–16. Massaux notes, "The letter of Clement of Rome reveals a special relationship to the Sermon on the Mount, which occupies a special place in the first gospel as it did in primitive Christianity," 7.

6 Farmer, *Jesus and the Gospel*, 149–50.

7   This point of view was first put forth by B. W. Bacon in "The Five Books of
    Moses Against the Jews," *The Expositor*, 8th series, Vol. 15, no. 85 (1918), 56–66.
    It was reaffirmed in a modified form by David R. Bauer, *The Structure of Matthew's
    Gospel* (Decatur, Ga.: Almond, 1988). Recognizing Bacon's contribution neither
    exhausts other structural possibilities for Matthew nor defines Jesus simply as
    another giver of the law like Moses. Davies and Allison note the five major dis-
    courses, but conclude they "do not add up to any grand scheme;" see *Matthew* 1,
    72. Dale C. Allison provides a critical and historical evaluation of Bacon's theory.
    Though he is not convinced, he notes that Bacon provided the impetus for seeing
    the Moses typology in Matthew; see *The New Moses: A Matthean Typology*
    (Minneapolis: Fortress, 1993), 293–98. As the title of Allison's book indicates, the
    person of Moses was foremost in the mind of Matthew in presenting the person of
    Jesus. Allison also shows that Moses was a type in presenting such Old Testament
    heroes as as Joshua, David, and Ezra (11–95). This was possible because Moses
    held such offices as leader or king, deliverer, prophet, and lawgiver (91). Allison
    calls attention to the fivefold division of Psalms in linking David to Moses (36).
    Bacon's theory about Matthew's five discourses means that a deliberate attempt was
    made by the evangelist to pattern his book after the Pentateuch. Even if this was not
    his intention, it certainly must have crossed his mind or those who heard it read the
    first time. After hearing the fourth discourse, the readers might have anticipated a
    fifth one. They were not disappointed. Jesus is such a thoroughly Mosaic figure in
    Matthew, the five discourses could only have recalled to the Jewish hearers the writ-
    ten revelation God had given through Moses.

8   Ulrich Luz sees nothing significant in the fivefold division, noting that Psalms and
    other books have five divisions, *Matthew 1–7* (trans. Wilhelm C. Linss; Minn-
    eapolis, Augsburg, 1989), 44. His explanation that Matthew uses the schema for
    the longer, but not the shorter and less arranged discourses is not completely con-
    vincing. Luz's noting the fivefold division of the Psalms would support that
    Matthew intends his gospel to supplement the Old Testament.

9   J. Armitage Robinson, gen. ed., *Texts and Studies: Contributions to Biblical and
    Patristic Literature*, Vol. 1, no. 3: *The Lord's Prayer in the Early Church* by Frederic
    Henry Chase (Cambridge: Cambridge University Press, 1891), 48.

10 Luz, *Matthew 1–7*, 213–14, holds that Matthew has supplemented Luke's Sermon
    on the Plain with material from Q and other sources. Davies and Allison,
    Matthew, hold that Matthew 5:21–6:18 is handed down. Luz does note that Hans
    Dieter Betz, *Essays on the Sermon on the Mount* (trans. L. L. Welborn; Philadel-
    phia: Fortress, 1985), recognizes "that the evangelist has used a Jewish-Christian
    Sermon on the Mount as a source without changing it during the integration into
    the Gospel."

11 Determining the oldest version of the Sermon is dependent on a theory of the
    origin of the Gospels. Davies and Allison, *Matthew*, present arguments for the
    commonly held two-source theory, which they favor, and the two-Gospel theory,
    commonly known as the Griessbach theory, prominently associated with Farmer
    1, 97–127. The two-source theory sees the Sermon evolving from several sources,
    but recognizes some of it, e.g., 6:1–18 and 5:21–37, as having their origins in
    "pre-Matthean 'cult-didactic'" (Davies and Allison, *Matthew*, 1, 126). Luz sees
    Luke's Sermon on the Plain as Matthew's outline, 213–14.

12 Luz, *Matthew 1–7*, claims that the phrase "this gospel of the kingdom" from
    Matthew 24:14 refers to "the gospel of Jesus contained in the whole Gospel of

Matthew" and though an identification between the word "gospel" and the written document has not been made, it has been foreshadowed. He also notes that Ignatius also understands gospel as a written document (208). Matthew's word for command is *entellomai* and not *keleuo* as found here in the *Didache*; however, *keleuo* is a characteristic Matthean word being used eight times. It is used only once by Luke. Thus the connection between the *Didache* and Matthew is reinforced.

13 Betz sees the Sermon on the Mount as composed by a redactor in the 50s; see *Essays on the Sermon on the Mount.*

14 Isabel Ann Massey, *Interpreting the Sermon on the Mount in the Light of Jewish Tradition as Evidenced in the Palestinian Targums of the Pentateuch*, Studies in the Bible and Early Christianity Vol. 25 (Lewiston, N.Y.: Edwin Mellen, 1991).

15 This observation was made by Jaroslov Pelikan in his introduction to *The Preaching of Chrysostom: Homilies on the Sermon on the Mount* (Philadelphia: Fortress, 1967), quoted in Kissinger, *The Sermon on the Mount*, 1.

16 Robert H. Gundry, *Matthew: A Commentary on His Literary and Theological Art* (Grand Rapids: Eerdmans, 1982), 136. Gundry calls attention to the concluding formulas in Numbers 16:31; Deuteronomy 32:45; and Jeremiah 26:8. See also the discussion of the structure of Matthew in Brevard Childs, *The New Testament as Canon* (Philadelphia: Fortress, 1984), 63. Childs notes that one objection to the fivefold scheme of Bacon is that the crucifixion-resurrection becomes epilogue; so also Douglas R. A. Hare, *Matthew: Interpretation, A Bible Commentary for Teaching and Preaching* (Louisville: John Knox, 1993), 2–3. This hardly has to be the case. Matthew's five discourses serve as explanations of Jesus' redemptive acts which they introduce. Bauer notes the development of the five discourses climaxing in 28:16–20, 134. Graham Stanton says of the Sermon that "for the evangelist it is only the first of five discourses to which he attaches equal importance." "The Origin and Purpose of Matthew's Sermon on the Mount," *Tradition and Interpretation in the New Testament* (ed. Gerald Hawthorne and Otto Betz; Grand Rapids: Eerdmans, 1987), 189. Luz notes the fivefold division but sees no theological significance in it, 44.

17 Gundry also includes chapter 23:16–17.

18 W. D. Davies, in his exhaustive study, *The Setting of the Sermon on the Mount*, has set forth a detailed analysis recognizing Pentateuchal motifs in the Sermon and seeing Jesus as the New Moses (Cambridge, England: Cambridge, 1964; Atlanta: Scholars, 1989), 14–108. John 1:17 has been used by Bultmann, for one, to contrast Moses and Jesus in terms of Law and grace. Raymond Brown finds this more Pauline than Johannine. Taken to its logical extremes it would be Marcionite. Hebrews 1:1 might provide the key in understanding both John 1:17 and the role of Jesus in the Sermon: "Long ago God spoke to our ancestors in many and various ways by the prophets, but in these last days he has spoken to us by a Son." Raymond E. Brown, "*The Gospel According to John I–XII*, Anchor Bible 29 (Garden City, N.Y.: Doubleday, 1966), 16.

19 So Gundry, as is evident in his title *Matthew: A Commentary on His Literary and Theological Art.*

20 The Sermon "is Jesus' teaching, not that of his disciples, which is contrasted with the teaching of the scribes. This is because Jesus and no one else is the source of the Christian *halakah*," Davies and Allison, *Matthew*, 1, 728.

21 Eduard Schweizer, *The Good News According to Matthew* (trans. David E. Green; Atlanta: Knox Press, 1975), 203.

22 So Stanton, "The Origin and Purpose," 189 and Luz, *Matthew 1–7*, 456.

23 Gundry, 469, favors Luke's "apostles" and not Matthew's "wise men and scribes" as original. Just the opposite may be likely. 1) It is unlikely that Matthew would have introduced the word "scribes" in a positive sense when in all other cases of his gospel with the exception of 13:52, it is used as a synonym for the enemies of Jesus. This would have been very confusing for the reader. 2) The designation of the twelve as apostles reflects a post-resurrection usage.

24 Krister Stendahl, following the lead of E. von Dobschutz that Matthew might have been a converted rabbi, suggests that the scribe of Matthew 13:52 "may be veiled reference to the author." See his *The School of St. Matthew*, 2nd ed. (Philadelphia: Fortress, 1968), 30. Davies and Allison, *Matthew*, 2, 446, point out the rare use of the passive in being made a disciple and not making oneself a disciple suggests the divine initiative in being called into the kingdom. While they dismiss that the Greek for being made a disciple, *matheteutheis* suggests that the author's name was Matthew (*Maththaios*), they are convinced that the scribe who is made a disciple for the kingdom "is probably something like a self-portrait." Whether or not the evangelist deliberately intended to make a connection between *Maththaios* and *matheteutheis*, it could have hardly escaped him and the first hearers. The evangelist similarly uses a wordplay in making the connection between Nazareth and Nazarene in 2:23.

25 Davies and Allison, *Matthew*, 1, 240, suggest that Matthew may have been a scribe, as Mark's disparaging remarks about them are missing in Matthew.

26 The suggestion that the tax collector is the author of the gospel is not without challengers. Davies and Allison, *Matthew*, 2, 98–99, among several options, favor seeing that the evangelist substituted Matthew for Levi (Mark 2:14) on the basis that among the apostles his name was as good as any other. But this solution does a disservice to the man who was chosen by Jesus as a disciple and recognized with honor as an apostle in the church (Matt. 10:1–2). Among those who honored the apostolic office or had any memory of Matthew such an act of defamation would have hardly been tolerated. In discussing Matthew's inclusion in the apostolic list with a reference to his being a tax collector, Davies and Allison claim that the evangelist did not know the occupation of the others, with the exception of those employed as fishermen, an item not worth mentioning, 2, 155. This approach supposes that after the evangelist substituted the name of Matthew for Levi, he adjusted the apostolic list to say that he was a tax collector. In need of further explanation is why Matthew and not another apostle was seen as its author as early as A.D. 125. No one is suggesting that the title "the Gospel according to Matthew" was part of the original autograph, but in some sense it had to be seen as related or even evolving from the two references to that disciple in the gospel.

27 Luz, *Matthew 1–7*, 208.

28 So also Davies and Allison, *Matthew*, 2, 184.

29 Davies and Allison, *Matthew*, 2, 183–84, avoid making specific historical identification with the reference of the kings and governors. This is remarkable as they date Matthew towards the end of the first century when Christianity was so widespread as to become "officially unrecognized" as a *religio illicita*. They do suggest that the Christians could have been flogged by the synagogues for speaking derogatorily of the Jewish leaders or because their claims for Jesus were seen as blasphemous.

30 Stendahl, *The School of St. Matthew*, 34, who, as mentioned, sees the possibility of reference to the author in Matthew 13:52, and who, along with other writers,

draws no connection between 13:52 and 23:34, though these are the only two positive references to the scribes, does mention that wise men and scribes as titles "can be said to determine the character of the gospel."

31 For a discussion of Christian prophets and scribes, see Farmer, *Jesus and the Gospel*, 65–68.

32 Gundry, *Matthew: A Commentary*, 192, mentions that Matthew has "their synagogues," pointing to a time when the church and synagogue were already estranged from each other. "Sanhedrins" are a reference to local Jewish councils.

33 Davies and Allison, *Matthew*, 1, 183.

34 The question of Paul's influence on the situation in which Matthew was written is one of debate. For a discussion of this, see Stanton, "The Origin and Purpose," 181–92. A post-70 date for Matthew raises the possibility of its being an anti-Pauline polemic, a position offered by Betz, *Essays on Sermon on the Mount*, 35. Stanton cautiously argues that "Matthew is simply un-Pauline," 184. The church to which Matthew is writing may not only have known, but some of its members may have gone through the persecution brought about by Paul (Saul). It would also have been a church which would have known about his missionary enterprises.

35 There is no substantial agreement on the meaning of these words, but as mentioned, both Farmer, *Jesus and the Gospel*, and Stendahl, *The School of St. Matthew*, see some sort of reference to early church structures. See also Farmer, *Jesus and the Gospel*, 89–90.

36 I offered this hypothesis in *James the Apostle of Faith* (St. Louis: Concordia, 1983), 28–31. The shared persecution experienced by the readers of James and Matthew might provide still another historical link between the communities.

37 Schweizer, *Good News According to Matthew*, 203.

38 So Stanton, "The Origin and Purpose," 188. "In short, the Christology of the SM is not unrelated to the rest of the gospel." Similarly Luz, *Matthew 1–7*: "The Sermon on the Mount does not presuppose the gospel of the kingdom but is this gospel," 208.

39 There is wide support for the view that the evangelist is responsible for the form and inclusion of the five discourses. Concerning the place of the Sermon on the Mount, Farmer, *Jesus and the Gospel*, 150, says, "It is harmoniously included in a whole that is greater than its parts. It is thus assured attention from *many* churches as a priceless pearl in a magnificent setting. When the evangelist writes, 'Go make disciples of all the Gentiles ... *teaching them to keep whatsoever I have commanded you*,' the reader is naturally reminded of what proceeded forth from the mouth of Jesus with astonishing authority when he began to teach the crowds at the beginning of the Sermon on the Mount."

40 Stendahl, *The School of St. Matthew*, 20–30, offers the hypothesis that the entire gospel of Matthew may have served as a handbook. It is therefore not unlikely that the five discourses of Jesus were used for catechetical purposes. The same seems also to be true of the *Didache*. Clayton N. Jefford places some of the material in the Didache as early as 50 with the final composition between 80–100, the same years in which he places the composition of Matthew. *The Sayings of Jesus in the Teaching of the Twelve Apostles* (Leiden: E. J. Brill, 1989), 145. It was not unusual to date it as late as 150. See Arthur Voobus, *Liturgical Traditions in the Didache* (Stockholm: Estonian Theological Society in Exile, 1968), 12–13.

41 For example, Georg Wunsch, *Die Bergpredigt bei Luther* (Tübingen: J. C. B. Mohr, 1920).

42 Kissinger, *The Sermon on the Mount*, 1–2. McArthur's categories are: "1) Absolutist, 2) Modification, 3) Hyperbole, 4) General Principles, 5) Attitudes-Not-Acts, 6) Double Standard, 7) Two Realms, 8) Analogy of Scripture, 9) Interim Ethic, 10) Modern Dispensationalist, 11) Repentance, and 12) Unconditional Will"; Henry's categories are: "1) Humanistic, 2) Liberal, 3) Dispensational, 4) Interim Ethic, 5) Existential, 6) Anabaptist-Mennonite, and 7) Reformed."

43 Views from Leo Tolstoy to Walter Staedeli are presented and critiqued by Clarence Bauman, *The Sermon on the Mount: The Modern Quest for its Meaning* (Macon, Ga.: Mercer, 1985). Those acquainted with this important and helpful work may rightfully conclude that the thrust of this present work is closest to that of Gerhard Kittel, and Joachim Jeremias, who interpreted the Sermon as Gospel, a position of which Bauman is highly critical.

44 Robert A. Guelich, *The Sermon on the Mount* (Waco: Word, 1982), 14; Kissinger, *The Sermon on the Mount*, 5–12.

45 Guelich, *Sermon on the Mount*, 15; Kissinger, *The Sermon on the Mount*, 12–16.

46 Guelich, *Sermon on the Mount*, 15; Kissinger, *The Sermon on the Mount*, 16–20.

47 Guelich, *Sermon on the Mount*, 16–17; Kissinger, *The Sermon on the Mount*, 20–23. Concerning the view of Lutheran Orthodoxy, D. A. Carson writes: "This claims that the Sermon is an impossibly high ideal to make men aware of their sin and turn to Christ for forgiveness. The sermon, then, is essentially a preparation for the gospel. This view does justice to some of the relationships between Jesus and Paul; but it sounds more like a conclusion of systematic theology applied a trifle too soon than the exegesis of the text," *Sermon on the Mount* (Grand Rapids: Baker, 1978), 153. The same dilemma between the Law or the Gospel as the correct interpretation of the Sermon was resolved by W. D. Davies by seeing it as a resolution of James (Law) and Paul (grace, Gospel). From this he concludes that the Sermon in Matthew is much later and serves as a bridge between the first and the second centuries, *The Setting of the Sermon on the Mount* (Atlanta: Scholars, 1989; 2nd printing), 414, 433–35, 440. Such a resolution puts the stress on morality and sees the Sermon as Law.

48 Guelich, *Sermon on the Mount*, 17–18; Kissinger, *The Sermon on the Mount*, 29–34. Belonging to Anabaptists are Thomas Muenzer, the Zwickau prophets, the Swiss Brethren, Hutterites, and the Mennonites.

49 Kissinger, *The Sermon on the Mount*, 52–56; Bauman, *The Sermon on the Mount*, 11–36.

50 Kissinger, *The Sermon on the Mount*, 40–44.

51 Kissinger, *The Sermon on the Mount*, 57–60; Bauman, *The Sermon on the Mount*, 111–27.

52 For a critique of the dispensational view of the Sermon, see Carson, *Sermon on the Mount*, 155–57.

53 Kissinger, *The Sermon on the Mount*, 87–91.

54 Schweizer, *Good News According to Matthew*, 193–209. See esp. page 197: "Probably we will not make any further progress until we take seriously the observation that the Sermon on the Mount is not a discourse delivered by Jesus but a veritable chorus of voices, some bearing the stamp of Jesus, the others assembled by the

evangelist to form a single whole that makes certain specific points." W. D. Davies
in his monumental study on the origins of the Sermon comes to a similar conclusion, but does not remain completely pessimistic about recovering the orignal
words of Jesus. "Far more likely is it that the Church inherited and preserved sayings of Jesus which floated in tradition, modified them for its own purposes, and
then again ascribed them to Jesus in a new form. The recognition of the original
form may not be easy, but is also not always impossible," 418.

55 Again Schweizer, *Good News According to Matthew*, 199–200. Also Guelich, *Sermon
on the Mount*, 33–36. For an extensive study of the sources for the Sermon, see
Davies. While not completely dismissing "Q" as a catechetical device in the
church, a view held by T. W. Manson, Harnack and Dibelius, Davies emphasizes
it as *kergyma*, *The Setting of the Sermon on the Mount*, 366–86.

56 This is Guelich's stated aim, *Sermon on the Mount*, 419. Attention must be called
to Joachim Jeremias, *The Sermon on the Mount* (trans. Norman Perrin; Philadelphia: Fortress, 1963).

57 Graham,"The Origin and Purpose," 188.

58 See Davies, *The Setting of the Sermon on the Mount*, 376, 460, and 461. For an
overview of the problems, see Carson, *Sermon on the Mount*, 139–49.

59 Kissinger, *The Sermon on the Mount*, 88.

60 "'For though it was spoken unto them, it was written for the sake also of all men
afterwards. And accordingly on this account, though he had his disciples in his
mind in public preaching, yet unto them he limits not his sayings, but applies all
his words of blessing without restriction' (XV 2)"; *The Preaching of Chrysostom:
Homilies on the Sermon on the Mount* (ed. Jaroslav Pelikan; Philadelphia: Fortress,
1973), quoted from Kissinger, *The Sermon on the Mount*, 11.

2

THE SPEAKER OF THE SERMON

Matthew places the Sermon on the Mount as the first extended discourse of Jesus to confront the reader. It follows shortly after the division describing the public ministry of Jesus which begins at 4:17, "From that time, Jesus began to preach, saying, 'Repent, for the kingdom of heaven is at hand,'" more literally, "Repent, for the kingdom of the heavens has come near."[1]

Though it is common to assume that the different lifestyles of John who fasted and Jesus who was accused of being a glutton and drunkard (Matthew 11:19–20) meant that each preached different messages, it cannot be supported from Matthew. The evangelist also says of John that he preached, "Repent, for the kingdom of heaven is at hand" (3:2). This phrase is intended more as summary of their common message rather than a phrase they constantly repeated. The phrase refers to Jesus' entire message as Matthew presents it in his gospel, especially the Sermon. The message of John is abbreviated in 3:7–12. Though it is impossible to reconstruct the totality of John's message from what is contained in Matthew, it may be assumed that it was not that much different from that of Jesus. Where they differ is authority: John's authority is derived like that of the prophets; Jesus' authority is inherited and belongs to his person (7:29). John's reference to the gathering of the wheat and the burning of the chaff (3:12) is similar to the parables of wheat and the weeds (13:24–30). From this one example, it seems that John may also have used agricultural parables. Matthew's purpose in his gospel is to preserve the teaching of Jesus and not of John for the church, as John points to the coming kingdom and Jesus points to himself as the coming of this kingdom. John belongs to Matthew's introduction of Jesus (1:1–4:16), whose teaching is presented first in the Sermon on the Mount. Considering that Luke places John's birth six months before Jesus (1:6) and that John was so effective as to have followers found in Ephesus years after his death (Acts 19:1–4), it appears that the ministries of John and Jesus were coterminous for an extended period. Since John earns the attention of Herod the Tetrarch and is imprisoned (Matthew 14:1–2), it seems unlikely that his ministry could have lasted only one year. Regardless of how long John worked, Matthew removes him from the scene (4:12) before he presents the teachings of Jesus. Though their ministries overlap, the older age does not survive into the newer one.[2]

THE USE OF THE PENTATEUCH IN PRESENTING JESUS

Many commentators have suggested that the five discourses in the gospel of Matthew, beginning with the Sermon on the Mount, are patterned after the fivefold arrangement of the Pentateuch (Genesis, Exodus, Leviticus, Numbers, Deuteronomy). In such a recapitulation many have also seen a parallel between Jesus and Moses.[3] This does not mean that a one-for-one equation has to exist between the Old Testament events and Matthew's account of Jesus, since for the faithful Israelite each prophet or specially chosen person recapitulates previous historical persons and projects that image into the future. To use the language of W. D. Davies, there is in Jesus a new exodus and a new Moses; the Mosaic categories are transcended.[4] Each historical person in himself and as part of a larger corporate image contributes to the picture of God's final Messiah. In contrast to the Old Testament, where a series of heroes are presented, each of the gospels, including Matthew, concentrates only on one person: Jesus. Though the lives of others are presented before Moses, e.g., Abraham, Isaac, Jacob and Joseph in Genesis, Exodus through Deuteronomy is the story of Moses, the man of God. Among these models it is not unexpected that the evangelist should pattern his picture of Jesus after the Exodus-Deuteronomy story of Moses.[5] From the persecutions in his infancy to his final commissioning of the Eleven, there are parallels between Moses and Jesus, through whom God is now speaking his final word, a word far superior to the Old Testament revelation (John 1:17). The image of Moses, of course, is not the only one used by Matthew, since obviously he sees the persons of Abraham, Isaac, David, Solomon, Jonah, perhaps even Elijah and others, represented in Jesus.

Matthew 1:1 is taken by the RSV as a title of the genealogy: "The book of the genealogy of Jesus Christ, the son of David, the son of Abraham." It has also been understood by scholars as the title of the entire book or the first section. It might be better to render this title as, "The Book of Genesis: The Account of Jesus Christ, the Son of David, the Son of Abraham." The evangelist has deliberately taken the common designation for the first book of Moses in the Septuagint and used it to begin his account about Jesus Christ.[6] This understanding is reinforced by v. 17, where Matthew recounts that between Abraham and Jesus there are three sets of 14 generations, reminiscent of Genesis 1 and 2, where the creation account given by Moses takes place in seven days. The first creation which spanned seven days is reflected in 14 plus 14 plus 14 generations of God's new creation. The total number 42 is the multiple of both six and seven, numbers reminiscent of the first Genesis account. The evangelist also wants the reader to understand that the book which he is writing is *The Book, The Bible (biblos)*; in the title he thus makes a claim to authority at least matching and perhaps exceeding the writings of Moses and the prophets. The authority of Matthew's gospel is superior to them because it is derived from the incarnate Son of God whose teaching it intends to preserve.

Unlike the Bible of the Old Testament, which presented any number of heroes, each of the four gospel accounts has its focus on Jesus Christ. The Sermon on the Mount stands as the longest, first, and hence most significantly placed discourse not only in Matthew but within the traditional arrangement of the books in the Gospel canon.[7] Matthew uses a genealogy starting with Abraham to introduce Jesus. This was certainly not uncommon in the Old Testament, where the lineage of David, for example, is traced back to Perez, the son of Judah (Ruth 4:18–22). His use of the genealogy here at the beginning may have also been motivated by his desire to pattern his work, as much as possible, after the encomium or biographical form of the ancient world.[8] The question is immediately raised why Matthew begins with Abraham and not Adam, a point noted by Luke and appropriately adjusted back to Adam (3:23–38). For Matthew God's history of salvation begins not with Adam, but with Abraham, who is developed as the major figure of the Book of Genesis. The story of Abraham is centered on the birth of his son Isaac under unusual circumstances and on God's command to sacrifice him. Matthew will introduce Jesus as one who like Isaac has an unusual birth and who is to be sacrificed by the divine will (16:21). Though the Book of Genesis told the story of Adam, the Jews see their history beginning with Abraham. The Jews recognize that the Gentiles are the descendants of Noah, but not Abraham. One of the themes of Matthew's gospel is that the Gentiles are taking the place of the Jews (8:11–12). Going back to Adam would not have served Matthew's purpose.

Placing the Matthean and Lucan pre-birth narratives side by side, it is soon evident that Luke is both longer and more descriptive. Luke offers several episodes centering around Zechariah and the angel (identified as Gabriel); Elizabeth, Mary and the Lord's angel again (the annunciation); a meeting between the two women (the visitation); and the birth of John. In contrast to Luke, Matthew offers only one pre-birth narrative, focusing on Joseph, not Mary. The angel, with no name, is presented as the Lord's angel, reflecting Genesis, where he comes to Abraham to announce the

birth of the promised child. While there is no suggestion in Luke of conception out of wedlock, the suspected adultery of Mary is Matthew's first
topic of discussion. It may be introduced here by Matthew as an apologetic
motif, since at the time of the gospel's writing, indeed during the lifetime
of Jesus, the charge may well have been made that he was conceived from
an adulterous union. In a way the genealogy prepares the reader for this by
including Tamar and Bathsheba, who is simply called the wife or woman of
Uriah, the Canaanite (Hittite) military officer, a mercenary who shows a
greater zeal for the God of the Israelites than does David, the Israelite king.

The supposed adultery of the mother of Jesus gives the evangelist not
only the opportunity to answer the Jewish critics of Jesus but to identify
him as God and his true origin from the Holy Spirit.[9] For the evangelist
there is no possibility that Jesus is derived from an adulterous union, since
in introducing the Joseph narrative he says that "before they came together she was found to be with child of the Holy Spirit" (1:18), and during the
narrative itself Joseph is informed that her child "is of the Holy Spirit"
(1:20). This would seem to indicate that Matthew had at his disposal information used later by Luke, since his accounts presuppose that Mary is
already pregnant by a special activity of the Holy Spirit. Though Matthew
does not give the Spirit the same prominent role as Luke does, it is the
Spirit who is responsible for the conception of Jesus, who comes upon Jesus
at his baptism (3:16), and who directs him (4:1). The Spirit also speaks
through the Twelve in their testimony to Jesus (10:20). He is placed alongside of the Father and Son at the gospel's climax (28:19).

If Matthew's birth narrative has an apologetic purpose, it also serves in
a positive way to present the one born from the virgin as God himself.
This theme that Jesus is God will be important for Matthew in presenting
him as the speaker of the Sermon on the Mount. Though the Mosaic
theme is evident throughout Matthew's presentation of Jesus, the speaker
of the Sermon on the Mount is presented as far greater than Moses; he is
God himself. On this mount God speaks not through his prophet, as he
did on Sinai, but directly with his people.

The virgin birth of Jesus would easily fit Matthew's and Luke's shared
theme that Jesus is a king. Neither Matthew nor Luke were ignorant of the
ancient world's accounts of great persons known as encomiums. These
were extant and available to educated persons among whom the evangelists
would be included. The account of Alexander the Great was commonly
known in the ancient world; and by this time the stories of Julius Caesar
and Augustus would also have been known. They were born under unusual circumstances through the assistance of the gods. All had been rulers of
Palestine, and through the processes of Hellenization such accounts were

known there. Luke's somewhat lengthier discourse between the angel and Mary about the possibility of a virgin birth may have indicated a concern greater than Matthew's in following the encomium model for the birth of Jesus. For Luke, Jesus was the king whose birth from Mary the virgin had historical and not simply legendary roots. His claim to kingship is substantiated by his birth from the virgin. As Luke makes mention of Mary after the ascension and before Pentecost (Acts 1:14), it is quite possible that he may have had direct contact with her. While Luke seems to have been concerned to show that Jesus was at least equal, if not superior, to the ancient world kings in their origins, he does not present Augustus and Tiberias or the imperial Roman system in an unfavorable light. Matthew makes no mention of Augustus and treats Herod and his son unfavorably.[10] Matthew ties his account of the virgin birth of Jesus in with the prophecy of Isaiah, a prophet who at several points has influenced Matthew's portrait of Jesus before the actual account of his ministry is begun (4:17). Jesus' designation as the Nazarene (2:23) reflects Isaiah 11:1, and his dwelling in Nazareth (4:13–16) reflects Isaiah 9. The virgin birth for Matthew authenticates that the final Son has been born to the house of David and in him the fullness of David's kingdom has begun. Where for Luke the unborn son of the virgin is the Son of the Most High (1:32) and the Son of God (1:35), for Matthew he is the Emmanuel child, for which Matthew provides a theological interpretation that Jesus is God with us (1:23). The theme that Jesus is God's Son will first be introduced by Matthew at the return from Egypt (2:15) and then again in his baptism by John (3:17). The Son of God theme is reinforced by the temptation narratives (4:3,6), so that there can be no doubt in the mind of the reader that the speaker of the Sermon is not simply the son of Abraham and David, but the Son of God.

In the introduction to the Sermon, Matthew presents Jesus in a way that suggests that he is at the same time both Moses and God. Jesus seeing the crowds and going up into the mountain suggests Moses, who left the crowds and went into the mountain of Sinai to receive God's revelation (Ex. 19:3). While Moses taught the people only after he had come down (Ex. 19:25), it is on the mountain that Jesus teaches the people. Matthew's placing Jesus in a seated position, not mentioned by Luke, puts him in the traditional position for the teacher.[11] The evangelist intends to present Jesus as the "one who is present with his community, instructing not only the twelve during his earthly ministry, but also the post-Easter church" (28:18–20).[12] Describing Jesus as opening his mouth and beginning to preach should not be taken as mere description, but as the presentation of God himself speaking. It carries the force of Isaiah's "For the mouth of the Lord has spoken" (40:5).

Though it is often held that the concept of Jesus' deity is not fully developed among the evangelists until John (who for that reason has been called "John the Theologian," i.e., the one who writes about Jesus as God), this theme is equally prominent and developed in the first gospel. The evangelist Matthew's understanding that the preacher of the Sermon is God himself is already developed in his theological explanation of Jesus' birth from the virgin. According to Isaiah 7:14 the promised child of the virgin is called Emmanuel, a passage which the evangelist uses and for which he provides the translation "God with us," which he purposely intends to be an explanation of who Jesus is, namely God. The concept that Jesus is God is introduced by the evangelist even before this, for the name Jesus is explained as the one who saves his people from their sins (1:21), an activity which the Jews saw as properly belonging alone to God. Only God can call the Israelites "his people." Thus in the birth narrative Jesus is presented not only as God, but as the God of the Old Testament who, unlike the gods of the Gentiles, is concerned for the salvation of his people.

In the original rendering of Isaiah 7:14 it is the mother of the child who names him. In Matthew the task is given by the Lord's angel not to Mary, as would be expected by the Isaiah text, but to Joseph, who like Jesus is identified by the messianic title "the son of David" (1:20) and through whom Jesus inherits the title by his being named and thus claimed as his own by Joseph (1:25). What is more striking is Matthew's changing of Isaiah's "*she* shall call his name Emmanuel" to "*they* shall call his name Emmanuel." By this adjusting of Isaiah 7:14 the evangelist sets forth his reason for writing his gospel in making it possible for his readers and hearers to recognize who Jesus really is, that is, God.[13] The purpose of the child's birth is fulfilled when God's people recognize who he is and he remains and dwells with them as God. The gospel's concluding verse, "Lo, I am with you always, to the close of the age" (28:20), is the fulfilling realization of the name Emmanuel. It seems reflected in Revelation 21:3: "Behold the dwelling of God is with men. He will dwell with his people, and they shall be his people, and God himself will be with them." Thus the Revelation citation reflects both Matthew 1:23 and 28:20 and by combining them suggests that the latter was seen in the early church as a fulfillment of the former. In Matthew 28:19–20 the promise of the presence of Jesus with his disciples follows directly after the command that they should teach the Gentiles all things. Those teachings are presented first and at greatest length in the Sermon on the Mount. Through the teaching of the Sermon, the presence of Jesus continues in the church.

In contrast to Luke, there are in the strictest sense no conception and nativity narratives in Matthew; rather, Matthew's Gospel contains post-conception and post-nativity narratives. The birth of Jesus is simply announced as occurring in the days of Herod the king. The coming of the Gentile magi is traditionally seen as reflecting the coming of vassal kings to Solomon (Psalms 72:10), who like Jesus is renowned for his wisdom (Matthew 12:42). Thus in the coming of the magi the general Davidic theme is furthered. The seeing of the star reflects Numbers 24:17, a Mosaic passage, where the Gentile prophet Balaam prophesied that the star will arise out of Jacob.[14] The Gentile magi, whose knowledge appears to be limited to the Pentateuch (Numbers 24:17), can on the basis of an abridged knowledge of the written revelation from Moses determine that the final messiah has appeared. This contrasts with the Jews who with a fuller canon do not recognize who Jesus is. Through this word from Moses, the magi believe in Jesus before they see him (Matthew 2:2).

The story of the stay of Jesus in Egypt reflects the accounts of the Joseph of Genesis, the 400 years of the Israelites in Egypt, and the return of the people to Canaan. Like the Balaam prophecy these are all found in the books of Moses. Matthew's Joseph, like the Genesis Joseph, is the recipient of dreams. Like Abraham he receives visits from the Lord's angel. The story of the child Jesus is very much like that of Moses.[15] Both are infants during a period when a king opposed to God's purposes is reigning. As pharaoh is intent on destroying God's people through a program of infanticide, so Herod, who is also a Gentile king, now intends to destroy God's Son also through a plan of general infanticide.[16] Both find refuge in the same place. Moses is rescued by the Pharaoh's daughter in Egypt and Jesus is rescued by the appearance of the Lord's angel who warns Joseph of the impending danger from Herod; Joseph with his family flees into Egypt. At the end of the Egyptian period, Joseph is again informed by the Lord's angel in a dream that he should now return into the land of Israel. All this resembles the Lord's leading the Israelites out of Egypt through the intervention of the angel of the Lord who passes before the people. Matthew's use of the Hosea 11:1 passage, "Out of Egypt I have called my Son," does not move his discussion out of the Pentateuch, since here Hosea is commenting on the Mosaic history by recalling the failure of the Israelites to obey God's summons to leave the land of Egypt for Canaan. Their failure to obey the divine summons means that they have forfeited the right to be called God's sons anymore, and they are slain in the wilderness. Jesus obeys the call and demonstrates that he is God's Son.[17] The slaughter of the holy innocents serves Matthew's themes of persecution and eschatological wrath for those who do not obey the message of Jesus,

the new Moses. In the ninth and final Beatitude, those who are persecuted for the sake of Jesus are called blessed (6:11). Matthew's gospel is the
account of the persecution and martyrdom of Jesus and also of those who
then share in his suffering. Like the pharaoh of the exodus, Herod moves
to destroy God's people, now present in Jesus, by killing the infants. At the
same time Matthew includes Jeremiah's description of the deportation into
Babylon of the residents of Jerusalem as an effective reminder of the seriousness which has been attached to the message of Jesus. In his genealogy
the evangelist makes a double reference to the deportation into Babylon
(1:11–12, 17), though it is clearly unusual to break a genealogy with such
an unflattering historical footnote. By this device the evangelist prepares
the readers for the prophecy of Jesus that Jerusalem will fall because it has
not taken his message seriously (23:27–28).[18] The threat found in the closing parable in the Sermon on the Mount of the man who builds his house
on sand, i.e., the man who has heard the words of Jesus in the Sermon but
has not ordered his life accordingly, carries the same message. But it is
within this eschatological theme with its threat of the removal of God's
people from Jerusalem into Babylon that the evangelist develops the
theme that the message is also intended for the Gentiles, a people other
than the Jews. The thrust of Jeremiah 32 is not merely the destruction of
the Jews, but the salvation of the remnant from which God will now construct his people. Jesus is that remnant, and those who are to be joined to
him are related to him not through blood but through faith. The slaughter of the infants is for Matthew God's preliminary warning of what he is
going to do with his own people for failing to recognize who Jesus really
is and to take his message seriously. The return of Jesus into Israel (2:21)
is the coming again of God's promised people into the land promised to
them through Abraham. Even in his return to the land of Israel, Jesus,
God's chosen and elect child, avoids Jerusalem and Judea to go into
Nazareth in Galilee. Here the evangelist delivers his message to the Jewish
population that God is on the verge of deserting them and going to the
Gentiles. The final command of Jesus to make disciples out of all the
Gentiles shows that the threat of divine displeasure against the Jews has
been carried out. While addressing an audience at home in the world of
the Old Testament, Matthew has in mind from the beginning that the
gospel is also intended for the Gentiles. The climax at the conclusion is
anticipated in the introduction.

Comparing how Matthew and Luke handle their introductions to
Jesus can be informative. In Luke's gospel the account opens in Jerusalem
where Zechariah is serving as priest and he returns to a village in Judea. In
Bethlehem, another Judean town, Jesus is born, and his birth is welcomed

by neighboring shepherds. To fulfill Jewish purification laws Mary and the child Jesus go to Jerusalem where they are welcomed and recognized by two elderly persons serving in the temple. The twelfth birthday is the occasion for Jesus to return there and to be received positively by those equipped to teach the Old Testament Scriptures. In handling the resurrection, Luke relates episodes that happen in and around Jerusalem. In Matthew, however, Jerusalem is the seat of hostility. From Jerusalem comes the first persecution of the child Jesus through the attempt of Herod to kill him through mass infanticide. Even Herod's death does not change the situation, as Joseph avoids Jerusalem to safeguard the young child's life (2:22). In the three predictions of the death of Jesus, Jerusalem is designated as the place where God's Son will meet those who will put him to death. Matthew's negative treatment of Jerusalem carries over into his Easter narrative, where Jesus appears only once in Jerusalem, then to the women, but not to the disciples, who see him first and only in Galilee. The only extended discourse about Jerusalem in the Easter narratives (28:11–15) is the account of how the Jews bribe the soldiers to say that the disciples have stolen the body of Jesus. Matthew sees the message of Jesus as first intended for the Jews.[19] In spite of the strong Jewish style of Matthew's message, foreign or at least difficult for the Gentiles, it is these non-Jews who believe.

John the Baptist is also used by Matthew to further the Mosaic themes which are used in presenting the person of Jesus as the speaker of the Sermon on the Mount. The Jordan River, where John is baptizing, was the last barrier to be overcome before the Jews entered the land promised to them through Abraham. Here in Matthew the river, where sins are confessed in John's baptism, is the last barrier to be overcome before entering the kingdom which has now arrived in the person of Jesus. The pro-Gentile and anti-Jewish tone, so prominent in Matthew's description of Jesus, is already clearly evident in the preaching of John preserved by Matthew. For Matthew John's claim that God can make children to Abraham out of the stones is no idle threat. Likewise, the request of the Roman centurion to heal his servant provides an opportunity for Jesus to say that the Gentiles coming from the east and from the west will sit down at the table with Abraham, Isaac, and Jacob and the sons of the kingdom shall be thrown into the outer darkness (8:11). The full impact of the threat and promise in John's preaching to replace the Jews with Gentiles as Abraham's children is placed by Matthew in his conclusion to make disciples out of all Gentiles, without any special reference to the Jews. Their uniqueness now belongs to the historical past.

The baptism of Jesus by John furthers the theme introduced by Matthew with the use of the Hosea passage ("Out of Egypt I have called my Son"): Jesus is God's true Israel and *true Moses*. The first Moses passed through the Red Sea and showed that he was God's faithful servant. The second Moses also came out of Egypt like the first one, but unlike the first one he is allowed to pass through the Jordan as Joshua did bringing the people to the land of promise. It seems unlikely that Matthew was unaware that Jesus and Joshua are the same names. Where he felt obligated to develop the connection between the names of Jesus and Emmanuel (1:21), he perhaps found an explicit discussion about Jesus and Joshua a bit too obvious, as Joshua in the Septuagint, Greek translation of the Old Testament used at that time, was *Iēsous*, Jesus. With Jesus passing through the Jordan, he shows that he has not only come out of Egypt across the Red Sea as did the first Moses, but has passed through the Jordan River into the land of promise. The words of Hosea, "Out of Egypt I have called my Son," referring to the exodus from Egypt, are supplemented by the voice from heaven, "This is my beloved Son in whom I am well pleased," signifying that Jesus, the true Joshua, has come into the land of promise. Matthew has shown that Jesus is the true Israel.

It cannot be known for certain why Matthew does not develop the theme of Joshua more explicitly, though it seems to be implied. It may be that for the Jews, Joshua, like the prophets, was only a slight reflection of Moses. Moses set the standard for Joshua, as he did for all the prophets. It was not the reverse. Matthew wants his readers to understand that Jesus is the *true* Moses and more. Presenting him as another Joshua and thus lowering his stature would hardly have served that purpose.[20]

Rather than advancing beyond Moses to another prophetic figure from Israel's history, Matthew in his presentation of the temptation of Jesus reverts back to Moses in ever clearer outlines. In the appearance of Jesus as the *true* Moses in the wilderness to be tempted by Satan (4:1–11) Matthew concludes his introduction of the person of Jesus. In 4:12 Matthew introduces the actual ministry of Jesus. Up to and including the temptation narrative, Jesus is the one who is acted upon. He comes from a long genealogical process, he is born, he is honored by the magi, he is persecuted and flees, he is brought by his father into Galilee, he is baptized by John, and now he is the one tempted by Satan. He does not initiate these actions.[21]

The reader is prepared for the appearance of Jesus in the wilderness by Matthew's placing the Baptist in the wilderness, where he conducts his preaching of repentance. The wilderness not only as geographical reference but as theological theme goes back earlier than to the account of the exodus out of Egypt. It has its roots in Genesis 3 and the cursing of the earth (3:18–19). The fertile Eden is replaced by the ground so cursed that man's every attempt to reestablish paradise is met by thorns and thistles. Noah's planting a vineyard (Genesis 9:20) and the Israelite spies returning with abundance of fruit (Numbers 13:23–24) suggest that God's people expected that in some way the original paradise of Eden would be reestablished among them. Matthew's message is that God's kingdom is not coming with the land but with Jesus, who by his 40-day exile in the desert identifies himself with Israel and more importantly as Israel.

The stay of Jesus in the desert is strongly impressed with themes prominent in the books and life of Moses. The desert, unlike the Genesis garden, is the place where God does not seem to be present. Here in the bleak desert Satan, not God, seems to be in control. Jesus is deprived of the presence of God as was the first Adam, who after the fall is left alone in the world without God. But if the first Adam faced Satan with the advantage of the garden and personal presence of God, the second Adam meets him in the desert.

The temptation of Jesus by Satan after the baptism by John provides a necessary introduction to the Sermon's discussion of evil. If the evangelist in some way wants the reader to understand that Jesus is Adam, he is equally intent in furthering his picture of him as Moses. The desert meant the 40-year period of trial before entering Canaan, the history of which is told in Exodus-Leviticus-Numbers-Deuteronomy, the time when Moses led them. Matthew's use of "forty days *and forty nights*" (4:2), which becomes significant when compared to the Markan and Lucan parallels which omit the reference to the forty nights, is a clear reference to Moses, who is 40 days and 40 nights with God on Sinai to receive the law (Exodus 34:28).[22] To all three temptations Jesus responds with words of Moses taken from Deuteronomy, the law of Moses: "Man shall not live by bread alone but by every word that proceeds out of the mouth of God" (Deuteronomy 8:3); "You shall not put the Lord your God to the test" (Deuteronomy 6:16); and "You shall worship the Lord your God and him shall you serve" (Deuteronomy 6:13). Even the attendance of angels at the giving of the law to Moses (Acts 7:53; Galatians 3:19) finds its parallel in Matthew, where at the end of the temptation angels come and serve Jesus (4:11).

So concludes Matthew's introduction of the person of Jesus as the true Moses. The promised prophet like Moses (Deuteronomy 18:15) has appeared. The hearer of the Sermon on the Mount has already been prepared by the evangelist to expect that in hearing the words of Jesus he will be receiving a revelation from God. The imprisonment of John the Baptist

(4:12), the last of the prophets, is the final step in Matthew's introduction to the ministry of Jesus.

To the disciples' question of when Elijah would appear, Jesus replied that he had appeared in John the Baptist (17:10–13). The Baptist is used by Matthew as the summary conclusion of the prophetic office established by and in Moses. Elijah like Moses had conducted the most effective part of his ministry in the desert region. John was now appearing as the eschatological Elijah. Matthew attributes to John and Jesus the same message, and some have concluded, not without good reason, that Jesus as a disciple of John was influenced by him. The imprisonment of John is used by the evangelist to inaugurate the preaching of Jesus, as with the removal of John, a prophet of the old order, the newness of God's kingdom in Jesus can now appear. Matthew does not intend to suggest that their ministries did not overlap in a historical, chronological sense. The evangelist brings John into the gospel at five strategic places. John's imprisonment (4:12) is placed directly before the Sermon on the Mount. His question to Jesus about his messiahship is placed directly after the second discourse, the one dealing with the apostolic office. John is said to bring a conclusion to the Law and the Prophets (11:13), but the one who sees and hears about what God is doing in Jesus has the advantage over him. (The office of the apostle is thus elevated over that of the prophet.) After the third discourse, Matthew places the account of the Baptist's martyrdom, beginning with a discussion of how Herod the Tetrarch feared that he had been raised from the dead (16:21). A fourth reference, to the suffering of John (17:10–13), is placed between the first and second prediction of the suffering and death of Jesus (16:21 and 17:22–23). A fifth, final reference to the Baptist is placed by the evangelist in 21:23–27 between the fourth and fifth discourses. During the final week of his life Jesus is asked by the religious authorities about his own authority for his teaching. Rather than respond, he puts to them a question about the Baptist's authority, whether it was from God or man. The confrontation ends with neither Jesus nor his adversaries answering the questions placed before them. The evangelist has Jesus answering the question in the gospel's conclusion (28:16–20) by saying that all authority has been given to him. Jesus implies that *God* has given him the authority.[23] The difference between the Baptist and Jesus is not that one has received his authority from God and the other not, but its extent and the manner in which it was given. John's teaching authority is partial and derived, while the authority of Jesus is complete and innate. It is with the question of authority that Matthew will conclude the Sermon.

"And when Jesus finished these sayings, the crowds were astonished at his teaching, for he taught them as one who had authority, and not as their scribes" (7:28–29). The Sermon of Jesus has God's own direct authority, and thus it supersedes the prophets' message. The superiority of Jesus to Moses and the prophets is found also in John (1:17) and Hebrews (1:1–2).

PLACING THE SERMON ON THE MOUNT

In his introduction to the Sermon on the Mount the evangelist has used the persons of Moses and of John the Baptist to connect it to the Old Covenant. The focus is not on the authoritative writings of Moses or the charismatic quality of the preaching of John. The evangelist's task is rather to shift the gaze of the listener to Galilee, as far away from Jerusalem as possible without leaving Canaan. This is part of his purpose to present the Gentiles as those who will soon replace the Jews as the recipients of the kingdom and as the sons of Abraham, a theme suggested in the coming of the magi but made explicit after the Sermon in conjunction with the healing of the centurion's servant (8:11–12). The city of Capernaum (4:13), Peter's home town, initiates for Matthew the ministry of Jesus. John chose Cana, also a Galilean city, to initiate the ministry of Jesus (2:1,11). In Peter's house in Capernaum the third-listed miracle after the Sermon on the Mount took place. This city took on added importance for Matthew's church since his gospel in several places singles out Peter for special attention, especially his receiving of the kingdom's keys in Matthew 16. Thus Matthew may have concentrated on Capernaum as the starting and major location of the preaching of Jesus because of Peter's continually zrecognized position of prominence and leadership in the early church. Equally important in singling out Capernaum over against Nazareth, which is prominent for Luke, is that, unlike Nazareth, Capernaum is a city by a sea and thus would fit the Isaiah 9 reference where the people who sit in darkness and see the great light dwell in the northern regions "by the way of sea, around Jordan." For Matthew, Capernaum with its location on the Sea of Galilee fulfills Isaiah 9:24. The people sitting in darkness are the Galileans; in Jesus the light has shined on them, a theme developed in the Sermon (5:14).

Matthew does not give the geographical location where the Sermon was given, but by placing Capernaum in his introduction to the ministry of Jesus (4:13) and then again shortly after the Sermon's conclusion (8:5), he suggests that the message of Jesus is for the Gentiles. Galilee, where Capernaum is located, is not simply Galilee for Matthew, but "Galilee of the Gentiles" (4:15).

THE HEARERS OF THE SERMON

Matthew divides his audience into the disciples and the crowds (5:1). Luke describes the hearers as "great crowds of his disciples and a great multitude of people" who originate from Judea and Jerusalem and the sea-coast of Tyre and Sidon. At the beginning of the Sermon Luke writes: "He lifted up his eyes on his disciples, and said..." (6:20). However, Luke concludes his version of the Sermon without distinguishing the two groups from each other (7:1). In Matthew Jesus is placed among the crowds, but the Sermon is directed primarily to the disciples. At the end of the Sermon the crowds are amazed at his teaching and follow him (8:1), but the sense of following here is not the kind of discipleship demanded for the kingdom. Stanton suggests that the dual audience of the Sermon is deliberate to indicate that while the entire Sermon is directed to the disciples, parts of it are appropriate for a wider group.[25] The "crowd" suggests a parallel between Jesus and Moses, who was surrounded by them in his descent from Sinai. Luke has "democratized" the teaching of Jesus, intended chiefly for the disciples in Matthew, and made it more accessible.[26] Matthew reports Jesus as working in Galilee, especially Capernaum, but the crowds following Jesus are from Galilee, the Decapolis, Jerusalem, Judea, and the area around Jordan (4:25).

An exact location for the Sermon cannot be determined. For Luke Judea and Jerusalem are treated more favorably and are placed first; Matthew has them last.[27] Matthew 4:23–25 is intended as an introductory summary of the entire ministry of Jesus which is conducted throughout Palestine and cannot be used to designate one particular place. Matthew wants to focus the ministry particularly in Galilee. He also wants to leave the impression that the Sermon is a compendium of what Jesus taught throughout his entire ministry and not just in one time and place, though it may have come to be associated more with one particular locale than others.

Before presenting the Sermon, Matthew introduces the call of four of the twelve disciples (4:18–22). The four—Peter, Andrew, James, and John—have several things in common. Peter and Andrew are brothers, as are James and John, and all in distinction from the others are identified as fishermen by trade. The Fourth Gospel may suggest that some others were fishermen (21:1–3), but this is not certain. All but Andrew, who no longer plays any significant part in the gospel, are given special status by Jesus. The other three observe the raising of the daughter of Jairus, the transfiguration and the appearing of Moses and Elijah, and the suffering of Jesus in Gethsemane. Peter is singled out for a special honor (16:18–19) and the other two, James and John, ask for special status through their mother (20:20–24). The question remains why Matthew did not place all twelve (eleven) as the hearers of the Sermon as he did for the other four discourses and the final commission. Luke has all the disciples as hearers of the sermon (6:12–17). At the start of his version of the Sermon Luke has the call of the Twelve (6:12–17) and not simply the four. Matthew places the call of the Twelve after the Sermon (10:1–2).

The problem of not listing all Twelve as hearers of the Sermon is not so troublesome when we recall that Matthew is writing as much a theology as he is a history. He does not intend that the reader should get the impression that only four and not twelve disciples heard Jesus preach the Sermon. The command to teach the Gentiles all things (28:16–20) implies that the Twelve had heard and learned all things, including those in the Sermon. Simply because the gospel places the call of Matthew (9:9–13) and the calling of all the disciples (10:1) after the Sermon does not suggest that they did not hear it, as Matthew is not here interested in a chronological ordering. With Luke the possible confusion for the reader is removed in placing the calling of the Twelve before the Sermon.

Still this does not entirely resolve why Matthew mentions the calling of only four disciples: Peter, Andrew, James, and John. Perhaps in comparison with the others they are more obviously Galilean. They are from Galilee, and there they are called as fishers of men. The Galilean origins of these disciples prepare for the preaching of the gospel among the Gentiles. As three of them, Peter, James and John, are singled out for special attention as witnesses of the divine acts of Jesus, the evangelist's use of them here may accentuate that the Sermon is the divine teaching, something which only God can reveal, not unlike the transfiguration appearance of Jesus. It also may be that the evangelist wants to avoid placing himself in such a prominent position. This would occur if the names of the Twelve were placed before the Sermon, as it is done in Luke.

Another solution, equally plausible, is that Matthew intended to focus on Simon, then known to Matthew's church as Peter (4:18). Mark and Luke list him only as Simon, with no reference to his later name of Peter in the parallel passages (Mark 1:16 and Luke 5:10). With the use of the name Peter from the outset, the evangelist is acknowledging his special position of authority in the church. As Andrew his brother and the two sons of Zebedee are called at roughly the same time, Matthew thought to include them, especially since they would share with Peter a prominent position in the ministry of Jesus. At the time Matthew was being written, James the son of Zebedee had already been martyred; John, if he was not still in Jerusalem, was remembered for the prominent role he played in the early church (Acts 12:2).

Thus if 4:17, "From that time Jesus began to preach, saying" is to be taken as the introductory title sentence of the first half of Matthew's gospel (following the introduction of the person of Jesus), the evangelist's intent in placing the call of the four disciples at this point is to establish their place as the first recipients of his message.

Though the disciples are the first recipients of the message of Jesus (5:2), they are also the trustees of the message for the Gentiles (28:19). For the evangelist the Twelve (later the Eleven) are those who first are taught and then teach. They are disciples and apostles (10:1–2). The reader of this gospel should not have to decide whether the message of Jesus which Matthew puts in the Sermon was given by him at one place or whether the evangelist, working within his community, arranged his material to fit its needs. This is not an either-or decision. The preliminary pericope to the Sermon (4:23–25) indicates that the Sermon was a characteristic summary of the preaching of Jesus. The commission to the Eleven (28:16–20) just as plausibly suggests that the evangelist understands his gospel, including the Sermon, as material intended for church use.[28]

The pericope before the Sermon (4:23–25) should be taken not as a reference to the first year or any other period in the ministry of Jesus. It is, rather, a division according to subject matter. It should be taken as a characteristic description of his entire ministry. Matthew wants the reader to understand that this ministry took place in Galilee, a theme which is restated in the Easter narrative (28:7, 10, 16), where Jesus appears to the Eleven in Galilee, the place where they were called (4:12, 15, 18, 23). The description of Jesus' ministry as "teaching in their synagogues and preaching the gospel of the kingdom" does not refer to two different aspects, teaching and preaching, but one. For Matthew Jesus is not the 'street corner preacher,' but the rabbi who follows the usual rules of protocol for one holding this position. The usual place for his ministry was the synagogue. His dialogue with the Pharisees, Sadducees, and scribes indicates that even though his message may have been found intolerable by them, they did not question his rabbinic credentials, though they did question his message and practice. By pointing to "the mount" as the place for the delivery of the Sermon, Matthew shows the superiority of its message over what the rabbis taught in the synagogues.

The reference to Jesus' teaching could possibly be taken only to his participation in regular services of the synagogue, but in Matthew's use of the word "teach" it also focuses attention on the content of that teaching.[29] For Matthew even the verbal form "teach" along with the reference to the position of teacher stresses the office of the divine revealer with his message. Thus Matthew wants to leave the impression that the substance of

Jesus' message has been given to the Jews. Matthew's concept that the message of Jesus is first preached to the Jews parallels his handling of the miracles. In the first recorded miracle of Jesus, placed after the Sermon, the healed leper is required by Jesus to inform the priest of his cure (8:1–4), not only to fulfill the ritual law but to announce to the Jewish people that the Messiah has come. Jesus later mentions the healing of lepers to indicate that the messianic kingdom has come (11:5). Essential for Matthew is that the message which the Jews have rejected was first proclaimed to them. The preaching of the kingdom in the synagogues everywhere in Galilee (4:23) means for Matthew that the material included in his gospel has been first delivered to the Jews. More specifically the message of the Sermon has also been delivered in the synagogues according to the usual, customary procedures. Jesus' preaching the kingdom is preaching about himself. This must be developed later in connection with the content of the Sermon itself.

The phrase "healing every disease and infirmity among the people" (4:23), like the reference to the preaching in the synagogues, is intended as a summary of Jesus' entire ministry of healing and not just one particular period. It would be wrong to conclude that since Matthew places only a few miracles in the last section (16:21–28; 20), that the second half of Jesus' ministry had fewer miracles (21:14).

In the style of the writers of the ancient world, Matthew has selected only several anecdotes from the life of Jesus to demonstrate his miraculous healings. Luke expands upon this list, and Mark often provides more description. Where Luke tends to be interested in the personal affliction of the sick and Mark concentrates on the miracle-working power of Jesus, Matthew sees the healing miracles as part of the theological announcement that the messianic kingdom has finally arrived. The summary description of the ministry of Jesus in 4:23, part of the introductory pericope to the Sermon, is repeated in 9:35, where it is part of the introductory pericope to the call of the apostles. The first case is followed by the giving of the Sermon and the second by the commission of the Twelve, who are empowered "to heal every disease and infirmity" and thus are like Jesus (10:1). The implication is that their message is that of Jesus, presumably in the Sermon. Where Matthew does supply anecdotes from the life of Jesus to show that he did in fact "heal every disease and infirmity," he gives no example of the disciples having done this successfully. Their attempt to exorcize the demon-possessed boy ended in failure. Primary for Matthew is that the apostles are exercising the authority that Jesus claimed for himself. They do not have this as an autonomous but as a derived authority from Jesus. Luke does present both Peter and Paul as miracle workers in Acts, perhaps to provide a real demonstration of the authority of the apostles.

Whereas the miracle working of Jesus is restricted by Matthew to the Jews, "among the people" (4:23), no restriction to work simply among the Jews is placed on the disciples. Their ministry includes the Gentiles (28:16–20).

Matthew intends that the preaching of Jesus should extend beyond the Jews. He indicates this by the reference to the hearing of the message "throughout all Syria" (4:24). It seems certain that Jesus publicly preached there, as in the case of the feeding of the 4,000 (15:29). Crowds from the Decapolis hear the Sermon Jesus preaches to the Jews; Gentiles hear it and believe. To demonstrate this, the evangelist offers the accounts of the two centurions and the Canaanite woman, whom Luke identifies more precisely as Syro-Phoenician. At this point the evangelist attributes to Jesus the healing of three types of afflicted people: demoniacs, epileptics, and paralytics. Matthew has other summary statements (8:16 and 11:5), where the types of healing are expanded. As mentioned, for Matthew the attention here is not on the miracle and the person on whom it is worked, but on the one who is both the new Moses and the servant who suffers for sins (Matthew 8:17, Isaiah 53:4).

Placing the healing of the leper immediately after the Sermon (8:1–4) reinforces Matthew's picture that in Jesus the new Moses has appeared. After the first appearance to Moses in the burning bush, God gives three signs to Moses to show that he is the special prophet: the rod becomes a serpent, Moses' hand becomes leprous, and the Nile's water can be turned into blood. (Exodus 4:1–9) Jesus' healing of the leper directly after the Sermon shows that Jesus is superior to Moses.

The message of the Sermon must itself now be presented. For Matthew, Jesus now appears as Moses but not simply as Moses; he is the God who once had spoken to Moses and to his people. The Sermon is the message which God has promised to kings and prophets and yet has hidden from them, but which is being revealed to the apostles (13:17). The Sermon is also the message for Matthew's church and for the church of all ages.

There is always the temptation to insist that the evangelist has written a chronological life of Jesus. Luke and John may have been more concerned in providing a chronological sequence of events than was Matthew, who remains of the synoptic evangelists foremost a theologian. This does not mean that he has no chronological awareness of events. For Matthew too, the ministry of Jesus begins with his baptism by John and Palm Sunday ushers in the final week, but a theological rather than chronological order motivates his gospel's outline. It is written in the post-Easter church for those who have already heard in some way most, if not all, of the teaching of Jesus. It is more a theological handbook than it is an evangelistic preaching document, even though it came to serve this purpose also. The evangelistic document would appear in Mark. What Jesus had said before his death took on a fuller meaning and newer dimensions for the post-Easter church. At least one generation passed between the life of Jesus and the writing of the gospel. Paul not only gave a new dimension to the Christian message in the post-Easter situation, but he supplied a vocabulary and a new way of speaking that was hardly identical with that of Jesus. Matthew goes back to the pre-Pauline church to preserve both the message *and* the words of Jesus. He gives us the message of Jesus in and for the post-resurrection church, the church which knows Paul and his mission to the Gentiles. The Sermon on the Mount is not merely the preaching of Jesus the rabbi, but the preaching of the Jesus whom God has made both Lord and Christ, as it was remembered by the church. This distinction is extremely important, because it was not simply a matter of what Jesus had taught the original Twelve, but what he was now teaching the post-resurrection community in the teaching, the *didache*, of the Eleven. Matthew did not create his gospel merely as a historical record, but as a teaching guide for his church.

NOTES

1 For a critical discussion on the structure of Matthew, see David R. Bauer, *The Structure of Matthew's Gospel, Journal for the Study of the New Testament Supplement Series* (Sheffield: Sheffield Academic Press, 1988). Also Brevard S. Childs, *The New Testament As Canon: An Introduction* (Philadelphia: Fortress, 1984), 63–64.

2 The similarity between Matthew's presentations of John and Jesus was noted by Pierson Parker in "A Second Look at the Gospel Before Mark," *Journal of Biblical Literature* 100 (1981) 389–413 (1979): 147–68. Compare 3:2 with 4:17; 3:7f. with 12:37f, 23:33; 3:10 with 7:19; 3:12 with 13:20. Though Matthew reports the imprisonment of John before Jesus begins his ministry, the evangelist refers to him in strategic locations throughout the gospel. Before Jesus' conferral of authority on the disciples in chapter 10, John's disciples come to him with a question about fasting (9:14–17). After the discourse, John through his own disciples asks questions about the messianic claims of Jesus (11:2–18) and thus anticipates the confession of Peter in 16:16. His execution by Herod prepares for Jesus' execution by Pilate and, like Jesus, he is buried by followers (14:1–12). John is even reported as raised from the dead (14:2) and this is implied in 16:14. Jesus' unanswered question about the authority of John anticipates his own claim to authority from God at the gospel's conclusion (28:18).

3 For a full treatment of this issue see W. D. Davies, *The Setting of the Sermon on the Mount* (Atlanta: Scholars, 1989), 14–198. See also B. W. Bacon, "The 'Five Books' of Matthew against the Jews," *The Expositor* VIII ser. 15 (1918): 56–66, and Bauer, *The Structure of Matthew's Gospel*.

4 For an extended discussion, see R. H. Gundry, *The Use of the Old Testament in Matthew's Gospel*, Novum Testamentum Supplements to (vol. 18; Leiden: E. J. Brill, 1967).

5 Martin Hengel, "Probleme des Markusevangeliums" in *Das Evangelium und die Evangelien: Vortraege von Tuebinger Symposium 1982, Wissenschaftlicher Untersuchungen zum Neuen Testament*, vol. 28 (ed. Peter Stuhlmacher; Tübingen: J. C. B. Mohr, 1983), 26.

6 The phrase *biblos geneseos* (Matthew 1:1) without the article is found in the Septuagint translation of Genesis, e.g., 2:4, 5:1. See Bauer, *The Structure of Matthew's Gospel*, 73–77. Davies and Allison see a multiple reference in *biblos geneseos* with the first referring to the title of the book, the second to a genealogy, and the third to the life story of Jesus. It would have reminded Matthew's audience of the first book of the Old Testament and Adam. They suggest this title, "Book of the New Genesis wrought by Jesus Christ, son of David, son of Abraham" (149–50); Matthew, 1, 149–50.

7 Though nearly all scholars in the last century have favored placing Mark as the first written gospel, the matter is hardly undisputed, especially in light of the early church testimony which gave first place to Matthew. In the formation of the gospel canon Matthew was given first place. The reasons for this vary. It could have been the first written gospel, the most thorough gospel, and/or the one unlike Mark and Luke, which bore an apostle's name. For whatever reason, the church placed it as its first gospel and within this gospel, the Sermon on the Mount possesses the place of honor. William R. Farmer points out that no other book could have served so well as the linkage between the Old Testament and the emerging New Testament canon. *Jesus and the Gospel* (Philadelphia: Fortress, 1982), 17.

8 See Philip L. Shuler, *A Genre for the Gospels* (Philadelphia: Fortress, 1982). Dale C. Allison, Jr., devotes an entire book to seeing Jesus in terms of Moses (*The New Moses: A Matthean Typology* [Minneapolis: Fortress, 1993]). So the Gospel of Matthew can be considered an enconium, a particular biographical genre common in the ancient world. In the case of Matthew, it centered around the person of Moses and was used before and after Jesus for other biblical and non-biblical figures. Picturing Jesus as a new Moses was problematic for those stressing the uniqueness of Jesus as divine. In translating Deut 18:15, Luther wanted to change "a prophet like me" to "a prophet unlike me" (267, n.). This hesitancy is derived partially from seeing Moses as a lawgiver and not a deliverer. It also reflects the tendency to apply the Law-Gospel distinction to the Old and New Testaments, even though both testaments contain both elements.

9 Origen replied to the claims of Celsus that Jesus was born of an adulterous union. That such claims were made in his lifetime and in the earliest church is not unlikely. Matthew's description of the angel's appearance to Joseph centers on the possibility of her adultery. John's gospel may also reflect a similar concern. In 6:42 the Jews suggest that Jesus is the son of Joseph and in 8:41 the Jews reply to Jesus that they are not the children of fornication, implying that perhaps he is.

10 The dependency on the form of our gospels on the encomium is not beyond debate. The Old Testament does contain the accounts of great men after whom the gospels could have been patterned. Still the evangelists lived and wrote in a world which was already Hellenized and would have known the encomium form. See Shuler, *A Genre for the Gospels*.

11 Robert H. Gundry, *Matthew: A Commentary on his Literary and Theological Art* (Grand Rapids: Eerdmans, 1982), 66. Gundry points out that in contrast to Luke, Matthew not only sees the sitting position as referring to the ordinary posture for teaching (23:2) but also for pronouncing judgment (19:28; 25:31).

12 Bauer, *The Structure of Matthew's Gospel*, 132–33.

13 Brevard Childs calls Matthew's method of Old Testament quotation "reflexion citation," i.e., the OT passage provides the theological context for the event in the life of Jesus and shows the unity of God's message. The original passage and the commentary are merged, *The New Testament as Canon* (Philadelphia: Fortress, 1985), 70–71. John by his saying that his gospel was written so that people might believe on Jesus as God's Son and have eternal life (20:30–31) may very well be providing a commentary on Matthew's rendition of Isaiah 7:14 where "she" is replaced with "they."

14 Gundry, *Matthew: A Commentary*, 26–32.

15 Gundry, *Matthew: A Commentary*, 34.

16 See Eduard Schweizer, *The Good News According to Matthew* (trans. David E. Green; Atlanta: John Knox, 1975), 39. "In this account Jesus is depicted as a new Moses, sent by God to be the Savior of his people but threatened from the very beginning by those in worldly authority."

17 Schweizer points out that Matthew's interpretation of Hosea 11:1 as applicable to the one man Jesus may have been made possible by the Greek text of Numbers 24:7–8: "A man shall come from his [Israel's] seed and shall rule [shall be the Lord over] many gentiles ... God shall lead him out of Egypt" (LXX, Numbers 24:7–8). Jesus is not only the Lord of the Jews, but of the Gentiles, *The Good News According to Matthew*, 39–42.

18 The slaughter of the holy innocents does not only serve as a historical reference for Matthew, but has a theological purpose. In the genealogy he has already alluded to the Babylonian captivity (1:11, 12, 17), and thus to the impending doom coming upon Jerusalem, Gundry, *Matthew: A Commentary*, 36.

19 For a discussion of the complementary harmony, see Childs, *The New Testament as Canon*, 156–65 for infancy narratives and 199–209 for the resurrection narratives.

20 The comparison between Moses and Jesus is a theme picked up elsewhere in the New Testament: Hebrews 3:5, 6; John 1:17; and Mark (Hengel, "Probleme des Markusevangeliums"). Matthew's conclusion where Jesus commands the disciples to observe all things (28:20) bears a clear resemblance to the Greek of Joshua 1:7–9 where Joshua is enjoined to follow everything which Moses had commanded. Jesus, however, is never put into a position subservient to Moses, as Joshua was.

21 Bauer, *The Structure of Matthew's Gospel*, 142–43, notes that the first main division, 1:1–4:16, "prepares the reader for the rest of the Gospel by, among other things, presenting directly the nature and identity of Jesus. By means of a series of reliable witnesses, including Matthew himself, Jesus is identified as 'Christ,' 'Son of David,' 'Son of Abraham,' and king." The division of sayings of Jesus into five sections, of which the Sermon is the first, does not conflict but can be harmonized with Jack Kingsbury's threefold division: 1:1–4:16; 4:17–16:20; 16:21–28:20. This structural division coincides with a theological division. Its theological implications are discussed by Bauer, 142–45.

22 Gundry, *Matthew: A Commentary*, 55.

23 See note 2 above.

24 Compare Farmer, *Jesus and the Gospel*, 138–39.

25 Stanton, "The Origin and Purpose," 25, Gundry, *Matthew: A Commentary*, 66 and

Schweizer, *Good News*, 79, virtually identify the disciples and the crowds. Robert A. Guelich also recognizes a dual audience, but in contrasting terms: whereas the disciples believe, the crowds do not, *The Sermon on the Mount* (Waco: Word, 1982), 59.

26 The issue of sources is handled in detail by W. D. Davies, *The Setting of the Sermon on the Mount*; perhaps the issue should be kept separate from the matter of one version of the Sermon interpreting the other. Guelich provides a detailed listing of the Q materials in the Sermon (*The Sermon*, 34.) Matters are made more complex by finding bits and pieces of the Sermon in Mark, which traditionally has been recorded as an independent source alongside of Q. For the sake of debate, just Matthew and Luke should be placed side by side without recourse to Q or the *Didache*. If there were indeed two different sermons or if each evangelist was working with entirely different sets of material, the discussion could be limited to literary similarities. The similarities force us at some juncture to open the thorny question of dependency. For example a comparison between Matthew 5:2 and Luke 6:17 on the question for whom the Sermon was intended might be enlightening in determining whether one of these evangelists possibily knew and used the other. Matthew's version limits the primary audience to disciples, more specifically to Peter, Andrew, John, and James with the crowds placed on the fringe. Without diminishing the significance of the apostles, whose calling is placed before his version of the Sermon (6:13–16), Luke overcomes the distinction by merging the disciples and crowds into one group who hear the Sermon. Matthew does not list the disciples until 10:1–2 as he has only the calling of Peter, Andrew, John, and James (4:18–22) before the Sermon. Luke clarifies the roles of the disciples and the crowds as hearers of the Sermon; these are uncertain in Matthew's version: 1) the Twelve do hear the Sermon and not just the four; and 2) the crowds hear its message.

27 The theological motifs of each evangelist can be detected in how they describe the origins of the crowds. For Matthew the order is Galilee, the Decapolis, Jerusalem, Judea, and the area around Jordan. Luke places Judea and Jerusalem first and adds Tyre and Sidon (6:17), and so he prepares for the command of preaching the Gospel first in Jerusalem and then to the end of the earth (Canaan). This may reflect Pauline influence that the gospel is to be preached first to the Jew and then to the Greek. Matthew on the other hand begins in those lands where the Gentiles live, Galilee and the Decapolis. The gospel is for the Jews, but it is the Gentiles who come and believe it.

28 Krister Stendahl, *The School of St. Matthew* (Philadelphia: Fortress, 1968), 20–35. Also Stanton, "The Origin and Purpose," 188: "The disciples are told by the risen Lord to teach those who have been 'discipled' from the nations to keep all that Jesus has commanded (28:18–20). Once again the SM is an integral part of the gospel."

29 The synoptics recognize Jesus as a synagogue preacher (Matthew 13:54; Mark 6:1; Luke 4:16). Luke's comment is the most explanatory as he adds that it was customary for Jesus to do this on the Sabbath. The less Jewish-oriented audiences of Mark and Luke would be less aware that teaching was a divinely appointed function and was not haphazardly carried out. Stendahl points out that Jesus was regularly addressed as "Rabbi" (*The School of St. Matthew*, 34).

PART 1

THE SERMON
AND ITS MESSAGE

MATTHEW 5:3–48

3

THE BEATITUDES—
CHRISTOLOGY AND ECCLESIOLOGY

MATTHEW 5:3–12

In the Lutheran church communion, the Beatitudes serve as a liturgical canticle and are set to music. While this may appear at first glance to
be a bit strange, using them as a canticle may reflect the role they played
as a hymn about Christ in the early church, not unlike Philippians 2:5–11.[1]
The Beatitudes, of course, come from the pre-resurrected Jesus; the
Philippians' hymn originated as a post-resurrection church hymn. But
each would have been used in the Jerusalem church to present the person
of Jesus, and each concentrates on the common New Testament themes of
humiliation-exaltation.

It is a common view that the Beatitudes are speaking primarily about
Christian lives. In other words, those are the ways the followers of Jesus
should act; they are instructions about the behavior of a Christian.
According to dogmatic categories, they would fit under ecclesiology and
sanctification. But does such a view of the Beatitudes as law or instruction
really fit the context? The evangelist has already introduced a high
Christology in his presentation of Jesus with the themes Jesus the Revealer
(Moses), the Redeemer of Israel, the Christ (the Son of David), and the
God of Israel (Emmanuel), all of which he has developed at some length
and woven intricately into certain selected events. It would seem strange
at this point that he would move abruptly into rules for Christian living.
The reader would hardly be prepared for such an abrupt literary tactic at this
point. He would, however, expect a further development of the christological theme introduced in 1:1–4:17. As Stanton notes, "The chap[ter]s which
precede and follow the SM are profoundly christological."[2]

In his introduction to the person of Jesus, Matthew has summarized
the messages of John and Jesus as a preaching of repentance with the
announcement that the kingdom of the heavens has come near. From the
place of the Sermon and the Beatitudes within the general arrangement of

the gospel, it would not be unexpected to find here the heart of that kingdom preaching. The reader is not disappointed.

The Beatitudes are so closely knit together that it is clear that they were received as a unit by the evangelist and were understood in the church as a unit.[3] They form a unit both in regard to structure and content, with each dependent for its meaning on the others. The nine sentences (Matthew 5:3–11) begin with the word blessed: *markarioi*. Each of these sentences has two parts. After the declaration of blessedness, a reason for this favorable condition with God is given. For example, the poor are blessed because theirs is the kingdom of the heavens.

In Matthew's gospel blessedness refers to the condition or state of an individual who has been favorably accepted by God and has received his divine approval.[4] In Matthew 16:17 Jesus uses the word in its singular form concerning Simon Bar-Jonah, who has recognized that Jesus is the Christ, God's Son. It is used in Jesus' reply to John concerning those who persist in the midst of persecution in believing that in Jesus God's kingdom is appearing (11:6).

It is less than completely satisfactory to understand the condition of blessedness as a reward, since the immediate implication is that those who are considered blessed have done something to deserve or merit God's approval. Even in Matthew 24:46, where it is used of the servant whom his master finds carrying out his responsibilities when he returns, blessedness does not refer to an earned reward. His faithfulness shows that he already belongs to God. His blessedness is seen in the faithfulness with which he carries out the responsibilities his master has given him. A parallel might be found in James 1:25, which seems to reflect the Beatitudes before they assumed written form in Matthew. The one whose life has been permeated by the Gospel, that is, "the perfect … law of liberty," shall be recognized for who he really is—blessed—by what he does.[5] There is no suggestion in the Beatitudes of a cause and effect.[6]

The first eight Beatitudes (5:3–10) are markedly different from the Ninth Beatitude. The first eight speak of "they" (third person plural), while the last one speaks of "you" (second person plural). The ninth Beatitude makes this division even sharper, because not only does it introduce the pronoun "you," but Jesus makes a specifically clear reference to himself: "Blessed are *you* when men revile *you* … on *my* account." At this point we note a subtle shift from Christology to ecclesiology, but in such a way that we can agree with Stanton that "christological and ecclesiological concerns are often inter-related."[7] The high Christology of the introduction to the gospel continues to permeate the Sermon. Thus only in the Ninth Beatitude does he distinguish himself from his followers. All of Luke's renderings of the Beatitudes have already been changed from "they" to "you." Matthew's "Blessed are the poor" becomes Luke's "Blessed are *you* poor" (6:20). These grammatical differences are not without theological significance.

The suggestion that the first eight Beatitudes may form a separate unit is supported by the fact that the First and Eighth Beatitudes speak of the kingdom of the heavens as a present reality, "for theirs is [now] the kingdom of the heavens." The intervening six Beatitudes all use future verbs in the concluding part of the sentences. The comforting, the inheriting the earth, the being filled, the receiving mercy, the seeing of God, and being designated as sons of God, all remain in the future. Thus the grammar and the structure of the Beatitudes suggest that the first eight should be understood as a unit and the Ninth with its deliberate use of *you* provides the connecting link with the remainder of the Sermon, which is directed to the original disciples and now through Matthew's gospel to his church.[8]

THE FIRST BEATITUDE

Together as a unit the Beatitudes have presented several problems for interpreters. Are they intended to make the requirements for the kingdom present in Jesus more severe than Moses (Law) or are they descriptions of what Christians already are in Christ (Gospel)? Calling them promises hardly resolves the tensions, since promises may suggest a reward for acceptable behavior. Of all the Beatitudes, the First, with its reference to "the poor in spirit," may be the most difficult, and so resolving its meaning may be the key to understanding all of them. The First Beatitude, "Blessed are the poor in spirit, for theirs is the kingdom of heaven" (5:13), may set the theme for the Sermon itself and perhaps for the entire gospel. It cannot be overlooked that the evangelist has chosen these words as the first recorded words of the public proclamation of Jesus. Thus the words "Blessed are the poor in spirit" summarize Jesus' preaching that "the kingdom of the heavens is at hand."

The phrase "the poor in spirit" presents the reader with a challenge. Economic deprivation is comprehensible, but spiritual deprivation less so. Luke changes "the poor" to "you poor," omits "in spirit," and substitutes "kingdom of God" for the "kingdom of heaven": "Blessed are you poor, for yours is the kingdom of God" (6:20). Luke uses examples of economic poor, e.g., Zechariah and Elizabeth, Mary and Joseph, the shepherds, the story of the rich man and Lazarus, all accounts missing from Matthew, not to show the religious advantage of being monetarily poor, but as signs of their refusal to make claims on God. Matthew's inclusion of "in spirit" makes clear that poverty acceptable to God is other than economic deprivation.

At the time of Matthew's writing, the word "poor" was used for the Christians in Jerusalem who had become economically dependent on the Gentile churches in the west (Romans 15:26; 1 Corinthians 16:3). The lack of material goods may have been the occasion for pointing to a more profound poverty. Matthew is obviously not negative to people of wealth. Such rich men as the Old Testament Abraham, Jairus, and Joseph of Arimathea receive favorable treatment. The addition of "in spirit" to poor may be the key not only to the interpretation of this beatitude but to the Sermon and perhaps even the gospel.[9]

The word "spirit" for Matthew can be used of the Spirit of God (i.e., the Holy Spirit), the soul, or the realm of God. Though it cannot be ruled out that the evangelist is referring to the soul in the body/soul dichotomy scheme, such an understanding would hardly come to terms with what he is saying. He also uses "spirit" in distinction to the flesh, man in his opposition to God. This is a dualism between good and evil where the flesh refers to man in his alienation from God and spirit as he has become an object of God's gracious working. For example, "the spirit is willing, the flesh is weak" refers not to the constitutional dichotomy of man as body and soul, but as creature divided by his loyalty to God and still tortured by his past association with his former life (26:41). The struggle between the two ways permeates the entire Sermon and is found in the *Didache* in its opening sentence: "There are two ways, one of life and one of death, and there is a great difference between the two ways!"

With this understanding of spirit as the life lived before God, "the poor in spirit" refers to those who make no claims on God for themselves. Before God they stand as destitute beggars. They make no claims in heaven and expect no rewards.

The Greek word for poor (*ptamochos*) resembles in meaning the words for meek (*praus*) and humble or lowly (*tapeinos*). These latter two words are used by Jesus of himself in 11:29: "for I am meek and lowly in heart." The Old Testament Hebrew word *nwm* is regularly translated in the Septuagint by the Greek word for meek (*praus*) except in Isaiah 29:19 and 61:1 where poor (*ptamochoi*) is used. The word "meek" is used in the Third Beatitude (5:5). *The three Greek words form a messianic constellation used in the early church specifically of the humiliation of Jesus.* Paul writes: "For you know the grace of our Lord Jesus Christ, though he was rich, yet for your sake he became *poor*, so that by his *poverty* you might become rich" (2 Corinthians 8:9). This may be Paul's exposition of the First Beatitude, known to him in oral tradition. Any reference to the poor in Matthew's church had christological implications, more specifically referring to the humiliation of Jesus.

Paul may not be the only one who comments on the First Beatitude. James 2:5–6, probably written before Matthew, may in fact refer to the logion which later was inscribed as the First Beatitude:[10] "Has not God chosen those who are poor (*ptamochois*) in the world to be rich in faith and heirs of the kingdom which he has promised to those who love him? But you have dishonored the poor man (*ptamochos*)." James' use of the plural and singular forms for the poor might provide a key for understanding how the First Beatitude was understood in the early church. The latter part, "you have dishonored (*atimasate*) the poor man," can be taken to mean that some early Christians, in shabbily treating the poor in the congregation, had by that act deprived Christ of the worship that was due him. The word honor (*timao*) is used of the believer's attitude to God (Matthew 15:8; John 5:23). Dishonoring would mean failing to give God the worship due him. This is implied in the judgment of the sheep and the goats where deeds done to the least of Jesus' brothers are done to him. Christ was understood as *the* poor man (singular), and those who suffered for Christ shared in that poverty and were called the poor (plural).[11]

The First Beatitude, along with the following seven, presents a problem in not clearly identifying the subjects. Who are the poor, the mourners, the meek, etc.? The Ninth moves to resolve the problem by distinguishing the disciples and Jesus. But what of the first eight? If it were not for the plural forms of the first eight Beatitudes, they could well be taken as referring to Jesus himself! They are marked by messianic, christologically-freighted language. James, by using the plural and singular forms of the word for poor side by side in the same context (2:5–6) provides an early church view of the Beatitudes. *The Beatitudes are markedly christological, but not in an isolated sense. They are descriptions both of Jesus and of those who have been joined by Jesus' Father to his kingdom.* For Matthew Christology and ecclesiology are interrelated.

Grammatically the Beatitudes may be seen as categories with indefinite references. They invite the reader to provide the subject that fits the category. The First Beatitude says that to the poor in spirit belongs the kingdom of heaven, but it does not tell us who these poor in spirit are. Matthew's gospel provides the historical answer in Jesus to the categories established by the evangelist in the Beatitudes. Thus if Matthew's gospel is christological, a theological life of Jesus, told to generate and sustain faith, the Beatitudes can be viewed as a summary introduction of this Christology as it is found in the rest of the gospel. The Beatitudes provide the *theological* contours for which the remainder of the gospel provides the historical answers by selecting certain episodes from the life of Jesus.

Of all the Beatitudes none describes this Christology better than does the First: "Blessed are the poor in spirit, for theirs is the kingdom of heaven." Here is the picture of Jesus. After the Lord's Prayer, the Beatitudes probably remain the most frequently used section of the New Testament. The First Beatitude presents a theological portrait of Jesus and those who have been confronted by his message.

Not only does Matthew present Jesus as the one who describes himself explicitly as meek and lowly (11:29), but he develops this theme from Herod's persecution of the infancy of Jesus to the abandonment by the Father in the hour of death. The Eighth Beatitude links the persecution of Christ with his poverty in the First Beatitude so that the first eight Beatitudes mark a unit, with the Ninth as a transitional appendix. The follower of Jesus is recognized as blessed along with him in the Ninth Beatitude. The blessedness of the follower of Jesus is seen in his persecution for the sake of Jesus.

Matthew's presentation of Jesus in his introduction is to a large extent dependent on Isaiah 7, 9, and 11. The evangelist also is dependent on Isaiah for his understanding of the Messiah's relation to his people (Isaiah 41:8–9). Isaiah, like the other prophets, can use messianic language with reference to all of Israel and to one particular messianic figure. Behind the First Beatitude is Isaiah 61:1.[12] Hosea, like Isaiah, sees the nation of Israel present as one person before God (11:1), and Matthew takes advantage of this in his own presentation of Jesus in 2:15: "Out of Egypt I have called my Son." For Matthew, Jesus is God's Israel who comes out of Egypt.

For those who stress the act of salvation as a divine activity outside of the Christian (*extra nos*), the concept of how the Messiah can be fully present *in his people* and his people totally present *in him* may be strange. Yet this is a predominating theme in the first gospel. Matthew does not present, for example, the birth of the Immanuel child as an isolated historical event or even mere theophany, an appearance of the divine, but rather as a birth that has for its purpose the salvation of his people. He is called "Jesus" since, as the evangelist says, "He will save his people from their sins" (1:21). Jesus performs miracles since he has taken the sicknesses and illnesses of his people upon himself (8:17).

The corporate inclusion of Israel in their Messiah makes their rejection of Jesus more serious for the evangelist. God's people in rejecting Jesus the Messiah have done the unthinkable, since they have in effect acted against themselves. As the Fourth Gospel says, "He came to his own home, and his own people received him not" (1:11).

This corporate nature whereby the Messiah and his people become one before God finds reflection in the Beatitudes. *The Beatitudes are the christological prism through which the followers of Jesus find their standing before God.* Seeing the Beatitudes as descriptions of Jesus alone would result in a dogmatic abstraction without salvatory significance for the people. Applying them to the church apart from Jesus raises the expectations of the people beyond what they can expect of themselves before God or their otherworldly character deteriorates into moralistic demands.

The corporate nature Jesus shares with his people also solves the problem as to how he could describe himself as "poor in spirit," which we have defined as "those who stand before God as destitute beggars." He is one with his people; he bears their sins (Matthew 8:17).

The First Beatitude can serve as an apt description of Jesus in his poverty not only in regard to God, to whose will he submits (Matthew 26:38–42), but also to all people, to whom he makes himself a servant (Matthew 20:25–28). Though the lowliest of the nonrational creatures have places which they can call their own, he has no place to lay his head (Matthew 8:20). In his death for sin, he is recognized as both servant and slave; he requires that his followers assume the same posture of servitude to all others (20:26–28). He who is poor in spirit is also the one who has become servant and slave. Those who are in him have assumed the same posture. Not only is he poor and has no possessions, but as slave he puts himself in debt to all men.[13]

In the First Beatitude "the kingdom of the heavens," a phrase peculiar to Matthew, cannot be taken as a kind of reward given the faithful at the time of death. "Heaven(s)" is commonly used to refer to the destiny of believers, life after death. But this meaning cannot be read into Matthew's use. For this evangelist "the kingdom of the heavens" refers to the salvation which God is accomplishing in Jesus, that is, in his death for sinners and its proclamation. "The kingdom of the heavens" is used to introduce the individual parables which are symbolic stories about what God is doing in Jesus. Those who are poor in spirit and make no claim upon him are those whom God has included in his work of salvation. The First Beatitude should not be taken to mean that *if* you are poor in spirit, God will reward you with heaven after death. "Blessed are the poor in spirit" is not a prescriptive commandment. Rather it means that among those who make no claim of righteousness for themselves, God's plan of salvation in Jesus is already effective.

The question then is: How does the First Beatitude apply to Jesus? In what way does the kingdom of the heavens belong to him? For him the kingdom of the heavens cannot be regarded as reward. For his death for the sins of the world the Father rewards him by raising him from the dead, but the kingdom of the heavens means more than his resurrection. Jesus in his person and in his work *is* the kingdom of the heavens. Through him God participates with human beings as a man and accomplishes his purpose of saving his people. "Blessed are the poor in spirit, for theirs is the kingdom of heaven" means in the first instance that Jesus' total submission to God by his death is where God's work comes to its first expression. It also looks forward to God's future vindication of Jesus when he comes as the world's judge.[14]

The phrase "the kingdom of the heavens" cannot be detached from Matthew's understanding that Jesus is king. The evangelist opens with the royal genealogy in which David is central. Joseph, the legal father of Jesus, is addressed as son of David (1:20), while Jesus is addressed throughout the gospel as *the* Son of David, especially in regard to the entry into Jerusalem (21:9). To the Gentile magi is given the honor of first explicitly asking for the whereabouts of the king of Jews (2:2). Matthew makes Jesus' kingship the cause of his death, and before his execution the royal robes are placed on him (27:11, 29). The culmination comes in the crucifixion, where Pilate affixes the kingly title to the instrument of execution and even the Jews in their taunting suggest that Jesus should demonstrate that he is their king by coming down from the cross (27:37, 42). While the concept of kingdom and kingship is descriptive of the entire ministry of Jesus, it comes to clear expression in his death. In his death, Jesus shows that he is God's king in giving his life for his people (1:20) and by that act establishes the kingdom. While the kingdom of the heavens points to God's continued rule in Jesus for his people, it comes to clearest expression in the suffering of Jesus as king. In the great judgment scene Jesus is both Son of Man and king (25:31, 34), but the kingdom for Matthew's church is found first in the suffering of the king and secondly in that of the church. The church's suffering convinces it that with Jesus they belong to those who are poor in spirit.

Suffering through persecution comes to explicit expression in the Eighth and Ninth Beatitudes. The connection between the First and Eighth Beatitudes with their themes of poverty and persecution was recognized as early as the first part of the second century where the church father Polycarp in his Letter to the Philippians (2:3) combined them into one: "Blessed are the poor and they that are persecuted for righteousness' sake for theirs is the kingdom of heaven."[15]

THE SECOND BEATITUDE

The Second Beatitude follows logically after the First, where the stress is placed upon the suffering of Jesus and his followers. Later Matthew describes Jesus lamenting over Jerusalem, which has rejected God's salvation (23:37–38). Here, in the Second Beatitude, Matthew reflects Isaiah 61:1–2, where the Suffering Servant is empowered by God's Spirit to bring good news to the afflicted and in particular "to comfort all those who mourn." While for Isaiah the immediate context includes the deliverance from the Babylonian captivity, for Matthew it takes on a deeper theological, salvific meaning of eschatological redemption. The future tense, used in the Second through the Seventh Beatitudes, points to an activity which God is about to do. The church's affliction shall be replaced by ecstatic joy in the sense of Psalm 126 where those who weep "shall come home with shouts of joy" (Psalm 126:6). The mourning of Jesus, not over his own death (26:38) but over unbelieving Jerusalem, is resolved by his constituting a people for himself from both Jews and Gentiles. The use of the passive voice in the future tense points to God's eschatological deliverance of his people.[16]

THE THIRD BEATITUDE

The promise of the land goes back to Abraham (Genesis 12:1), an Old Testament patriarch given a prominent role in the gospel of Matthew. Jesus is introduced in the gospel's title as the son of Abraham (1:1), and the Gentiles sit down with Abraham, Isaac, and Jacob in the kingdom of heavens (8:11). While other New Testament writers speak of a renovation of the heavens and the earth, a cosmic restoration (2 Peter 3:13; Revelation 21:1), the promise of the Third Beatitude is made with language reminiscent of Caanan as the promised land. What was originally promised to Abraham had not become the permanent possession of the Jews, especially in the situation of the first century where Roman rule was seen as an imposition on God's people and an unacceptable inter-vention into the promise. The evangelist does not here speak of a polit-ical or Zionistic recapture of the land, as the future tense here also points to an eschatological reality, not a historical event in time. Just as the kingdom for Matthew does not mean the restitution of the Davidic or Solomonic rule ("Behold, something greater than Solomon is here" [12:42]), so the promised land takes a meaning beyond ordinary geo-graphical understandings. Hebrews 4:1–10 speaks of the promised rest which goes beyond the land conquered by Joshua. In the judgment scene the word "inherit" refers to what the Son of Man gives his followers on the Day of Judgment (25:34). Though Matthew does not use the word "grace," he expresses the thought of unmerited and unearned reward with the word "inherit." The followers of Jesus inherit a land which they did not earn. In the final judgment scene none makes claim to reward for what they have done.

Meek and poor are synonymous terms referring to those who because of their degraded state dare make no claim on God. Jesus uses meek specif-ically of himself in 11:29, "I am meek and humble in heart." "In heart" modified his meekness as much as his humility. The meekness of the Third Beatitude refers to an internal condition of a person before God and known only to him. The invitation to come to him is offered by Jesus in his humility (11:29) and is shared with those who place themselves under that burden. In Jesus' inheriting the land, the promises made to Abraham finally come true. He shows that just as he is the *true* Moses and the *true* David, he is also the *true* Abraham.[17] For this reason and not simply because of lineal descent, which is no longer valid in the new kingdom (3:10), the evangelist calls Jesus the son of Abraham. Abraham received the promise of the land, but never took actual possession of it. Though rich before God, he was so poor in regard to possession of the land that he had to purchase from the Hittites a burial plot for Sarah from those who had legal title to it (Genesis 23). Now Jesus, as the true son of Abraham, takes full possession of the land for his followers. He appears as the final Joshua who has come into Canaan, a thought presented above in the discussion of his baptism.

THE FOURTH BEATITUDE

Hungering in the Fourth Beatitude, "Blessed are those who hunger and thirst after righteousness, for they shall be satisfied," refers not to a physical hungering, but to an internal longing of the soul in its relationship to God. In the first three beatitudes the evangelist has spoken of the individual's relation before God, and the hungering and thirsting should be understood in the same way. The background is Israel's sojourning in the wilderness where for both food and water they were completely dependent upon God. The hungering and thirsting suggest that a person's total existence is dependent for life upon something outside of him. This theme has already been introduced by the evangelist in the temptation of Jesus, where in Satan's desire that he should change stones into bread, he responds: "Man shall not live by bread alone, but by every word that proceeds from the mouth of God" (4:4). In the Fourth Beatitude the blessed long for something which only God can satisfy. Again the passive future form of the verb, they shall be satisfied or filled, points to something which God is going to accomplish eschatologically, though he has already begun to do it. Whereas Jesus says that man shall live by God's Word, the Fourth Beatitude states that the believer's hungering and thirsting for righteousness will be relieved by God. Taken together they comprise one meaning: man longs to hear the word of God's completed righteousness.

Of the seven appearances of the word "righteousness" in the gospel, five are found in the Sermon. In none of these places can the meaning of righteousness be the fulfillment of God's legal demands in the sense of the commandments. In Jesus we are dealing with a figure entirely different from the Teacher of Righteousness in the Qumran sect. Whereas the Teacher of Righteousness required his followers to keep all the commandments as interpreted by him, Jesus required that his disciples follow him.[18] By his baptism, Jesus responds to the Baptist's reluctance to baptize him. Jesus' ministry and life, beginning with his baptism, bring God's plans of righteousness to completion. "Thus it is fitting for us to fulfill all righteousness" (3:15). There is no reason to understand righteousness here in any other way than the Pauline sense of what God accomplishes for people in Christ.[19] We should not be bound to understand righteousness in terms of legal perfection, since the view that righteousness has to do with a legal fulfilling of the law has led interpreters to understand the Sermon in moralistic terms. By recognizing the similarity of the meaning of righteousness in Matthew and Paul, two insights emerge. First, Paul was not an unknown factor in Matthew's church, regardless of when this gospel is dated.[20] Second, it is not impossible that Paul was developing an Old Testament thought, expounded by Jesus, and his vocabulary was already part of the church's language.

Without Jesus' being baptized and being placed with sinners (3:14), God's plan of righteousness cannot be brought to completion. Those who hunger and thirst after righteousness desire nothing else than to receive God's righteousness now revealed in Christ.[21] The righteousness for which the blessed hunger and thirst is not adequately described simply as an ethic superior to that of the scribes and Pharisees (5:20), but one which is essentially of a different type; it is derived from God *alone*.

The concept of righteousness will be discussed again in its other appearances in the Sermon (5:20; 6:1, 33), but even in its use to describe the work of the Baptist, that he came "in the way of righteousness" (21:32), it does not refer to an ethical, moralistic type of righteousness, a fulfilling of commandments, but a proclamation of righteousness. The chief priests and the elders could not accept the preaching of John (21:23), but tax collectors and prostitutes could (21:32). The way of righteousness could not refer to ethics or morality without presenting a glaring contradiction. Even Matthew's use of the adjective "righteous" (or just) seems to correspond with this view of righteousness. Joseph and Jesus are called just men, that is, men whom God has found to be just or righteous, and not men who have made themselves righteous before God. Matthew's church has felt the influence of Paul. It was a church which already was understanding the terms "righteousness" and "righteous" according to Paul's distinctive usage. The proper sense for "righteousness" (justice) and "righteous" (just) as references to people whom God finds just and not those who make themselves righteous before God goes back to the Old Testament, and therefore it is not surprising that the Sermon should use it in what is considered a Pauline sense.

If the follower of Jesus longs for this imputed righteousness from God, the evangelist portrays Jesus himself as the one who first longs for righteousness as the Lamb of God who has taken upon himself the sins of the world (John 1:29). He is against those who are righteous in themselves and who oppose the manifestation of God's righteousness in him. His desire to be baptized by John to fulfill all righteousness is his own hunger and thirsting after God's plan of salvation so that through and in him it can be brought to completion.

THE FIFTH BEATITUDE

Whereas the first four beatitudes describe the blessed as under stress and suffering, the next three beatitudes, the Fifth through the Seventh, omit these themes. Mercy is a divine quality which God exercises over those who are in his debt.[22] It is expressed in the Lord's Prayer, where those who are forgiven by God respond by releasing those who are obligated to them (6:12). The explanation following the prayer also expresses that God expects a forgiving attitude from those whom he has forgiven (6:14–15). The matter is taken up later in the parable of the unforgiving servant (18:32–34) with the concluding warning of Jesus, "So also my heavenly Father will do to every one of you, if you do not forgive your brother from your heart" (35). The Fifth Beatitude is presented positively without any reference or threat to those who will not forgive.

While in the Old Testament mercy describes Israel's God who, without limitation, forgives his erring people and always restores them to their former fortunes and status as his own people, in the New Testament mercy finds its purest expression in Jesus. He answers the cries for mercy from the blind men (9:27), Canaanite woman (15:27), and the father of an epileptic son (17:5). His gospel proclaims that in him God has forgiven and is having mercy on all. The question remains that if the beatitude applies to Jesus, how is it that he also receives mercy? His cry from the cross to God that he has been forsaken is a plea for mercy. The crowd believes that he is asking for deliverance though they understand "Eli," God's name, as a request to Elijah (27:49). The account of the resurrection is the story of God's having mercy on the one who had mercy on all men. "Blessed are the merciful, for they shall obtain mercy" describes the community of Jesus as a forgiving one.[23]

THE SIXTH BEATITUDE

Though it is tempting to understand the Sixth Beatitude as a plea for moral or ethical purity, its meaning is of another, higher dimension. The attention here is not on the outward behavior in the sense of the Pharisees who perform their righteousness before men, but on the inward condition, which is known only to God (6:1). The pure or clean in heart are those whose existences are totally committed to God without any ulterior motives or thought of personal benefit. As one commentator says, this beatitude "speaks of total integrity, without dissimulation, totally committed to God."[24]

The seeing of God is reserved for Moses in the Old Testament (Deuteronomy 34:10), and Matthew claims that only the Son knows the Father (11:27). The Fourth Gospel may be reflecting on this Beatitude in saying that the only begotten Son (God) has seen God (1:18). The seeing of God in the Sixth Beatitude is reserved as an eschatological reward for the person who has committed himself without deviation to God.[25] What is impossible for man by himself (such as purity of heart) becomes possible for him as he is in Jesus. The qualities of Jesus become those of the followers of Jesus. The plural forms of the Beatitudes have their own theology! Only Jesus sees God directly and as the Son he knows the Father immediately, but he gives the revelation of God and the Father to whomever he wills (11:27). This revelation is not theophanic, a glorious appearing of God, but a revelation of God seen in the humility of Jesus. The Fourth Gospel provides this commentary on this beatitude in the reply of Jesus to Philip: "He who has seen me has seen the Father" (14:9). The Messiah remains one with his people, as the evangelist has explained the name Immanuel, and the christological perogatives become theirs. They see God.

THE SEVENTH BEATITUDE

In Isaiah 9:5–6, part of a pericope which Matthew has used in placing the ministry of Jesus in Galilee (4:15–16), the messianic child is called the Prince of Peace. The peace described in Isaiah 9 is supernatural and not earthly. In Zechariah 9:9–10, which Matthew uses to usher Jesus into Jerusalem (21:5), God's deliverer commands that peace be proclaimed to the Gentiles. This Beatitude is the only place in the New Testament where the word peacemaker is used, but Paul uses its verbal form in Colossians 1:20 of Christ's work in reconciling all things in heaven and earth to himself. The title of peacemaker is clearly a redemptive term applicable to God's Messiah as the Reconciler. The christological intent of this Beatitude is furthered by the peacemakers being called the sons of God.

Since Matthew is circumspect in applying such an overtly divine title as the Son of God to Jesus, (only eight times in his gospel), it is amazing that he uses the title here in the plural form: sons of God.[26] No other evangelist does this. Three times Son of God is used by Satan to refer to Jesus (4:3, 4) and once by the demons (8:29), by the disciples (14:33), by the crowds who taunt him (27:40–43). The Fourth Gospel will call Christians children of God (*tekna*; 1:12), but not sons of God.

How can this Beatitude, with its future tense, be applied to Jesus? For the evangelist Jesus *is being revealed* as the Son of God through a series of events beginning with his being called from Egypt (2:15) and including his baptism (3:17) and transfiguration (17:5). God has demonstrated that Jesus is his Son by what he has done. In the role of peacemaker, the atoner, Jesus gives the clearest indication of his special relationship with God. In this task he really shows who he is and what he has done. His resurrection is God's final confirmation of his identity. Paul says that through the resurrection God designated Jesus as his Son (Romans 1:4). While Matthew 11:27 speaks of a preexistent relationship of the Father and Son in terminology characteristic of the Fourth Gospel, the use of the word "sons" here in the Beatitudes, as well as "son" in the call from Egypt, the baptism, and the transfiguration puts the stress on Jesus as the Son *in a functional sense as one who shows that he is the Son by what he actually does.* The reader is to become convinced who Jesus is first by what he does. Function precedes essence. Matthew uses a similar argument in 23:31–32 where the Jews' desire to kill Jesus is proof positive that they are the sons of those who killed the prophets. Their murderous desires serve only to confirm that they are sons of murderers. The fourth gospel uses a similar argument where the Jews' desire to kill Jesus is seen as proof that they could hardly be the children of Abraham who had no desire to kill him. Jesus' Sonship is evident in his making peace and reconciling all things (Matthew 20:28).

Then in what sense can the plural "peacemakers" be explained? It means that the followers of Jesus become in him God's instrument of reconciliation with the world.[27] Again, this beatitude is preparatory for the Lord's Prayer, where the follower of Jesus forgives as he has been forgiven. The Christian is not only committed to preach the message of God's reconciliation but must in fact be reconciled to all. Again we are at the heart of the Sermon on the Mount and the evangelist's message. Reconciliation is the theme of not taking retaliation for evil done and of doing all in one's power to bring about peace with the offended brother (5:21–26; 38–48; 6:14–15). On this account Paul can call his message one of reconciliation.

THE EIGHTH BEATITUDE

The Eighth Beatitude is pivotal, as it reaches back to the First with its repetition of the phrase the kingdom of the heavens and it prepares for the Ninth Beatitude by speaking of persecution. The poor in spirit of the First Beatitude are defined more precisely as those who are persecuted for righteousness' sake in the Eighth Beatitude. Matthew has introduced the theme of persecution into his gospel as early as the birth narratives, where Herod seeks out the life of the child Jesus (2:20). Jesus is for the evangelist the Righteous One (27:19) and it is precisely because of this righteousness that he is persecuted and eventually put to death. The mark of the true disciple is that he like Jesus becomes a target of the world's hatred and for the same reason.

In the second discourse (the establishment of the apostolic office; 10:16–39), and in the third discourse (the parables), the topic of persecution is discussed further by the evangelist. The seeds which fall on the rock are those which fall away on account of persecution (13:21). The task of understanding the Eighth Beatitude as applying to both Jesus and his followers in a double sense is made somewhat easier, as the Ninth Beatitude explicitly makes the connection. While the First Beatitude dealing with an inward poverty towards God speaks of a hidden condition, the Eighth Beatitude speaks about the blessed as those who are receiving hostile activity.[28] The poverty of the spirit is neither visible nor tangible, but the persecution does serve as a kind of sacramental mark for the inward poverty of the spirit. It is the mark of God's activity in the world. The Eighth Beatitude, "Blessed are those who are persecuted for righteousness' sake, for theirs is the kingdom of the heavens" easily applies to Jesus who in his persecution even to death reveals God's salvific working among people. As persecution is a central theme of the entire gospel, it is appropriate that the Ninth Beatitude is made to serve by the evangelist as a commentary on the Eighth Beatitude.

THE NINTH BEATITUDE

The final beatitude is markedly different from the previous eight. The indefinite *they* of the first eight is now replaced with a clear distinction between *you* and *me*, that is, between the disciple and Jesus. The disciples are going to be persecuted on account of Christ, a theme which reappears in 10:17–18. The "on account of me" is rich in christological content, as it connects the Beatitudes with the person of Christ.[29] The first eight beatitudes describe the blessed by either a condition (poor), an activity which they do (peacemakers), or as recipients of an action (persecuted). The Ninth Beatitude introduces another group of persons known by their being reviled, persecuted and identified as targets of evil speaking. Those who revile, persecute, and speak evil are in league with Satan and are the enemies of the blessed, including Jesus. In this subtle way the evangelist refers back to the God and Satan controversy which has been introduced explicitly into the gospel in the temptation account. The disciple of Jesus will be like him in being Satan's target.

The cause of the believer's difficulty is Jesus, for whose sake they are persecuted. The cause of their persecution is identified by the evangelist in the second discourse as the preaching and confessing of him (Matthew 10:32–33). Followers of Jesus are accused of being in league with Satan. In the first eight beatitudes a promise is made to the blessed; the Ninth Beatitude is followed by a command. "Rejoice and be glad, for your reward is great in the heavens, for so men persecuted the prophets which were before you" (5:12). The persecutors do not understand Jesus' message and hence did not believe the prophets. The persecution that the believers are undergoing is diametrically opposed in its outward appearance to what God will eventually do for them. The miseries of the current persecution give no hint of their favored position with God. Though the thought of reward in the Ninth Beatitude is clearly in the future, it is already a reality in the heavens. "In the heavens" is Matthew's reference to the presence of God. For proof of God's favorable attitude to them in spite of the persecutions, they are asked to recall the plight of the prophets. In several other places Matthew mentions them as having been persecuted (23:35). The evangelist's church is a persecuted one.

There is no suggestion that the disciples suffered before the crucifixion of Jesus happened, though the predictions of their suffering (5:11; 10:38) precede the first announcement of his coming death (16:20). This is of course the editorial arrangement of the evangelist. Even if the Fourth Gospel mentions that the disciples after the resurrection were behind locked doors because of the fear of the Jews, Matthew offers no examples of their being persecuted, though he promises it will happen (10:17–22). Jesus' words are addressed to a persecuted church. The cross has now become a burden for the disciples (10:38). Christ's death, the Gospel's content, is now involving those who heard and believed his message in their own sufferings. In Matthew's church these words of Jesus took on more realistic meaning as they experienced their own persecutions.

The commands to rejoice and be exceedingly glad are directed by Matthew to people who had no obvious reason for joy. The first eight Beatitudes reminded these persecuted Christians of the example of Christ, who had endured affliction, a theme taken up explicitly in Hebrews 12:2–4. The Ninth Beatitude, which is directed specifically to them, points definitely to a reward, already present in heaven, and calls to their memory those who had undergone and endured similar situations.[30]

The phrase "for so men persecuted the prophets who were before you" may have been set down by the evangelist with double intent. While Jesus can use the example of the Old Testament prophets as those who endured the affliction, for the evangelist the word "prophet" could be used in the sense of those church leaders, particularly the preachers (Matthew 23:34), as they were called prophets in the early church (Acts 13:1). The church in Syria-Palestine, where Matthew probably wrote, already knew of the deaths of Stephen and James, the son of Zebedee (Acts 6; 12:2). A date after 70 would also allow for the death of James, the Lord's brother. The reader would first think of the Old Testament prophets and then of the church's prophets, some of whom were martyrs.

The Beatitudes in their portraying an abstract picture of the Messiah, that is, a Christology, along with the picture of the church, comprise the essence of the message of Jesus.[31] They must be considered some of the most mysteriously sublime literature of the entire New Testament. Certainly no other section brings us as close to the mind of God as revealed in the person of Jesus as do the Beatitudes. For the most part, the rest of the Sermon will be more of an ecclesiology, but always an ecclesiology which reflects a definite Christology. The church remains church only insofar as she reflects the suffering of Jesus.

NOTES

1 David Daube cites as a parallel a hymn to God from Rabbinic Judaism. *The New Testament and Rabbinic Judaism* (London: Athlone, 1956), 198. The first line, characteristic of the entire hymn, is "Blessed be he who spake and the world existed, blessed be he." Eduard Schweizer points out that beatitudes and blessings are found in the Old Testament, occurring chiefly in wisdom literature but also in the Psalms (84:5–6, 12; 128:1). *The Good News According to Matthew* (trans. David E. Green; Atlanta: Knox Press, 1975), 80ff. This would also support the view that the Beatitudes may have already been used as a hymn in the early church when Matthew was writing. For a literary analysis of the Beatitudes see Guelich, *The Sermon on the Mount* (Waco: Word, 1982), 66–68. Hans Dieter Betz, *Essays on the Sermon on the Mount* (trans. L. L. Welborn; Philadelphia: Fortress, 1985), 28, also notes the liturgical function of the Beatitudes.

2 Graham Stanton, "Matthew's Sermon on the Mount," 187.

3 Betz, *Essays on the Sermon on the Mount*, 23, sees the number of Beatitudes as a deliberate attempt to express perfection. William Farmer also sees the Beatitudes as a literary unit. "These verses seem to constitute a single literary unit." See his "From Oral Tradition to Written Tradition; A Source, Form-Critical, and Redactional Analysis of Matthew 5–7" (Dallas: Perkins School of Theology, n.d.), 93 (mimeographed).

4 Guelich, *Sermon on the Mount*, 66–67, Betz, *Essays on the Sermon on the Mount*, 23–25.

5 The value of James in understanding the Sermon cannot be underestimated. "But it is in the Epistle of James that the words of Jesus break through more often than in any other document outside the Synoptics, while at the same time they are subsumed under a single principle, the law of love." W. D. Davies, *The Setting of the Sermon on the Mount*, 402.

6 Betz, *Essays on the Sermon on the Mount*, 26–36. It is not as though some will receive the kingdom of the heavens because they have managed to be poor in spirit.

7 Stanton, "The Origin and Purpose," 188–89.

8 Guelich, *Sermon on the Mount*, excludes the Ninth Beatitude from the first eight.

9 Davies, *The Setting of the Sermon on the Mount*, argues that Matthew's "poor in spirit" and Isaiah's "poor" (61:1) and Luke's "poor" are equivalent, but Matthew's "in spirit" makes the meaning of "poor" more precise in a pointing to a religious and not an economic connotation. Betz, *Essays on the Sermon on the Mount*, 34, holds that the addition of the words "in spirit" is a deliberate attempt to nullify the idea that the economically poor are blessed.

10 David P. Scaer, *James the Apostle of Faith* (St. Louis: Concordia, 1984), 74–76.

11 Eduard Schweizer, *The Good News According to Matthew*, 68, says: "Only in the emotional transaction occurring between Jesus and his hearers do his words become true."

12 So Davies, *The Setting of the Sermon on the Mount*, 251. William R. Farmer, *Jesus and the Gospel* (Philadelphia: Fortress, 1982), 11–15, notes that no other gospel was so influenced by Isaiah as was Matthew.

13 For a discussion of poor in spirit, see also Guelich, *The Sermon on the Mount*, 67–75.

14 Guelich, *The Sermon on the Mount*, 78.

15 So the discussion in Betz, *Essays on the Sermon on the Mount*, 24.

16 Guelich, *Sermon on the Mount*, 81, points out that this mourning is not over sin but "refers to the disenfranchised, contrite, and bereaved" and thus this beatitude serves as a continuation of the first.

17 "In the language of Jesus, the word (meek, humble) can hardly be distinguished from 'poor,'" See Schweizer, *The Good News According to Matthew*, 89. Gundry points out that "poor" and "meek" go back to the same Hebrew word for "poor" (*nwm*). Bauer, *Structure*, 61, recognizes the christological significance of this beatitude: "Jesus declares that one of the characteristics of members in the eschatological community is 'meekness' (5.5), a term which Matthew connects 'humility' or 'lowliness' (11.29); apparently, these terms are at least generally synonymous for Matthew. Jesus demands lowliness of his followers in 18.3–4 and 23.12. But Matthew presents Jesus as the prime model of meekness and lowliness."

18 Davies, *The Setting of the Sermon on the Mount*, 213.

19 There is no need to follow Betz's suggestion that Matthew's church is anti-Pauline; see his *Essays on the Sermon on the Mount*, 20.

20 It is a thorny question to what extent Pauline influences can be detected in such an obviously Syro-Palestinian document as Matthew, a view held, for example, by Farmer (*Jesus and the Gospel*, 135). In a discussion on whether or not Paul knew of the empty tomb, W. L. Craig points out that the apostle was already in Jerusalem six years after the resurrection ("The Historicity of the Empty Tomb," *New Testament Studies* 31/1 [1985] 39–67). Thus the influence of Paul on Palestinian churches cannot be ruled out. In fact it seems probable, since he was not an infrequent visitor there and consulted with Peter, who plays a prominent part in Matthew's gospel.

21 Schweizer, *The Good News According to Matthew*, 53–56 and 91–92.

22 Guelich, *The Sermon on the Mount*, 104: "In other words, the merciful are those who demonstrate the God-like conduct of forgiving those in the wrong."

23 This Beatitude is also found in Luke 6:36 and in a briefer form in 1 Clement 13:2 and Polycarp 2:3. It is reflected in James 2:13. If the writer of Hebrews knew Matthew, then his reference to the mercy of Jesus (2:17) could indicate that this beatitude was interpreted christologically very early. See Schweizer, *The Good News According to Matthew*, 92.

24 Guelich, *The Sermon on the Mount*, 105.

25 Schweizer, *The Good News According to Matthew*, 93, rightfully speaks of the vision of God promised for the eschatological age, a vision which now angels enjoy. He fails, however, to see here the implicit christological reference.

26 Schweizer, *The Good News According to Matthew*, 94, calls attention to the great reserve with which the Bible, with the exception of Paul and John, refers to people as children or sons of God.

27 Guelich, *The Sermon on the Mount*, 92.

28 Guelich, *The Sermon on the Mount*, 93.

29 Stanton, "The Origin and Purpose," 187–88, uses the "on account of me" phrase to demonstrate that the five discourses are not only from the hand of Matthew, but are intimately related to the high Christology of the rest of the gospel.

30 Guelich, *The Sermon on the Mount*, 95, understands the reason for their joy is first their persecution and secondly their following in the prophets' footsteps.

31 Guelich, *The Sermon on the Mount*, 108, sums it up. "In brief, Matthew's Beatitudes are a declaration of the present and future aspects of the Kingdom of Heaven in the ministry of Jesus."

4

THE PRESENCE OF CHRIST
IN HIS CHURCH

MATTHEW 5:13–16

The sayings on salt and light are parallel to each other. Earth here refers to the world, not to Canaan (as in Matthew 5:5). Davies notes that the language points to the universal character of the disciples' task,[1] a theme that will reach its climax in the gospel's conclusion to make disciples out of the nations (28:19). The followers of Jesus are called the salt of the earth and the light of the world. In the ancient world salt was used not only for taste, but also as a preservative. This logion addresses the church's redemptive importance for the world, followed by a threat if that redemptive function is not carried out.

It stands in sharp contrast to Matthew's introduction of the person of Jesus in his gospel, through selected episodes and the Beatitudes. The focus is now shifted from Jesus to the disciples. The indefinite subject of the first eight Beatitudes comes to definition (after the Ninth Beatitude) as the hearers begin to recognize themselves as the objects of persecution. "You are the salt of the earth" takes the attention further away from Jesus and places the responsibility for the world on the disciples. The reference here is to the believers and not the crowds. The disciples continue in Jesus' place as God's redemptive agents in the world. The saying on salt thus anticipates the commission to make disciples out of the Gentiles given by Jesus, yet carried out by the Eleven. Through the disciples' preaching of the words of Jesus, the world will be preserved and saved from God's impending judgment.

While it cannot be known for certain why salt was chosen as a metaphor to explain the disciple's relationship to the world, salt is a substance known by its function. The question "how can salt be salted?" stresses salt's function. The disciple's function is to proclaim the message of Jesus. Unless he performs this function, he is no longer a disciple. The salt, that is, the disciple, has become foolish; this is what the original words of Matthew suggest. This may well have a deeper meaning, since Matthew uses the word "fool" of those who are aware of Jesus' message but have not taken the action it requires.[2] The man who hears the words of Jesus but ignores them (7:26) and the five virgins who are not prepared for the bridegroom (25:2) are called fools. Salt which has become foolish represents those disciples who refuse to act according to the purpose for which they were created, to preach the message of Jesus. The evangelist also has a theological purpose in saying that the salt is trodden underfoot, not disposed of as common garbage. The fate of the salt being thrown out and being trampled underfoot by men is the threat of eschatological punishment. Being thrown out is the fate of the Jews who are thrown out of the kingdom for not believing when the Gentiles do (8:12). The trampling underfoot by men resembles 6:7, where the swine turn on those who have thrown the pearls before them. Jesus is using very stern language to say that the person who does not carry out the kingdom requirements, which have become his through incorporation into Jesus, shall not escape the final judgment. This theme is repeated at the Sermon's conclusion in the parable of the house built on sand (7:24–26) and in the judgment scene, where those who failed to see Jesus in his brothers are thrown out of his presence (25:46).[3]

Luke has a slightly different version of the salt logion, which he puts not in his rendition of the Sermon but after the stories of the tower builder and one king assessing another king's forces (14:28–33). This theme of renunciation, understood in taking up one's cross (27), agrees substantially with Matthew's theme, which places the reference to the disciples as salt right after the prediction of Jesus that they will be persecuted like the prophets. Luke differs not in the persecution theme, but in the awareness of the commitment which the candidate for discipleship is making. Mark's version of the salt parable seems to be placed in the midst of a real, historic situation of persecution that may have existed at Rome. "For every one will be salted with *fire* and every *sacrifice* will be salted with salt. Salt is good; but if the salt has lost its saltiness, how will you season it? Have salt in yourselves, and be at peace with one another" (9:49–50). Mark, by describing the persecution with the words *fire* and *sacrifice*, closely resembles Matthew in referring to a real persecution. Luke stresses what Christians will have to do rather than what will happen to them. While Matthew points to general persecution, Mark's reference to the salting by fire could refer to the specific historical situation of Christians being put to death by fire as burning lamps under Nero in the Coliseum in Rome. Believers

were actually being *sacrificed* with and *for* Christ, a thought developed by
Paul (Romans 12:1; Galatians 6:17). The persecution promised by Jesus
in the Sermon has realized itself in fiery death for those in Rome. Mark's
strange command to have salt among yourselves may be the command
for Christians to encourage each other with their examples of martyrdom.[4]

No eschatological threat is connected with the disciples being the light
of the world. The theme of Jesus as the light of the world is developed in
the Fourth Gospel at some length, where he makes the claim explicitly that
he is the light (8:12; 9:5; 12:46). There is some indication that John's development of the theme may be dependent on Matthew's introduction of
Jesus as the light for those in darkness. Just before the evangelist introduces the work of Jesus with a title-like sentence in 4:17, that he began to
preach the kingdom, he uses Isaiah 9:2, where the people sitting in darkness see the great light; the light has arisen on those who have been seated in the shadow of death. Immediately after this, the evangelist says that
Jesus began to preach.[5] For the evangelist the preaching of Jesus is the
light's rising. John in his prologue with its reference to the light shining in
a dark place (1:5) could be dependent directly on Matthew's introduction.
Whereas Matthew stresses Jesus and his preaching as the light, John pin-
points the light concept more directly on his person. This difference is
more apparent than real, since John uses the works of Jesus to show that
he is the light. Jesus can no more be separated from his works than the disciple can be from his. Matthew has in fact already identified Jesus as the
light in his preaching of the good news which removes the darkness of
man's plight under Satan.

Jesus' description of his disciples, "You are the light of the world,"
expresses their relationship to him and their function to preach his message. The church's function as a light is explained by the illustrations of the
city on a hill and the putting of lights on lampstands. The city on the hill
is probably a reference to Jerusalem, a fortress city.[6] Though its location
contributes to its unassailability, its location is seen by everyone. Even on
a dark night it is silhouetted against the sky and it can be seen for miles
around. The background for this saying may be the imagery of God's people as Zion, that Davidic fortress which is high above everything else. The
church by its nature is recognizable; as Jesus says, "it cannot be hid." The
second illustration of light speaks of placing a light not on a lampstand but
under a bushel. It is not unlike the illustration of the salt losing its flavor.
The light hidden under the bushel can no longer carry out its purpose. For

practical purposes the light is no longer light. Hiding the light is as absurd as salt losing its saltiness. Jesus here puts forth no threat that the light will be put out or taken away as with the seven churches in the Book of Revelation (1:20), but requires that the light should be put on a lampstand to light the entire house, a reference most likely to the world. The word for lampstands is used in Revelation 1:20 for the churches. The lampstand can be taken away. *The church failing to carry out its purpose of preaching Jesus will no longer be church.*

The word *oikos* for house is used elsewhere in the New Testament for church; but in Matthew's language it can refer to the world. A usual Greek word for world, *oikoumene*, is related to the word for house, *oikos*. Luke substitutes bed for bushel as the place where men do not put light, but he maintains the parabolic concept of light. The light on the lampstand which lights the whole house is the church's preaching of the Gospel in the world. The sermon's "all in the house" prepares for the gospel's conclusion of making disciples out of "all Gentiles (nations)." The preaching function is suggested in 4:16–17. Such an interpretation would also fit the immediately following verse (5:16), which closes this section with the request that the disciples should let their light shine.[7]

The concluding verse of this pericope, "Thus let your light so shine before men, that they may see your good works and glorify your Father who is in heaven," flows out of the previous section as referring to what Christians do by nature. It should not be seen as a command or threat and should not be interpreted within Paul's concept of faith vs. works (as if Matthew is offering a theology of works in contrast with Paul's theology of grace). When the message of Jesus is proclaimed by the church, the works will be seen flowing from the preaching. Works here cannot be taken to refer to mere moral or ethical behavior, as this is constantly scored throughout the gospel by Jesus as unacceptable among the Pharisees. The good works which men see are the works of mercy which Jesus also did among the people. These works, suggested in the Beatitudes, are works of those who are merciful and serve as peacemakers among men. These works thus bring the reality of the redemption into the world. The works that serve the church's preaching of the Gospel are the church withstanding persecution and exercising love to all people. The followers of Jesus stand in his place in the world.[8] When the church suffers, she exemplifies Christ's suffering which she preaches.[9] This does not mean that morality is a matter of indifference, as Jesus reserves some of his most severe words for immorality. Simple ethical morality, however, does not begin to approximate what the evangelist intends by the words "good works." What impresses the world in distinction to Judaism, as Davies points out, is the higher righteousness of the Christian community.[10]

This is the only place where the evangelist speaks about glorifying the Father, more expressly "your Father." In other places after the performance of miracles the crowds are said to glorify the God of Israel (9:8; 15:31). In these citations there is no suggestion that the crowds have recognized who Jesus is, but only that God has accomplished something extraordinary. They can come no further than recognizing that God is operative in some special way in Jesus, and can come to no conclusion on who he really is and what is his real relationship to God. "Glorifying your Father," on the contrary, suggests belief. The one who hears the message of the followers of Jesus and sees their works of mercy will understand that God has established a special relationship with the followers of Jesus so that now Jesus is recognized and acknowledged as God.[11]

NOTES

1 *The Setting of the Sermon on the Mount* (rpt; Atlanta: Scholars, 1989), 249. See also Robert A. Guelich, *The Sermon on the Mount* (Waco: Word, 1982), 121. How salt loses its saltiness is unimportant. But when or if it does, it is no longer salt. When it no longer carries out the function for its existence, it has lost it and must be disposed of. The disciple of Jesus faces the same either-or situation.

2 Guelich, *The Sermon on the Mount*, 121, favorably mentions Joachim Jeremias' position that the use of the word foolish suggests that the disciple should take his role seriously.

3 Just how salt loses its saltiness might at first glance have a note of absurdness or impossibility about it. Jesus may have exaggerated in the style of the rabbis. According to Guelich, *The Sermon on the Mount*, 121, Rabbi Josua B. Chanaja (ca. 90) noted the nonsense of the phrase. If this is a direct reference to the Sermon on the Mount, it would point to a relatively early date for the Gospel of Matthew and its circulation in a Jewish community that was separate from the church. Robert H. Gundry offers three possibilities for the loss of saltiness: 1) fraudulent adulteration of the salt; 2) dissolving away of the sodium chloride; and 3) masking the taste of the salt with gypsum; see his *Matthew: A Commentary on his Literary and Theological Art* (Grand Rapids: Eerdmans, 1982), 75–76.

4 Agreement is lacking in both the textual evidence and the interpretations of this salt and fire passage in Mark. Where some see it as a reference to internal purification, others see it as a reference to preservation in hell. See C. S. Mann, *Mark*, Anchor Bible (Garden City, N.Y.: Doubleday, 1986), 383. The textual variants indicate that from the first the scribes attempted to relieve the difficulty of interpretation by additions. One school of variants offers this additional phrase "and every sacrifice will be salted with salt." Just how one is to take this phrase is hardly obvious. The introduction of the word "sacrifice" may indicate that the copyist

understood the salt and fire passage as a reference to an actual martyrdom in
Rome. It could also suggest that participation in the Christian liturgy had resulted
in the persecution of the most hideous kind. Lighted Christians were actually living sacrifices!

5 Stanton, "Matthew's Sermon on the Mount," 188. Guelich, *The Sermon on the
   Mount*, 122.

6 Guelich, *The Sermon on the Mount*, 122; also Eduard Schweizer, *The Good News
   According to Matthew* (trans. David E. Green; Atlanta: Knox, 1975), 99. In one
   papyrus and the Gospel of Thomas, the city on the hill was extended to include
   the community of Jesus.

7 Schweizer, *The Good News According to Matthew*, 102, astutely points out that it is
   not the disciples who are to shine, but the Father who is to shine through them.
   The lampstand refers to the preaching of Jesus. Instead of Matthew's having the
   light shine on all who are in the house, Luke renders this saying that "those who
   enter may see the light (11:33)." Gundry, *Matthew: A Commentary*, 123, notes two
   things about Luke: 1) the Palestinian house was generally one room and thus it
   seems that Luke's house had a vestibule, and 2) people slept on the floor, and thus
   Luke's reference to putting the light under the bed (and not the under the bushel)
   is problematic at first glance.

   Comparing Matthew and Luke at this point can divulge the motives of each.
   Matthew's "the whole house" anticipates the Gospel's being preached in all the
   world (28:19–20). Luke's reference to those coming in are to the Gentiles who see
   and come to the light (2:32). Matthew's bushel is the more awkard and suggests
   an older form of the saying. Luke's house where the light is hid points to a situation outside of Palestine where people did not sleep on the floor. Davies, *The
   Setting of the Sermon on the Mount*, 249, also sees the house in Matthew's Sermon
   as a reference to the world and the universal obligation of the disciples.

8 Schweizer, *The Good News According to Matthew*, 103.

9 Guelich, *The Sermon on the Mount*, 124–25, rightly shows that the evangelist is not
   intending to put a higher value on deeds than words.

10 Guelich, *The Sermon on the Mount*, 196. Davies points out that this phrase is not
   directed against Gnosticism which replaced actual deeds with words, but to the
   Jewish community surrounding the Christian one.

11 The disciple is the agent of God, since through his deeds God and not the disciple
   is glorified, Guelich, *The Sermon on the Mount*, 125.

5

OLD TESTAMENT AS AUTHORITY FULFILLED IN JESUS

MATTHEW 5:17–20

This section is without parallel in the other two synoptic gospels, except the reference to the impossibility of the passing away of the Old Testament revelation, which is placed by Luke in the context of John the Baptist, who is named as the last of the prophets (16:17). Matthew's pericope should be taken as Jesus' own explanation of his ministry in relationship to the Old Testament. The new understanding of the Old Testament is its *fulfillment* in Jesus; the obligation of the disciples is not to the Old Testament as a separate, independent revelation but to its message now fulfilled or completed in Jesus. The last verse of the pericope, v. 20, refers to the content of the message, now fulfilled in Jesus, as the new righteousness, that is, the righteousness which is superior to that of the scribes and Pharisees.

There is no suggestion that Matthew's church was on the verge of antinomianism, a more characteristic sin among Gentile Christians.[1] His church may have had to address the question of what role the Jewish Scriptures, that is, the Law and the Prophets, had to play in the Jewish Christian synagogues. Alongside the reading of the Old Testament Scriptures, here referred to as the Law and the Prophets, the deeds and words of Jesus were being recited in their services before the gospel was written. This may have given the suggestion to some that the older written revelation of the Old Testament was no longer valid. In fact these early Christian communities might have been aware of the evangelist's writing a new "Bible" (*biblos*; Matthew 1:11) and could have come to the conclusion that the older written revelation had lost its purpose. The reverse may have also been true. The words of Jesus may not have been given the same force as those of the Old Testament. The improper relationship between the testaments found its classicial expression in Marcionism which devalued the older revelation and Ebionism which could not go beyond seeing

Jesus as a prophet. In any event, the evangelist was addressing the issue of the authority of the older written revelation in the church. It was not simply a matter of having 'old' and 'new' testaments and putting the proper value on each, but more importantly seeing the Old Testament coming to a conclusion in Jesus so that the church could have a 'new testament.' The Old Testament would still have validity in the church, but no longer as an autonomous source. The coming of Jesus would not allow for this. It was in the sense of this new understanding that the early church fathers understood this passage against Marcion.

For Matthew the Old Testament has undergone a fundamental change with the coming of Jesus. The problem was not the danger of adding anything to the written revelation, but that of removing part of it; "not an iota, not a dot, will pass from the law until all is accomplished" (5:18). The fundamental change brought about in the written revelation is achieved by Jesus who fulfills it. In the Easter narratives Luke twice makes the point that the entire written revelation of the prophets deals with Jesus (24:26, 27, 44). In contrast to Luke, who places the specific fulfillment idea in detail at his gospel's end, Matthew throughout his gospel presents Jesus as the one whose birth, childhood, miracles, preaching, death, and burial fulfill certain Old Testament requirements.[2] There is no summary conclusion of the fulfillment idea in Matthew as Luke has it. Luke in his prologue refers to a document or documents which make references to the events of Jesus' life as fulfillment. Matthew's gospel is exactly this kind of document. More than the other gospels it showed step by step that what Jesus said and did had been predicted by the prophets.

For Matthew, the entire written revelation has undergone a fundamental change with the coming of Jesus; the Law is fulfilled, but in such a way that all of its words and letters stay in place. The fulfilled Law, that is, the Torah now completed in Jesus, has assumed the new form of Matthew's written gospel. For this reason he calls his gospel a *biblos* (5:19). The warning about breaking or relaxing the least of the commandments should be taken not as a reference to the binding nature of the Old Testament's laws, whether they are moral or ritualistic, but as an admonition to take seriously the words of Jesus, which in Matthew's gospel had become fulfilled Scripture. The Greek word for commandments (*entolai*) refers not to a law in the sense of prohibition and threat, but to any divine word, now written, regardless of its content. The Gospel is commandment (*entolē*) because of its origin with God, not in the sense of forbidding or demanding something from the hearer. A disservice is done to the Sermon when the Law-

Gospel paradigm is superimposed in its interpretation of the words law and commandments. Though it is recognized that Marcion's distinction of seeing the older revelation as Law and the newer as Gospel is simplistic and wrong, it is difficult for some interpreters to free themselves from these categories. The end result is that the stern God of the Old Testament is replaced by a loving one in Jesus. For both exegetical and dogmatical reasons such a view must be challenged. The contrast is between the written word of Moses and God's living word in Jesus, not between Law and Gospel.

The warning about tampering with the commandments (*entolai*) applies to everything which Jesus has said[3] and in the context of Matthew's gospel to that gospel itself as written document. The reader of Matthew's gospel could come to no other possible conclusion. The warning about the failure to give full attention to the words of Jesus, with total sincerity, is parallel to the gospel's conclusion, where Jesus instructs the disciples to teach the Gentiles all things whatsoever he has commanded (28:19–20).

Jesus directs this part of the Sermon specifically to his disciples as the first teachers of the church and then to the teachers addressed by Matthew.[4] The warning is against those who fail to understand the commandments (Word) of Jesus and then proceed to teach this misunderstanding to others. Matthew is already operating with a canonical norm, a standard of orthodoxy for his church. This part of the Sermon is anticipated by James 3:1: "Let not many of you become teachers, my brethren, for you know that we who teach shall be judged with greater strictness." The James passage comes before the writing of Matthew's gospel and reflects the logion as it may have been used in oral form.[5] In neither James nor the Sermon is there the threat of a final judgment to damnation for the careless teacher, as there is in Matthew 7:21–23 and 25:41–46, which are universal in scope. There is the real danger of being called least in the kingdom of the heavens. In turn the one who does them and teaches them correctly shall be called great in the kingdom of the heavens. The Sermon distinguishes the teachers of the Sermon from its hearers, just as it from the beginning distinguishes between the disciples and the crowds.

Matthew's church already has a recognized group of leaders, known as teachers, stressing their role in preserving the gospel in its most primitive form as *didachē*. The church already has a structure. This gospel comes out of a similar situation to that of the Epistle of James, where these men were called teachers, a term commonly used in the New Testament for those now known as pastors or ministers. Other indications show that they were also called prophets in Matthew's church. The teaching function in Matthew involves both receiving the message in its form and passing it on without deviation. This warning about the iota and dot is contained in none of the other three canonical gospels. Matthew's gospel has a more "professional," clerical tone about it and points to itself as being a compendium of Christian doctrine for the preparation of not only catechumens but perhaps also the church's leaders in the second generation.[6]

This pericope concludes with the warning that unless the righteousness of the disciples exceeds that of the scribes and Pharisees they will not enter into the kingdom. In comparison with the teacher who lapses in one point, but still manages to share in Christ's work, the person without the righteousness higher than that of the scribes and Pharisees has no part in Jesus. For the person without the higher righteousness there is no chance of eschatological redemption! While Luther thought this was a preaching of Law with such severity and no possibility of accomplishing it that the believer would have to thrust himself on Christ, nothing here suggests this meaning. While this is a legitimate New Testament theme (e.g., Romans 3:20–26), Jesus is holding out to his followers a righteousness which does not originate with them, but is still not beyond their grasp. Jesus holds up the Pharisees as examples who fulfill all the Law's requirements and still are unacceptable to God. Paul also claims that if righteousness were by the Law, he as a Pharisee would have been the one who could be most assured of his salvation (Philippians 3:5–6). From the context of the Sermon, the higher righteousness here cannot mean a quantitatively superior righteousness in that the followers of Jesus are to do more of what the Pharisees are doing. Such a meaning would suggest that the followers of Jesus were simply to be better Pharisees.

The higher righteousness of this pericope, the one that exceeds that of the scribes and Pharisees, is not one that exceeds in quantity but quality.[7] In 5:37, "more" (*perisson*), a cognate of "exceeds" (*perisseuō*), is used. Here it is used as an activity motivated by Satan (Greek: the evil one) and must carry with it the idea of qualitative and not just quantitative differences. The righteousness required for the kingdom of the heavens is of a different and higher kind than that of the Pharisees.[8] The righteousness of God is revealed in Jesus, who accepts humankind's burden (3:15); it has already been proclaimed by the Baptist (21:32). For this righteousness the ones who are blessed long (5:6); it is known only to God (6:1). The person with a righteousness of works as exemplified in the scribes and Pharisees is forever excluded from participating in Jesus' work of salvation. That the evangelist here is speaking of the higher righteousness, the one that comes from God and is revealed in Jesus, is reinforced by the strong double negative in the Greek language (*ou mē*). Thus the meaning would be that the one who presumes on his own righteousness shall absolutely never share in what Christ has done. Since the higher righteousness is not one that reaffirms a more meticulous morality, but one which has its origins in God's work in Jesus, it could be logically expected that the next section 5:21–26, should be related to this.[9] It is!

NOTES

1 George Strecker understands Matthew's use of righteousness as strict ethical command, see *Der Weg der Gerechtigkeit* (Goettingen: Vandenhoeck & Ruprecht, 1962), 155.

2 For a discussion of a variety of understandings of fulfillment, see Robert H. Guelich, *The Sermon on the Mount* (Waco: Word, 1982), 138–43. He puts it well when he says, "Matthew's use of the Old Testament is foundational for his christology that perceived Jesus to be the Messiah Son of God who comes as the fulfillment of God's promise to his people for the end times. The evangelist is most concerned to demonstrate that Jesus stands in line with the prophetic promise of Scripture, but only as the ultimate fulfillment of that promised, the new, final chapter in God's redemptive plan for history" (142). This includes but certainly goes beyond matching New Testament texts with Old Testament ones.

3 This view is supported by Eduard Schweizer, *The Good News According to Matthew* (trans. David E. Green; Atlanta: Knox, 1975) and Ernst Lohmeyer, *Das Evangelium des Matthaeus* (Goettingen: Vandenhoeck & Ruprecht, 1962), 111.

4 Guelich, *The Sermon on the Mount*, 150, notes that in Matthew the verb "to teach" is ascribed of Jesus in all but two places (5:19 and 28:20).

5 The question of dating and the ordering of the New Testament books can never be settled to everyone's satisfaction. Note can be made of Gerhard Kittel's threefold distinction in citations. At the first level, the words of Jesus are cited without ascription to him. At the second, they are ascribed to him as in 1 Cor. 7. Finally in the church fathers an explicit ascription is made. With this scheme James would be the earliest. See his discussion in "Der Geschichtliche Ort des Jakobus briefes," *Zeitschrift für die neutestamentliche Wissenschaft* 41 (1942): 71–105. This is a helpful distinction only if for example James 2:8 does not contain a reference to Jesus as the speaker of this words. See David P. Scaer, *James, the Apostle of Faith* (Saint Louis: Concordia, 1984), 81–82.

6 Aloys Grillmeier properly calls Matthew "the Book of the Church," *Christ in Christian Tradition* (trans. John Bowden; Atlanta: Knox Press, 1975), 11.

7 William Farmer, "The Sermon on the Mount: A Form-Critical and Redactional Analysis of Matthew 5:1–7:29," *SBL Seminar Papers* 25 (Atlanta: Scholars Press, 1986), 68. Farmer notes "Taken as an original saying of Jesus the import of v. 20 would be to emphasize that the righteousness of the Scribes and Pharisees must be exceeded in a qualitative sense, such as is suggested in the antitheses which follow. Or if we disallow the exegetical claims that 5:21–48 may have on the inter-

pretation of v. 20 because of their proximity to it, and view this saying against the background of Matthew 23:23, the sense would be that our righteousness must exceed that of the Scribes and Pharisees in not neglecting the 'weightier matters of the Law,' 'justice, mercy and peace.' Still again, if this saying be viewed against the background of Luke 18:9–14, it would suggest that *the righteousness that exceeds that of the Pharisees is a gift of God that is appropriated by faith*" (emphasis added).

8 As mentioned in note 1, George Strecker supports the view that righteousness here refers to ethical demand. Supporting the view that righteousness is God's act in Jesus is Schweizer, *The Good News According to Matthew*, 109. Combining righteousness both as gift and corresponding conduct is Guelich, *The Sermon on the Mount*, 172. For a thorough study of the matter, see Cameron A. Mackenzie, "Matthew 5:17–20: Crossroads of Gospel" (S.T.M. Thesis, Concordia Theological Seminary, Fort Wayne, Ind., 1984). He agrees with Guelich in seeing both christological and ethical implications in righteousness.

9 W. D. Davies notes that Jesus comes not to destroy the law, but to bring it to its ultimate purpose; *The Setting of the Sermon on the Mount* (rpt; Atlanta: Scholars, 1989), 101–2.

6

NECESSITY OF RECONCILIATION

MATTHEW 5:21–26

To put this pericope into actual practice according to what it requires presents so many problems that it is no wonder that if Luke knew of it that he retained only the last two verses dealing with practicalities of reconciliation. How does one carry out reconciliation? The complexities involved in the Matthean version would give any interpreter good reason for avoiding them.[1] It is unlikely that the evangelist was laying down the procedures for a specific judicial proceeding, since the three 'crimes' of being angry with the brother and calling him *raca* and *fool* are hardly punishable offenses according to any known standards.[2] Certainly anger is not. The *Didache* omits references to these sins altogether.[3] The previous pericope spoke of the superior righteousness of God revealed in his redemptive reconciling work in Jesus. In regard to the new righteousness now brought in Jesus, simply refraining from murder does not meet God's requirements. The purpose here is not to transform the law's power from an external to an internal force in the life of the church. Israel's real sins were of the heart. The Old Testament was also directed to the condition of the people. Jesus goes beyond the external and ethical issue. He speaks of the universal sin of anger to introduce the atonement as the underlying principle for behavior in the community and to prepare his disciples for the universal preaching of the gospel.

The focus here is on the judicial proceedings that the one who murders must face. The one who is angry has equally great problems. Jesus' logion on forbidding anger is spoken from God's perspective. God sees the brother who is angry with another one and brings him to judgment. Though some have attempted, not without good reason, to see here an early church court proceeding,[4] what is going on is beyond the human level. Only God knows who is angry with his brother, and the offense of insulting someone else could hardly be carried out for each case in the courts, especially the Sanhedrin. No human court, even a religiously constituted one, would have the right to consign someone to hell, especially in matters of the heart. The evangelist has in view a supernatural tribunal over which God presides. *Raca*, which the RSV renders as "whoever insults," is a translation as good as any other. Since its exact meaning is not known, it is taken by some scholars to mean "empty-headed." "Fool" is used elsewhere by Matthew to mean someone who knows Jesus but remains ignorant or unaware of God's salvation accomplished in him.[5]

Both *raca* and fool are to be taken in a religious context. This is not to suggest that disciples have license to insult others within a secular, nonchurchly context, but the force of this logion is that a member of the Christian community dare not call a brother ignorant and take an unforgiving attitude toward him. Jesus is talking about a word of condemnation in the fellowship of the redeemed. The offender has deliberately labeled his brother as one who by nature is ignorant of what God is doing for salvation. Such a charge of ignorance is particularly serious in an early church community where a careful and frequently long period of instruction was required. The meaning therefore goes beyond merely insulting another person to that of condemning another follower of Jesus as being unaware of God's salvation. It comes close to making oneself the eschatological judge in discerning who is and who is not worthy of salvation, the position reserved for Jesus. The references to the court, the Sanhedrin (RSV: council), and hellfire point to no human judicial procedure—though the terms are taken from the world of jurisprudence—but to a divine process. It could be that Matthew's process refers first to the judgment at the time of the offense, second to the final judgment, and last to the consignment to hell.[6] This may be the pattern in Matthew 25:40–41. Determining exact referents here is not as important as knowing that this judgment is being carried out before and by God and that the end result is consignment to hellfire.

The purpose of this pericope is not to frighten the hearer into fear of God's severe law, but to impress upon him the necessity of making reconciliation in the community of Jesus with a grieved brother. Thus the center of the pericope is the command to make reconciliation with the brother, even if one is in the middle of performing his religious duties. The breaking of fellowship and restoration by reconciliation in the early church was done in the context of the eucharistic celebration (1 Corinthians 5:6–8).

The offense here is not simply a moral infraction. Such infractions are forgivable and must be forgiven according to the Lord's Prayer (6:12). What makes the offense totally intolerable is that one who is angry has taken to himself the prerogative that belongs to God alone. The phrase "without cause" does not belong to the original reading.[7] Even if there is a cause for anger, anger must be put aside among the followers of Jesus. There is *no* cause for anger. Though anger is the prerogative of God alone, in his work of reconciliation in Jesus he has set aside this anger. This makes the offense of anger even more repugnant. By becoming angry the one who claims to belong to Jesus and to know his mind takes an attitude diametrically opposed to God, who is no longer angry. The refusal to be reconciled is the sign that the person no longer belongs to Jesus and from God's point of view is no longer a member of the community. Here is where excommunication becomes operative. Though it may be difficult to demonstrate that Matthew here describes a process of removal from the early Christian community, it is true that the refusal to be reconciled identifies one as no longer belonging to Jesus and no longer his follower and a member of his community.

The heart of the pericope is that the one who is angry with his brother denounces his right to be angry and reconcile himself. The word for "reconciliation" belongs to a family of words used elsewhere in the New Testament for God's reconciling activity in Jesus Christ (2 Corinthians 5:10; Romans 5:10). The reconciliation between brothers and followers in the community of Jesus reflects the higher reconciliation that God has made with all people, a theme taken up elsewhere in the Sermon (6:45). The reconciliation among brothers is the *sine qua non*, without which the church no longer exists as church. Reconciliation is the higher righteousness.[8]

But what religious responsibilities were interrupted to carry out his reconciliation? At first glance, Jesus is referring to the carrying out of the sacrifices on the altar in the Jerusalem temple, as there is no other place where sacrifices could be offered up. Yet such an interpretation hardly squares with Jesus' lack of interest in Jerusalem and its temple, both of which have only temporal significance and are destined for destruction. While Luke has favorable uses for Jerusalem and the temple, Matthew does not.

Here and elsewhere in the Sermon, however, there are indications that the evangelist is directing these words to procedures which were taking place within the congregation at the time of his writing. The *Didache*, a near contemporary of Matthew, contains a strikingly similar parallel.

> And on the Lord's own day gather yourselves together and break bread and give thanks, confess your transgressions, that your sacrifice may be pure. And let no man, having his dispute with his fellow, join your assembly until they have been reconciled, that your sacrifice may not be defiled (14:2).

Matthew's procedures, as those of the *Didache*, require reconciliation among the members of the community before completing the act of worship. Matthew's word is "gift" (*dōron*); the *Didache* has "sacrifice" (*thysia*), in the context of the breaking of the bread and the giving of thanks—a reference to the Lord's Supper. In addition, the *Didache's* word for "sacrifice" (*thysia*) is related to Matthew's word for "altar" (*thysiastērion*), the place where the gift is sacrificed. The *Didache's* reference to a eucharistic setting may point the way to a similar understanding of the Sermon at this point. If Matthew 5:23–24 was not understood eucharistically at the time of the gospel's writing, its language soon was used for this purpose. If the *Didache* and Matthew were contemporary or drawing from the same source, it would be difficult not to understand this section in Matthew as eucharistic. Matthew's church would understand the references to the altar, the gift, and the reconciliation as descriptive of their own eucharistic situation. Further help is offered by 1 Corinthians 10:18–20 where such terms as sacrifices, altars, and Communion, applied to the Sacrament, support the view that used together they form a constellation of eucharistic language, already familiar to the early Christians.

The sayings on reconciliation and punishment (25–26) reinforce the seriousness of the matter, just as the threat about failing to attain the higher righteousness did at the conclusion of the previous pericope (20). The accuser is the brother within the community to whom reconciliation is refused or who remains alienated. Again, this is not a reference to a human judicial procedure. This is not a trial whereby guilt is determined (22), but a description of the execution of the penalty necessitated by a preceding trial. He is put in the hands of the judge, the guard, and finally he is put into prison until he should "pay the last penny."

The penalty of imprisonment resembles that given the unforgiving steward, who is confined until he pays his total debt (Matthew 18:21–32). When the indebted steward in the parable is ordered to be sold into slavery so that the master can retrieve his money, he asks for and receives the master's mercy. When the master learns that he has not forgiven the small debt of a fellow servant, he orders the steward to be handed over to the jailers until he should pay the entire debt. In the Sermon the one who refuses reconciliation must pay to the last penny. The parable reinforces the Sermon on the necessity of forgiveness. The word for "debt" is the same that is used in the Lord's Prayer, "And forgive us our debts, as we forgive those who are in debt to us" (6:12). While 5:26 uses the word for penny or farthing and 18:34 uses the more general term for debt, both pericopes place the victim in a financially impossible situation from which he can never extricate himself.[10] The failure to reconcile is the refusal to forgive. The one who does not have the higher righteousness, the righteousness of reconciliation, which forgives, will absolutely never enter the kingdom (5:20) and the one who refuses to be reconciled will remain in prison until he pays the last penny. The pericope in the Sermon of requiring reconciliation and then failing to seek it makes no mention of how the indebtedness was acquired. The Sermon's saying is filled out and further explained not only by the Lord's Prayer but by the parable of the unforgiving steward. The concept of debt owed and debt paid reaches its culmination in the words of Jesus that he came to serve by offering his life as a ransom for many (20:28), i.e., the community. Refusing to forgive another member of the community becomes more onerous, since the community has its origin in the redemption of Jesus whose death remains its constitutive authority.[11]

NOTES

1 Luke 12:57–59 parallels Matthew 5:25–26.

2 Guelich mentions that some commentators take "Sanhedrin" to be a reference to an early church council of elders with judicial powers. Though the word is sometimes used of a council of elders (Irenaeus), there is no reference to such rigorous discipline being carried out; see his *Sermon on the Mount* (Waco: Word, 1982), 186–187. Gundry, while holding that this lays down no pattern for civil cases, sees such sins as punishable within the brotherhood of disciples; *Matthew: A Commentary on his Literary and Theological Art* (Grand Rapids: Eerdmans, 1982), 85. The exclusion of this material in Luke and the *Didache* points to their authors' awareness of the possible danger of misapplying such procedures in a church situation of discipline. If Luke's church or the community around the *Didache* had known of such church trials, they would have probably included Matthew's materials.

3 *Didache* 2:1–5; 14:2; 15:3.

4 Gundry, *Matthew: A Commentary*, 84, Guelich, *Sermon on the Mount*, 186. See n. 2.

5 Gundry, *Matthew: A Commentary*, 84–85. Massaux notes that Justin Martyr abbreviates Matt. 5:22, eliminating the words "brother," "*Raca*," and "Sanhedrin." He keeps the word "fire," but not "Gehenna"; Edouard Massaux, *The Influence of the Gospel of Saint Matthew on Christian Literature before Saint Irenaeus*, 3 vols. (trans. Norman J. Belval and Suzanne Hecht; ed. Arthur J. Bellinzoni; Leuven: Peeters and Macon, Ga.: Mercer, 1990), 3:222. "Brother" was eliminated because it would be disconcerting to the pagan mind; the other Aramaic words would be unintelligible. This process of interpreting the Sermon by simplification began already with Luke and was carried over by the church fathers. It is also done wherever the Sermon is preached. Since Justin wrote at the mid-second century, a date for Matthew at the beginning of that century, a popular view, is problematic.

6 The words of Jesus reflect the legal system of Palestine where a trial was first conducted at the local level and then by appeal before the Sanhedrin, a supreme court, which gave the final sentencing. See Guelich, *Sermon on the Mount*, 187.

7   Guelich, *Sermon on the Mount*, 185. The "without cause" was probably added because Matthew's statement in not allowing anger in any circumstances was found too sweeping.

8   Some contemporary commentators catch the true meaning of this pericope by calling it "The New Righteousness," Schweizer, *The Good News According to Matthew*, 110, "The Greater Righteousness," Guelich, *Sermon on the Mount*, 175, and "The Righteousness that Surpasses that of the Scribes and Pharisees," Gundry, *Matthew: A Commentary*, 82.

9   Geoffrey Wainwright sees the same connection made in the early church. See *Eucharist and Eschatology* (New York: Oxford University, 1981), 142 and 175, n. 186.

10 Matthew's payment, a *kodranten*, is worth ¼ cent, twice as much as Luke's *lepton*, worth ⅛ cent. This is confirmed by Mark's account of the widow's offering where two copper coins are given the worth of a penny (12:42). Gundry, who does not recognize Luke's dependence on Matthew, concedes that Matthew here has an older tradition. Luke thus intensifies the severity of the judgment on the offender.

11 C. S. Mann, *Mark*, Anchor Bible (Garden City, N.Y.: Doubleday, 1986), 415–420, has an extended discussion on understanding "the many" in Matthew 20:28 and 26:28 and Mark 10:45 and 14:24 as the community. His arguments are based on texts from Isaiah and Daniel and their understanding in the Essene community of Qumran. The use of "the many" historically has been the center of debate about the extent of the atonement. That question can be addressed by other texts and not these as they look at Jesus' death as performed for the community without reference to those outside. The new understanding provides further reasons for seeing this section in the Sermon as applicable to the community's eucharistic functions. The blood of the Eucharist is shed so that the community of Jesus may be forgiven their sins (26:28). Within this community each member must be reconciled with each other before he approaches the altar (5:24). The divine reconciliation accomplished by Jesus is foundational for the community's life and understanding the Sermon.

7

ADULTERY, EVIL THOUGHTS, AND EXCOMMUNICATION

MATTHEW 5:27–30

Unlike the previous pericope, where anger is to be replaced with reconciliation, this section contains a blunt condemnation of adultery but no suggestion on how to overcome the adulterous thoughts of the heart. Adultery in thought or action is forbidden. It will not do to suggest that Jesus has intensified the original prohibition, which applied to an outward act of illicit sex, by making it applicable to man's internal condition. The last of the Ten Commandments forbids coveting the neighbor's wife. Coveting is a sin of the heart. In the Old Testament adultery takes on a deeper theological meaning, going beyond illicit sexual relationships to refer to Israel's unfaithfulness in her relationship to God. Yahweh, God, was the husband, and Israel, the bride, on account of her unbelief was regarded as adulterous. Jesus speaks of the Jews who desire a sign from him to demonstrate who he is, as "evil and adulterous" (Matthew 16:4). They failed to recognize that they belonged to him and by requiring proof before they would extend to him their "marital" loyalty showed they had already gone over to Satan (*ponēros:* the evil one). Their cavorting with Satan was adultery, as they had been pledged to God. As with the sin of being angry with the brother, adultery in the heart is known only to the person and to God. No possibility of civil penalty exists for adultery in the heart, as it did for adultery as an act. Though it is generally pointed out that adultery referred specifically to an illicit act between a man and a married woman, placing the sin in the heart makes it applicable to any illicit sexual thought.[1] The *Didache* places other sexual sins alongside adultery.[2]

What is striking is that this particular commandment should be so forcefully stated in the Sermon by its prominent location and the severity of the suggested penalties. The Jews at the time of Jesus were influenced by the Pharisees, who were zealously puritanical in their sexual ethic. The inclusion of the pericope of the woman caught in adultery, whatever its

precise origins (John 7:53–8:11), may have been retained by the early
Christian communities to demonstrate that this zeal may have been more
apparent than real. The Jews were guilty of the very things which they
condemned in others. The evangelist, however, has recorded these prohibitions against adulterous thoughts as normative for his community.
Proper outward sexual behavior is self-understood for the church, but
above and beyond that, God is judging the heart. "In the heart" is the
reverse side of "before your Father in the heavens." Life for the follower
of Jesus is not only lived face-to-face with others in the Christian community and church, but also directly before God.

Since the sin of adultery in the heart is known only to the individual
and to God, no punishment from the community is suggested by Jesus. The
individual afflicted with the inward sin is himself required to take the necessary steps to overcome it. The attention to the inward adultery of the
heart does not relieve the community of dealing with flagrant, public violations of this command. What is problematic is that the remedy offered by
Jesus requires putting out the right eye and cutting off the right hand and
throwing it from you. Some commentators avoid completely interpreting
this section.[3] The easiest solution would suggest that this is a form of
Semitic exaggeration or hyperbole to show what drastic steps should be
taken to avoid eternal condemnation. Avoiding the sin of internal adultery is no more possible than actually requiring the most horrid amputation. Origen, the early Alexandrian church father and theologian, muti-
lated himself, only to find that he was still beset by the same problems.
Luther says that this is another proof that the Sermon offered a Law
more impossible than that offered by Moses. Since the penalty is so hor-
ridly impossible, it may be best simply to give minimum or no attention
to it at all, as some commentators have done. Others suggest that it does
not fit.[4]

The matter is further complicated in that the evangelist elsewhere in
the gospel places the origin of the sins of evil thoughts, adulteries, and for-
nications in the heart (15:19) and not in the eyes or the hands. Even in the
Sermon on the Mount the sin is located in the heart (5:28) and not in the
limbs or extremities. The more elaborate discussion of man's corruption as
coming from within and not from without (15:19–20) seems to be a brief
commentary on the Sermon's pericope.

One possibility is that the evangelist's command to gouge and amputate is a word of Jesus directed to the community on the necessity of maintaining its own discipline. Matthew's situation might have been similar to

Paul's in Corinth. That congregation had an open case of fornication in
their midst for which he commands excommunication (1 Corinthians
5:1–5). In the same epistle he speaks metaphorically of the church as the
body (10:17) and the responsibilities of community members in terms of
the parts of a body, with foot, hand, and eye specifically mentioned
(12:14–26). In 6:15–16 Paul speaks about the impossibility of being a
member of Christ's body and at the same time being of one flesh with a
prostitute. Idolatry along with the accompanying adultery appears most
offensive at the Lord's Supper where it is a defiant act against the meal and
the church, both expressions of Christ's body. Outside of a brief note to the
church as body in Romans (12:4–5), only in the Sermon and 1 Corinthians
is there such attention given to the body and its parts.

The church for which Matthew is writing is a eucharistic community
like Corinth, a church in which the Lord's Supper is celebrated, as he
retains the words of the Supper's institution (26:26–30). The previous pericope in the Sermon, 5:21–26, has, as other sections of the Sermon certain
characteristic eucharistic language, used in the early church. The commands to rid oneself of the offending eye and hand may come from an
understanding of the body, characteristic of Paul, and thus be an admonition to the church to practice excommunication against those who are
committing public adultery. Left unchecked, the public adultery is entic-
ing others. The word (*skandalizō*) which is translated by the RSV as "cause
to sin," has a more precise and narrower meaning for the evangelist than
just general sin.[5] It means to fall away or to cause to fall away, in this case,
from the faith. Sinlessness in the sense of total abstention from sin is not a
real goal in the message of Jesus, even as a preaching device. If the
Christian must ask for bread each day, so he must also ask for forgiveness.
What is a concern of the evangelist is that Christians can cause others to
fall away or renounce the faith. Christians are capable of causing believing
children to fall away from the community and its faith by despising them
(18:6); the Twelve will fall away from the faith because they are offended
at Jesus (26:31). The word for "to throw away," as used of throwing away
the eye and limb, is related to another word which is used for a kind of
excommunication (*ekballō*), removal from the redeemed community (8:12).
At the end time the unbelieving Jews are thrown into the outer darkness,
as is the wedding guest without a garment (22:13). Taken literally, pluck-
ing out one's eye is sufficiently horrid, without having the added agony of
throwing it away. The same is true for the amputated right hand. But how
is one to do this? The problem is removed if the pericope about the body

and its limbs is taken as a picture of the church, very much like Paul's in 1 Corinthians, where the presence of an adulterer, especially in the service which contained the Lord's Supper, was seen as injurious to their religious health. Davies does recognize that Matthew has a theology of the community as the body of Christ in the reception of the child (18:10–14) and the little apocalypse (25:21–46; esp. 40, 45).[6] The suggestion that the evangelist is speaking of a body other than a physical one may be the most plausible, especially in the light of the problems of interpretation.

The public adultery, left unattended, so contaminates (Paul's word is "leavens"; 1 Corinthians 5:6) the entire community that they soon find it acceptable for themselves and the whole body (Matthew 5:30; that is, the church), with the result that the adulterous member goes to hell (Matthew 5:29–30).

Regardless of whether this pericope is interpreted as requiring drastic action in the personal life of the believer or the corporate life of the church, in both cases the sin of adultery is equally threatening and must be removed.

NOTES

1 Before the coming of Jesus, the Jews were aware that the commandment against adultery was not limited to the physical act. Women were considered dangerous because they could lead men to sin. Jesus himself saw the man and woman as partners in marriage (19:4–6). As Schweizer points out, adultery with a woman threatens her future as a wife. The prohibition of Jesus does not forbid looking at another woman, but looking at her with the intent to commit adultery. See his *The Good News According to Matthew* (trans. David E. Green; Atlanta: Knox, 1982), 121–22.

2 *Didache* 2:2. The reference to pedophilia or homosexuality in the *Didache* points to the origins of his document in a community more Hellenized than Matthew's. Such errant practices were common among the Greeks, but not the Jews who comprised Matthew's audience. Therefore we would not expect that they should be addressed either in the Sermon or elsewhere in this Gospel. These other sins, however, are not unknown in the New Testament. 1 Timothy 1:10 condemns slave dealers who were notorious in providing boys and adolescents for indecent purposes. They are the corruptors of youth. See J. Albert Harrill, "The Vice of Slave Dealers in Greco-Roman Society: The Use of a Topos in 1 Timothy 1:10," *Journal of Biblical Literature* 118/1 (Spring 1999), 108–12.

3 I find no reference to the issue in W. D. Davies' otherwise monumental work, *The Setting of the Sermon on the Mount* (Atlanta: Scholars, 1989).

4 Nothing similar appears in Mark, Luke, or John. Schweizer, *The Good News According to Matthew*, 122, finds that the saying does not really fit. Guelich is also uncertain of the exact origin of the phrase, *The Sermon on the Mount* (Waco:

Word, 1982), 195. Guelich says that phrase requires drastic action. The question of how the second hand is to be amputated is so absurd as to suggest that actual physical amputation is not in view. Hans Dieter Betz, *Essays on the Sermon on the Mount* (trans. L. L. Welborn; Philadelphia: Fortress, 1985), 239, has a full discussion of this phrase in Judaism and suggests that in the Sermon it carries the idea of gaining control of one's entire being to avoid falling under God's judgment.

5 So Guelich, *The Sermon on the Mount*, 195.

6 Davies, *The Setting of the Sermon on the Mount*, 98. Davies supports his argument by citing the unpublished doctoral dissertation of Dan O. Via, "The Church in Matthew" (Durham: Duke University, 1955) and C. H. Dodd, "Matthew and Paul," *Expository Times* 58 (1946/47): 296–97. The issue of the relationship of Matthew and Paul cannot be avoided.

8

A HARD SAYING—
THE MARRIAGE ETHIC

MATTHEW 5:31–32

This section deals with actual adultery and not simply the intention. It is not difficult to see how this has become one of the most controverted sections of the Sermon as divorce in the church remains prevalent. The Sermon's ideal is one marriage without divorce (19:4). The Sermon has been taken to allow divorce and presumably remarriage for the offended or innocent party if adultery has taken place; but Mark (10:3–4, 11–12) and Luke (16:18) do not seem to make this allowance.[1] The matter of divorce and remarriage is sensitive and historically may be a factor in interpretations of this pericope which go beyond the apparently unfair strictness of its surface meaning.

The evangelist Matthew provides additional theological elaboration for this section of the Sermon in 19:3–12, where the Pharisees raise the question of whether divorce, as outlined in Moses, for any cause is acceptable. Jesus responds that the basis for marriage was the Genesis account where marriage constituted one flesh and was not subject to human disruption. Moses' divorce ordinance was for man *as sinner*. Only in the world of unbelief is divorce permissible. The reason for Matthew's inclusion of the prohibition against divorce in the Sermon is not difficult to determine. The church, for which the Sermon is being written, is the place where the kingdom of the heavens is going to be manifest. The situation of the original paradise in Genesis is being reconstituted in Jesus, who has appeared as the new Adam. The relationship between a husband and wife will follow the prototype of man not in his fallen condition, but in his pristine state where male and female constituted one flesh or person. Genesis 1–2 and not Genesis 3 is normative. A community tolerating divorce would seem to be an open denial of that community's purpose as God's *new* creation.

Determining the theological motivation of the prohibition against divorce and the inviolate character of marriage is easier than explaining

why Matthew allows divorce apparently where adultery has been committed, though there is some division on what precisely is meant, as will be
shown below. The other two synoptic evangelists have no exceptions. This
remains a controverted issue over which there is no solid agreement. The
Roman Catholic Church does not allow divorce, though its practice of
annulment asserts some liaisons were never properly marriages.[2]

A comparison of the synoptic gospels is used to point to the priority of
Mark and then Luke. It is argued that the absolute prohibitions against
divorce of these two evangelists were found to be so severe that Matthew
found it necessary to allow remarriage for those men whose wives had
committed adultery. The posteriority of Mark can be argued in that he
condemns *both* husband and wife for divorcing their spouses, reflecting the
Roman law which permitted both spouses to divorce. Matthew gives the
right of divorce only to the husband, reflecting the earlier Jewish situation
in the church. Regardless of whether Matthew omitted the reference to
the wife's divorcing her husband so as not to offend Jewish Christians or
whether Mark allowed her privilege to stand is a debated question among
scholars. The real problem is whether remarriage after divorce was permissible in the earliest Christian community.[3] J. Duncan M. Derrett claims
that it was not and offers a uniquely new interpretation of the controverted passage. He interprets "on the ground of adultery" as the husband's
divorcing his wife to avoid his committing adultery with her.[4] This might
sound somewhat complex, but Matthew 19 is informative. The basis for
marriage is not a contractual agreement but God's creative act whereby
man and woman become one flesh (5, 6). When one of the marriage partners has a sexual union with a third party, the original union is broken, but
not in such a way that a new one is established. A man and his wife who
has committed adultery can still live under the same roof, but not
together in the original union. By having relations with his adulterous
wife he in fact is entering into an arrangement with his adulterous wife's
illegal partner.

Behind this line of argument is the one-flesh principle that forbids
marriage between certain persons, not on the basis of sanguine affinity
alone but on the basis of the one-flesh rule which also includes those related through marriage. A person is one flesh with his wife, father, mother,
sister, brother, daughter, and son. Outside of his wife, to whom he is
already married, he may not enter into marriage with any of these *or* with
those that are one flesh with any of them. Thus he cannot marry his wife's
sister or his sister's daughter. By his wife's adultery a new link, though illicit, has been established through the one-flesh principle. His sexual union

with his unfaithful wife would establish an intolerable link between him and his wife's new companion. He is still obligated to provide for his adulterous wife, but he must forego the otherwise expected and usual marital relations. If he cannot avoid these, he may give her a divorce to remove her from his house but he still is financially responsible for her.

This is M. Derrett's view of giving her a divorce on account of adultery, the "except-clause." Such an interpretation sounds overly severe, especially within a community that is marked with forgiveness, but it does focus on the ideal of the one-flesh principle. His interpretation may find some support in the pericope's final phrase, "whoever marries a divorced woman commits adultery" (5:32).

It may be that the severe word against divorce can only remain an ideal goal for the church as God's community, which can only approximate the original Paradise situation but cannot begin to replicate it. It must remain a goal because of man's persistent, sinful imperfection. Divorce without remarriage, though not ideal, is preferable. The one-flesh principle is not violated, even though it is not practiced.

The forbidding of divorce and remarriage sounded so severe to the disciples that the evangelist included their response: "If such is the case of a man with his wife, it is not expedient to marry" (19:10). The prohibition against divorce with remarriage may have instigated celibacy as an alternative for the clergy. The next pericope, 19:11–12, dealing with eunuchs, may suggest this. For Matthew and his church remarriage was not an ideal alternative for the divorced. The problem is whether the ideal can be made binding today or even whether it was ever in fact carried out to the letter. Even Guelich, who sees Jesus as removing the Levitical permission for divorce, offers the exegetical opinion that divorce is allowed for those Gentile converts who are involved in incestuous marriages. The Roman Catholic Church, which does not allow divorce, nevertheless permits annulments. The Eastern Orthodox Church permits divorce and remarriage in some cases. The church in this sinful world is caught in the tension between the sacredness of marriage and the fact pronounced by God in Genesis that it is not good for man to be alone.[5] If this was true in the sinless situation, how much more is marital companionship necessary for us fallen creatures today![6]

Notes

1   Guelich understands the "except" clause as a concession to the Gentile converts who were allowed to terminate their inter-family marriages which were no longer acceptable in the church. Thus divorce is not allowed except for an incestuous marriage existing prior to the conversion and baptism of the Christian. See his *Sermon on the Mount* (Waco: Word, 1982), 210. Such a view presupposes that the Matthew was addressed to a Gentile audience. Mann contests the view that the most Jewish of the gospels would address a Gentile problem; see his *Mark* (Garden City, N.Y.: Doubleday, 1986), 388. Davies makes no further comment than seeing vows in marriage connected with the next section on vows; *The Sermon on the Mount and Its Setting* (Atlanta: Scholars, 1989), 140. This would point to their indestructibility.

2   Eduard Schweizer lists several interpretations of what may be permissible. See *The Good News According to Matthew* (trans. David E. Green; Atlanta: John Knox, 1982), 125.

3   Guelich believes that Matthew is setting aside the Levitical provision for divorce, with the exception mentioned in the previous note. See his *Sermon on the Mount*, 197–211.

4   J. Duncan M. Derrett, *Law in the New Testament* (London: Darton, Longman, and Todd, 1970), 363–83.

5   Mann provides an excellent overview of the historical and exegetical problems of divorce and remarriage (*Mark*, 386–389). Whereas the Roman Catholic Church allows for no divorce because of the indelible sacramental marks of marriage, the Orthodox and most Anglican churches recognize adultery as an acceptable cause for divorce. Protestant churches see other causes besides divorce. He finds it impossible to see what situation in the early church the evangelist was addressing. A discussion on how this passage reflects on the synoptic relationship is also included, 393–94.

6   Schweizer comes as close as anyone to expressing the frustration over divorce among Christians, *The Good News According to Matthew*, 126: "Once more he [Jesus] takes into his protection primarily the helpless party, the woman who is driven into adultery. The danger in the exception Matthew makes for the case of unchastity does not reside in the exception itself. Precisely for the sake of the other party divorce can sometimes be the better solution.... In the final analysis, all we can say is that under certain circumstances two people must go the way of divorce, experiencing God's forgiveness because the other way would have been more culpable."

9

SPEAKING IN GOD'S PRESENCE

MATTHEW 5:33–37

This pericope has caused no little problem since the Reformation period as some Protestant groups, beginning with the Anabaptists, have understood this pericope as an absolute prohibition against the taking of all oaths.[1] As society and government required oaths, other interpretations had to be found. Some commentators have also understood this as an absolute prohibition which describes an ideal situation but not one lived out in the real world. But if the evangelist intends to outlaw all oaths, especially those required in giving testimony before a court of law, then how can it be explained that Jesus is required to give testimony under oath and actually gives it: "And the high priest said to [Jesus]: 'I adjure you [or: I put you under oath] by the living God, tell us if you are the Christ, the Son of the living God." Jesus said to him, 'You have said so'" (Matthew 26:63). This confession proposed to Jesus in the form of the question by Caiaphas is virtually identical to the one made by Peter in the form of an answer in 16:16. Jesus acknowledges *under oath* that he is the Christ. If the Sermon disallows oaths of any kind, Jesus would be breaking his own command at perhaps the most crucial moment of his life.

Oaths in the Sermon are condemned for two reasons. First of all, an oath made by the heavens or the earth is the same as one made in the name of God. Heaven is the throne of God; Jesus felt no compulsion to avoid the divine name through circumlocution, an explanation frequently offered for Matthew's use of "the kingdom of the heavens." The earth is his footstool. Jerusalem is the city where God as king rules his people.[2] There is no part of this world's existence which is not permeated by the presence of God. Swearing by any part of the creation is swearing by the creation's Creator.

Second, swearing about the future is forbidden. An example of such swearing is given: the changing of the color of a white or black hair. It seems as if the evangelist is speaking of oaths whereby the oath-taker promises to take some kind of action in the future. As a security for his doing this, he calls upon God as his witness that he will accomplish this. The example of the hairs is trivial, perhaps even absurd, but it demonstrates that the prohibition against such oaths covers everything including the most insignificant things. The forbidden oath would be similar to those common oaths that go something like this: "I swear to God that I will...." Or, "By the grave of my mother I will...." Not included here are oaths whereby a person is required by a court of law to testify to the actual events or words from the past, as in the case of Jesus' own oath before Caiaphas.[3] In confronting a future action with its possibilities, a simple yes or no that something will or will not be performed will suffice.

The question remains: why are oaths promising to do something forbidden in the Sermon? The answer is that followers of Jesus live their entire lives exposed to God. No moment is less or more sacred than another. God knows the thoughts of the heart; sins of the heart fall under his condemnation and are to be avoided. Good works are to be performed secretly because God sees the secret things (6:4). Since the follower of Jesus already lives his life entirely before God, taking oaths becomes unnecessary. By taking an oath that he will perform a certain act, he is at the same time asserting control over his own life and denying God's direction of it. The future is no longer in God's hands, but his own. Anything more than a simple yes or no about the future is motivated by Satan (5:37), who attempts to usurp God's place in the lives of his disciples.

James writes: "But above all, my brethren, do not swear, either by heaven or by earth or with any other oath, but let your yes be yes and your no be no, that you may not fall under condemnation" (5:12). His words reflect this part of the Sermon before it was written down. In the context of the epistle, it appears to speak to those people who with oaths were determined to decide their own futures (4:13–17). They should preface their plans for the future not with oaths but by saying, "If the Lord wills..." (15).[4]

NOTES

1   Warren S. Kissinger, *The Sermon on the Mount: A History of Interpretation and Bibliography* (Metuchen, N.J.: Scarecrow, 1975), 33–34.

2   Dennis C. Duling has taken this as reference to Herod Agrippa I, ca 40. "[Do not swear....] by Jerusalem because it is the City of the Great King," *JBL* 110 (1991), 291–309. Thus it was seen as a warning to recent converts not to swear by an earthly monarch. While the argument that Agrippa was understood as a "Great King" can be historically supported, is it likely that any Christian community let such an ambiguous title stand?

3   For an extended discussion of oaths see Robert A. Guelich, *Sermon on the Mount* (Waco: Word, 1982), 211–19, 248–50.

4   See also my discussion of the parallel passage James 5:12 in *James the Apostle of Faith* (St. Louis: Concordia, 1983), 129–30. Mention should also be made of Peter's taking an oath in his denial of Jesus, though he was not legally or by the situation required to do so. In Matthew 26:72 he is described as denying under oath that he knew Jesus, and in v. 74 he denounced Jesus with oaths. The oaths served only to make Peter's lying and denial of Jesus more severe.

10

RETALIATION MADE
IMPOSSIBLE BY ATONEMENT

MATTHEW 5:38–42

"An eye for an eye and a tooth for a tooth" is commonly known as the *lex talionis*, which permitted retaliation for the offended party, but such compensatory retaliation could not exceed the worth of the damage inflicted.[1] In the pericope dealing with swearing, the evangelist has already introduced the concept that the universe is God's courtroom, heaven is the throne, and earth is the footstool. All words spoken by the followers of Jesus are spoken in the presence of God, who as the King is the Judge. In the ancient Orient the king was also a judicial figure. Even in the most advanced democracies the head of state still possesses the right of judicial review by pardoning or commuting sentences. In the pericope of retaliation the judicial imagery of God as King and Judge is furthered. In Matthew the emphasis seems to be on the Christian's renouncing his right to take his enemy to court to seek restitution.[2] He addresses the question of "seek(ing) legal vindication against an evil person."[3] Luke stresses foregoing the right of personal retaliation in the case of physical injury (6:29); the response is made right on the spot.

Matthew gives three examples of giving up the right of legal redress: 1) when struck on the cheek, the offended disciple is to avoid going to court to seek vindication, and is to let the offender insult him again; 2) when the disciple is forced to give up his body shirt, the garment worn closest to the body, he is to give up the outer, coatlike garment also;[4] 3) when Roman occupation troops forced the disciple to carry their loads one mile, he should do it for two.[5] In all of these cases the disciple of Jesus surrenders his legal rights for the benefit of the offender. Finally the disciple is not to turn away the one who asks and the one who desires to borrow money. The reference here is lending to a poor man.

Unlike the sections dealing with adultery and divorce, positive suggestions are made for the Christian conduct of life. Even though the instructions given here concerning behavior are explicit, they are less important than the principles which lie behind the prescribed actions. The examples offered by Jesus would have been pertinent only in the first century and then hardly everywhere. It is even doubtful whether retaliation was actually carried out by removing eyes and teeth, but the principle was recognized as valid and carried out according to the specific circumstance. Seeking revenge for public insult could hardly be adjudicated in every case. Being robbed of one's clothing does not seem a common occurrence.

What is important is the overarching principle behind these examples. The disciple of Jesus must act like the God who has become his Father in Jesus. The "eye for an eye" principle of retaliation for personal offense is no longer valid in the new age, because the atonement of Jesus has brought in a new dimension of reality. The principle of revenge can no longer reign in the church because in the atonement of Jesus God has surrendered that right by satisfying it.

The phrase "eye for (*anti*) an eye" closely resembles the great atonement pericope of Matthew 20, where the Son of Man gives his life as a ransom (*lytron*) for (*anti*) many (28). The death of Jesus is the climax of the gospel and his suffering necessarily becomes evident in the community of those who follow him. This Matthew has introduced into the Sermon in the Ninth Beatitude with Jesus' discussion of the disciples' suffering for his sake. Jesus' death has redemptive value that never becomes characteristic of those of his followers, but their death participates in his and becomes like his.

Understanding Jesus' death in the place of or for (*anti*) many in terms of the *lex talionis* of the tooth for (*anti*) tooth may be open to a certain misunderstanding if it suggests that in the atonement God limits himself to doing only that which is absolutely necessary for salvation and nothing more. Surrendering the outer garment along with the inner garment required of the followers of Jesus points to a God who exceeds his own demands. Jesus' death for sinners stands behind the disciples' returning good for the evil done to them. Jesus' death for sins makes the law of retaliation inoperative, since all claims that men have against each other have been satisfied by his death. Becoming a disciple of Jesus brings about this awareness.

In the four instances given by the evangelist, the law of retaliation has been replaced by a generous attitude of the offended party to the offender. As Jesus says to Peter, he must forgive his brother "seventy times seven" (Matthew 18:22). Here in the Sermon the Christian is dealing not with a brother but with one who is recognized as being God's enemy by his opposition to God's purposes. The Christian begins to share God's perspective on reality. He shares with the one who does not have anything, because his possessions are not really his. This pericope is really preparatory for the words of Jesus to love the enemy. Here we come closer to the mind of God, who loves all his human creatures and yearns for their salvation.

NOTES

1   Robert A. Guelich, *Sermon on the Mount* (Waco: Word, 1982), 219. "In either case, it guaranteed the injured person legal justice while protecting the offender from undue penalty."

2   William Farmer catches the spirit of these words. "To 'turn the other cheek' and to 'give one's cloak as well' thus means to refuse to be provoked into retaliatory action. Taken in connection with the teaching 'an eye for an eye,' which means: 'be sure your retaliatory response does not exceed what is commensurate with the injury that has been inflicted upon you,' Jesus teaches that one should not allow himself to be provoked into any form of retaliatory response, even in the face of the most abusive and insulting response, even in the face of the most abusive and insulting treatment." See his "The Sermon on the Mount: A Form-Critical and Redactional Analysis of Matthew 5:1–7:29" *SBL Seminar Papers* 25 (Atlanta: Scholars Press, 1986), 68.

3   Guelich, *Sermon on the Mount*, 219.

4   Both Matthew and Luke speak of inner and outer garments; however where in Matthew the inner garment is surrendered first and then the outer, in Luke the order is reversed (6:29). First the thief takes the more valuable outer garment and then the shirt. Davies and Allison explain that Matthew's example is that of a court in which the inner but not the outer garment can be requisitioned. Luke portrays an actual robbery in which the outer garment must be taken first (1:45–46). He cites Ex 22:25–27 and Deut 24:12–13. Betz has no explanation for it (*Essays on the Sermon on the Mount* [trans. L. L. Welborn; Philadelphia: Fortress, 1985], 290). Davies and Allison argue for the originality of Matthew. Luke's audience would hardly have known of the Jewish custom of giving your cloak as a pledge. What is a legal action in Matthew becomes an actual theft in Luke. Matthew's version allows for a deeper theological meaning. In being asked for the garment of lesser value, the follower of Jesus also surrenders the more valuable one. Here is the picture of the God who when he is offended by sin offers more grace than what is required.

5   The Romans derived the practice of the native population assisting soldiers from the Persians. Betz, *Essays on the Sermon on the Mount*, 291 n.

11

THE COMPLETE
RECONCILIATION

MATTHEW 5:43–48

This portion of the Sermon has been frequently used to teach moral perfection. In the Lutheran tradition it was seen as a preaching of the Law which was impossible to accomplish and thus was served only as a prelude to the Gospel. For others this moral perfection was an obtainable goal either partially or completely. Monastic Christianity and Protestant perfectionism moved in that direction. Whether moral perfection was completely attainable or not in this life, very few would have quarreled with seeing a moral imperative here that required a certain ethical response.[1] Apart from the question of determining what the word "perfect" (*teleios*) means, the command to be perfect does not appear in a pericope dealing with moral behavior in the sense of living life according to regulations, but with loving one's enemies. If it is a command for moral perfection, it seems strangely out of place. The *Didache* merges this pericope, the one about praying for the persecutors, with the previous one about the Christian's renunciation of his right to retaliation.

> "*Bless them that curse you, and pray for* your enemies and fast for *them that persecute you; for what thank is it, if ye love them that love you? Do not the Gentiles do the same? But do you love them that hate you,* and ye shall not have an enemy. Abstain from fleshly and bodily lusts. *If any man give thee a blow on thy right cheek, turn to him the other also,* and thou shalt be perfect [teleios] *if a man impress thee to go with him one mile, go with him twain; if a man take away thy cloak, give him thy coat also.*"[2]

Perfection in the *Didache* is understood within the context of loving those who hate you and returning good to those who abuse you. The perfection required of the Christian is not a moral one, though moral and ethical conduct is self-understood for those in the community. The *Didache* provides this interpretation when it says that if the Christian loves those who hate him, he will not have any enemies. By turning the other cheek—

renouncing his right of retaliation and doing good to the offender—he reaches a perfection that cannot simply be measured by ethical regulations. This perfection of forgiving the most objectionable becomes the description of the righteousnesss which is superior to that of the scribes and Pharisees.

The previous pericope in the Sermon gives four examples of how the disciple following the higher righteousness is to act: he does not go to a court of law against the adversary; he surrenders his coat when his inner garment is taken; he goes one more mile; and he provides the one who asks for money. This pericope, dealing with love for one's enemy, provides the theological basis for this extraordinary ethic.

Scholars are uncertain about the origin of the command to hate one's enemy. There is nothing precisely like it in the Old Testament or the rabbis. Is it a command or a deduction from Israel's religious isolation? Also debatable is the precise identification of the enemy. From the Old Testament background the enemies would most likely be religious enemies, that is, those who espouse a religion different from Israel and who threaten the nation's existence.[3] As the Israelites became frequently entangled with other gods and thus surrendered their faith in the God of Abraham, they were commanded to separate themselves from foreign people and in certain cases to exterminate them. Their national political enemies were frequently seen as their religious enemies because foreign governments would superimpose their own religion on the people. Religion and political causes were not distinct in the ancient world, where the kings served as religious leaders. The Jew was to love the fellowship of his own people, where the true God was worshiped, and was to shun religious and social commerce with the pagans (Gentiles). Davies favors connecting a reference to the Essenes who in spite of their non-violence cherished a hatred for the sons of darkness.[4] Thus it is not improbable that Jesus was addressing the ethic of the Essenes who made a distinction between themselves and those outside their community. The former were to be loved, the latter hated. This ethic could have remained influential into the earliest church and had to be refuted on the basis of a higher righteousness.

Within the context of Matthew's gospel, the enemies would be understood as those who are still under Satan's influence, as the same Greek word (*echthros*) is used in the parable of the wheat and the tares to explain his role of placing unbelievers among believers in the congregation (13:25). Without downgrading the need for loving one's personal enemies, the Sermon's command points explicitly to loving those who are opposed to the community of the followers of Jesus. The enemies are the world which has rejected the community's claims that Jesus was the Christ. The commands to love the enemies and pray for the persecutors are parallel, so that the enemies and the persecutors refer to the same group. The same can be said about the evil ones upon whom God causes his sun to rise (45). In the parable of the sower, the Evil One (singular) is Satan, who comes and snatches the Word out of the heart (13:49).

This pericope about praying for the persecutors points to the origin of Matthew's gospel within a persecuted church. This is the gospel's first command to pray, with the second coming as the imperative to pray the Lord's Prayer (6:9). Luke retains the examples of both Jesus (23:34) and Stephen (Acts 8:60) who pray for their enemies. Matthew may be referring to more than casual prayer in his command and suggesting a more formal prayer for the church's persecutors that was to be included in their regular services. The petition in the Lord's Prayer that the one offering the petition would forgive the debtors might have included the thought of forgiving the persecutors. The prayer on the lips of Jesus to forgive in Luke (23:34) seems to reflect the same imperative found in the Lord's Prayer. Rather than asking the Father to forgive him, Jesus, the petitioner, asks God to forgive others the wrong they have perpetrated against him. Thus Luke provides an example of how one is to love one's enemies and how the petition for forgiving others, required by the Lord's Prayer, is carried out.

Essential to the world view of the Sermon is the division of mankind into two groups, one that recognizes the God of Jesus and responds to him and the other that does not recognize the God of Jesus or, recognizing him, fails to respond.[5] They are under the control of Satan, whom Matthew also calls the Evil One, the enemy, the one who opposes God's purposes in Jesus. This pericope centers on God's universal love, in that in his care of people through nature he does not discriminate. They are his enemies, but he is not theirs. The animosity is from their side, not God's. They are his enemies only because they stand in opposition to him, not because God has an evil disposition towards them. It is not that God is only ready to bestow favors on them when they meet his conditions, but rather as the redemptive God he is already bestowing favors on all men. He is not waiting for their response to confer on them those good things to which the redemption entitles them. The disciple of Jesus adopts the same attitude as does God. The member of the community of Jesus does good and forgives before and apart from any gratitude or expression of appreciation. Others may make enemies of the disciple of Jesus through the persecution of the church, but they are not his enemies. The *Didache* reflects this when it offers this paraphrase of the Sermon: *"But if you love them that hate you, and ye shall not have an enemy."*[6] The category of enemy no longer exists for Jesus' disciples.

In loving the enemy and praying for the church's persecutors the disciples are said to become sons of the Father in the heavens. This should not be understood in a causal sense, so that their loving the enemies is the reason that God makes the disciples his sons. Rather the meaning here is that in their love of the church's enemies, they are recognized as the sons of God their Father. They share with God the trait of being impartial and showing no discrimination among other men. The Seventh Beatitude, "Blessed are the peacemakers, for they shall be called the sons of God" (5:9), comes to expression when God's initial making of peace with the world in Jesus is realized in the lives of Jesus' followers who make peace with their enemies. God cares for the followers of Jesus just as he does for those who have not only failed to recognize his work in Jesus, but who have become its opponents. The Father's causing the sun to rise and the rain to fall are part of God's redemptive or reconciliatory concern for the world and finds a parallel in Paul's sermon at Lystra where the sending of the rains and the fruitful seasons are a witness to him to which the beneficiaries are to respond (Acts 14:17). The sending of the rain and the rising of the sun refers to God's providing food for all men, regardless of their attitude to him.[7] Elsewhere in the Sermon anxiety about nourishment for the body is the mark of unbelief, as the unbeliever does not recognize the Father of Jesus as the provider of life's necessities. If God cares for the nonrational creatures, he will be even more concerned for human beings (6:25–33).[8]

At first glance, placing God's continued creative concern for the world under his redemptive purposes would seem to run squarely against a tripartite creedal Christianity which places providence along with creation under the First Article and thus makes it an activity of the Father. It might also suggest the validity of the concept of creative grace, that is, that people can be and are saved by God's grace in nature. This would be a modified form of universalism and a denial of the unique role that Jesus has in coming for salvation. What God is revealing in Jesus can be found neither in the teachers of old nor by the observation of the order of nature, the mark of the pagan religions. The Sermon stresses Jesus as God's only authoritative representative on earth.

On the surface, the meaning of the Sermon here is that God shows his love for all men in his providential care for them. In turn, his love for them is also his redemptive love that is reflected in the lives of the disciples of

Jesus. They reflect the Father's love for his enemies by loving those same enemies. Just as God is constant in his love to humanity by providing for them in nature because of the higher righteousness of the atonement, so the Christian follows this pattern in continually doing good to all without distinction.

Luke's version of the Sermon actually introduces the word grace (6:32–36).

> If you love those who love you what credit [*charis*: grace] is that to you.... And if you do good to those who do good to you what credit [*charis*: grace] is that to you.... But love your enemies, and do good, and lend, expecting nothing in return; and your reward will be great, and you will be sons of the Most High; for he is kind [*chrēstos*: gracious, showing grace] to the ungrateful (*acharistos*: those who are without God's grace) and the selfish [*ponēros*: evil, those under Satan's control].[9]

By his introduction of the word "grace" into his version of the Sermon, Luke is bridging any perceived differences between the Sermon and Paul. Paul is recognized as the apostle of grace for introducing the term into theology.[10] There is no thought of universalism in Luke. God is gracious (*chrēstos*) to those whose lives are still controlled by Satan, the Evil One (*ponēros*), though they do not respond in kind. The evil and unjust are identified more explicitly as those who are evil and unthankful, i.e., they are without God's grace (*acharistos*). They are ungrateful in the sense that their failure to respond indicates that they have not recognized that God has revealed himself in Jesus. God's grace in his life now means that the disciple treats with extraordinary and unexpected kindness and love those who reject him. The disciple who responds with good only to those who have first done good to him shows no evidence of God's grace working in him. A disciple not responding with the gracious attitude that God has demonstrated is devoid of grace. Justin Martyr combines Matthew's sermon and Luke's interpretation and offers this rendering: "And be gracious (*chrēstoi*) and merciful, as your Father is gracious and merciful, and causes the sun to rise on sins and just and evil men." For Justin Martyr God's care of all men is motivated by his grace; the apologist follows Luke in interpreting God's love as grace.[11]

Matthew's unfavorable use of tax collectors and Gentiles as examples of those who should be removed from the community (18:17) is similar to the Sermon's derogatory references to them. Tax collectors love only those who first love them and Gentiles greet only their own kind. Both groups, Gentiles and tax collectors, exhibit a righteousness unacceptable to God.

Unless these words come from Jesus, it is hard to explain how a church reaching out to Gentiles would have preserved them.

The absence of both Gentiles and tax collectors in Luke and his designation of what appears to be the same group as "sinners" (6:32–33) is not difficult to explain. (Luke has "sins" [11:4] for Matthew's "debts" [6:12] in the Lord's Prayer.) Though Luke's church would have understood what Gentiles and tax collectors were as designations of groups of people, they would not have known at first reading that for Matthew these terms were theologically freighted in a negative sense as outcasts from the community of the redeemed. Matthew's use of these terms was not preserved in the church's liturgies and any explanation of these terms by Luke would have caused confusion and perhaps resentment. Thus it is defensible to suggest that by his use of "sinners" in the place of "tax collectors" and "Gentiles," Luke preserves the original sense but without these terms. Another reason Luke avoided the term "tax collector" may be deference to Matthew, the tax collector. In his characteristic self-effacing style Matthew retains the original words of Jesus about the exclusion of tax collectors because of the word's association with him. In Matthew's world "tax collector" not only suggested a financially and perhaps politically corrupt person, but one opposed to God's people. Thus it also carried a certain theological weight. For Luke's church this was not so.

Matthew 5:20 demands a righteousness which exceeds that of the scribes and Pharisees, that is, a higher righteousness. While it presupposes outward morality and an intensification of the Law to the heart of man, its chief characteristic is that like God's love, the higher righteousness encompasses those who hate and persecute the church. The Christian loves all people from the heart and treats everyone alike, whether or not they belong to the fellowship of Jesus. Unless the disciple of Jesus acquires this higher righteousness, he becomes like those who do not belong to Jesus, because they do not exhibit that righteousness. In greeting only those who are like you, Matthew asks, "What more are you doing than others?" (5:40). The "doing *more* (*perisson*) than others" is related to the word for "exceeds" used in describing the righteousness which "*exceeds*" (*perisseue*) that of the scribes and Pharisees."[12] The higher righteousness goes above and beyond the ordinary ethic to the forgiving and universally embracing divine love that permeates the entire essence of the follower of Jesus. "You, therefore, must be perfect, as your heavenly Father is perfect," summarizes the higher righteousness.

Without denying the concept of morality in the Father's perfection, the stress here is on completeness and wholeness. Perfect does not adequately carry into English what is intended in the Greek word *teleios*. The verb related to *teleios* means to complete or bring to a goal. God's perfection means that God has no unfinished business with the world. The account is cleared. Nothing is pending. It is unconditional grace with no strings attached. God's gracious attitude (to borrow Luke's terminology) is recognized by its inclusiveness. It is no longer a matter of recognizing the rigid demands imposed by the moral commandments of God. The Pharisees did this by regulating the people's external behavior. But the disciple must be convinced that God's higher righteousness is seen in his redemptive love. Historically the command for perfection has been used to demonstrate both man's total capability to carry out the law and ironically his total incapacity for good. The Pelagian tradition finds here the foundation for man's total moral capability to please God. *Possibility* of moral perfection means it can be realized. The Lutheran tradition sees here a command whose ultimate purpose is to push man to despair in order that he might more desire the Gospel. Both traditions understand the required perfection solely as a moral quality, whether or not it is ever fully attainable. In favor of the Pelagian view, it would be difficult to demonstrate that Jesus never intends his imperatives in the Sermon to be followed and realized. The imperative is more than a simple oratorical device to convince the hearer that just the opposite of what is commanded is intended. In favor of the Augustinian and later Lutheran view, the Sermon's anthropology is pessimistic as it speaks of men as evil, hypocrites whose righteousness is never really acceptable. The real good comes only with the righteousness appearing in Jesus. Even the precise morality of the Pharisees is judged completely unacceptable. The Augustinian tradition is right in viewing man's nature as incapable of pleasing God when left to its own devices and abilities. The scrupulous righteousness of the Pharisee and Essene has nothing to do with the higher righteousness required in the Sermon. If humans were capable of self-redemption, as the Pelagians held, the command to seek the higher righteousness would be without purpose. But the Pelagians are right in taking the fulfillment of the imperative not only as a possibility but a necessity. Obeying the imperative to the higher righteousness cannot be grasped according to ordinary human understanding of how laws are kept. The required higher righteousness does not mean more of the same, but involves God's intervention. The commands to love the enemy and pray for the persecutors are given with the express intent that they must and can be fulfilled in the community of Jesus (5:11). These are not optional. If these commands are not carried out, this community is no longer recognized as belonging to Jesus. When the Greek word for "perfect," *teleios*, is understood not as only referring to moral perfection but to completeness, the command of Jesus is no longer a remote unattainable possibility but a necessary reality in the disciple's life. The follower of Jesus adopts the attitude of God in being content with the world. There are no incomplete ledgers. As no one is in debt to God, no one is in the debt of the followers of Jesus. This is repeated in the Lord's Prayer, "as we also have forgiven our debtors." His love, like God's love, becomes all-embracing. It shows no discrimination. It accepts those whom God has accepted and this means all people.[13]

Luke's rendition is so simple that it cannot be avoided in trying to resolve the riddle in Matthew. Matthew's "You, therefore, shall be [RSV: must be] perfect, as your heavenly Father is perfect" becomes for Luke: "Be merciful, even as your Father is merciful" (6:36). In Luke the saying follows admonitions against loving only those who love you and the command to love the enemies (6:32–35). God's mercy is seen in that he loves those who are opposed to his will. Matthew's perfect (*teleios*) has a more profoundly embracive meaning, but not as easily recognizable as Luke's merciful (*oiktirmos*). Justin Martyr, in perhaps the earliest and only citation of this passage in the early church (*Apology* 1:15, 13; *Dialogue* 96:3), depends on Matthew's version of the Sermon with its references to the sun and rain, but substitutes Luke's merciful for Matthew's perfect. "Be gracious and merciful as your Father is gracious and merciful," (*Apology* 1:15). *Dialogue* (96:3) is the same but concludes "as also your Father in heavens," preserving a characteristic Matthean phrase. In combining Matthew and Luke, Justin recognizes each as equally authoritative and speaking to the same situation. He seems to be quoting Matthew, but switches to Luke's command "to be gracious and merciful" to avoid Matthew's requirement for perfection. Together Luke and Justin Martyr show that an early church interpretation of Matthew's call for perfection was a plea to be merciful, that is, forgiving, as God himself was. Speaking of the righteousness higher than the one of the Pharisees may have led the later hearers to think that Jesus was simply giving more regulations. Such a misunderstanding became the basis for much false thinking in the church, something that both Luke and Justin may have recognized. Matthew's requirement for perfection seems the older of the phrases and the more profound. Understood as embracing the atonement, it provides a basis for God's mercy.

The only other place in the synoptic gospels, outside of the Sermon, where "perfect" is used is in the pericope of the rich young man, who is told by Jesus to sell everything and to give to the poor. In this way he will be perfect (*teleios*). Mark 10:17–22 and Luke 18:18–23 resemble Matthew's pericope (19:16–22) with the command to give to the poor and follow Jesus; Mark and Luke, however, omit Matthew's "if you want to be perfect." The same problem confronted by Luke in the Sermon may have risen in his and Mark's rendition of the pericope of the rich young man. Here "perfect" cannot be an ethical or moral perfection, as Jesus holds out perfection as a goal still to be grasped, even after the young man has claimed to have followed all the commandments. Jesus' demand for further perfection is not disputed. The perfection must be beyond a moral one, otherwise the phrase "if you want to be perfect" is without meaning or misplaced. Perfection is specifically attached not so much to the selling and giving up all as it is to the helping of the poor. Caring for the poor is exemplary of the higher righteousness which exhibits itself in giving to the one who begs and not refusing a loan to the one who wants to borrow (5:42). In helping the poor—a word for Matthew with christological overtones—the rich young man can attain perfection.[14]

Not only is this pericope noteworthy because it introduces a theology of grace without the use of the word, but also because its introductory clause "but I say unto you" implies a specific Christology which, as William Farmer says, "sets Jesus in a special relationship to God." This relationship demands that the hearer or reader realize that the Mosaic revelation was not intended to be final, as it finds perfection and completion in Jesus. Jesus' messianic claims were present in his preaching.[15]

NOTES

1   For a summary of the variety of historical viewpoints, see Warren S. Kissinger, *The Sermon on the Mount: A History of Interpretation and Bibliography* (Metuchen, N.J.: Scarecrow, 1975). Aquinas, the medieval theologian against whom Luther stated his own position, understood the Sermon's command to perfection as "evangelical counsels." Also called "counsels of perfection," they were distinguished from the commandments. While the commandments were for all, the "evangelical counsels" were for those who voluntarily took the obligations of the monastic life (16–18). John Wesley interprets the Sermon, beginning with the Beatitudes, as a progression towards perfection (37–40). See also Tore Meistad, *Martin Luther and John Wesley on the Sermon on the Mount* (Lanham, Md.: Scarecrow, 1999).

2   *Didache* 1:3, 4. Italics indicate correspondence to the Sermon on the Mount.

3   Robert A. Guelich, *The Sermon on the Mount* (Waco: Word, 1982), 227–29; 252–53.

4 Eduard Schweizer discusses the concept of hatred in the Qumran community, and notes that such hatred was not directed against persons individually, but against the causes they represented; see *The Good News According to Matthew* (trans. David E. Green; Atlanta: Knox Press, 1975), 132. Betz sees hatred of one's enemies as a logical conclusion of loving one's friends and so at best it is a rhetorical device. See a full discussion of the problem in his *Essays on the Sermon on the Mount* (trans. L. L. Welborn; Philadelphia: Fortress, 1985), 392–409.

5 This is caught by the *Didache* (1:1) first line: "There are two ways, one of life and one of death, and there is a great difference between the two ways."

6 *Didache* 1:3. Citing Gal 1:13, 23, 1 Cor 15:9, Phil 3:6, and 1 Tim 1:13, Betz notes that persecutors for whom the first Christians prayed included Paul; *Essays on the Sermon on the Mount*, 313. At one of the stages of the oral development of the Sermon on the Mount, the followers of Jesus in Jerusalem actually had Saul in mind when they heard these words. The mention of the disciples as the Eleven and not the customary Twelve in Matt 28:16 seems also to exclude Paul. Thus Matthew and his audience were well aware of that apostle who next to Jesus became the most influential person in giving form to Christianity.

7 Guelich, *The Sermon on the Mount*, 254–55.

8 See chapter 17 below.

9 Guelich, *The Sermon on the Mount*, 231, notes that Luke uses *charis* eight times and Matthew not at all. The *Didache*, which generally follows Matthew, at this point follows Luke: "for what grace (*charis*) is it, if you love them that love you (1:3)." Though Guelich favors the originality of the form found in Luke, the absence of *charis* in Matthew and its predominance in Luke suggests that Matthew's Gospel preserves the original and that both Luke and the *Didache* are dependent on Matthew.

10 See also Robert H. Gundry, *Matthew: A Commentary on His Literary and Theological Art* (Grand Rapids: Eerdmans, 1982), 3.

11 Apology I, 15, 13.

12 Guelich, *The Sermon on the Mount*, 234, recognizes that righteousness (5:20) and wholeness, perfection (5:48), hold the key to grasping Matthew's understanding of Jesus' demand. It *is* the key to Matthew's Christology. Benno Przybylski, among others, understands Matthew's concept of righteousness in a purely moral, ethical sense, which does not distinguish it from that of Jesus' opponents among the Pharisees. *Righteousness in Matthew and His World of Thought* (Cambridge: Cambridge University Press, 1980), 80–87. If Jesus and the Pharisees had the same understanding of righteousness, then another reason for their opposition to him must be found.

13 For a discussion of *teleios*, see Guelich, *The Sermon on the Mount*, 235–37. Betz notes that it is difficult to determine whether *esethe* is an imperative or a future with the force of a prediction or a promise. Rather than resolve the grammatical issue, the ambiguity describes both what God expects of Christians and what will indeed happen. See *Essays on the Sermon on the Mount*, 321.

14 In the monastic morality of the evangelical counsels, the stress was on the renunciation of wealth and less on its distribution. Economic deprivation was in itself virtuous. See note 1.

15 William Farmer, "The Sermon on the Mount: A Form-Critical and Redactional Analysis of Matthew 5:1–7:29," *SBL Seminar Papers* 25 (Atlanta: Scholars Press, 1986), 68.

PART 2

LIFE WITHIN THE COMMUNITY OF THE FOLLOWERS OF JESUS

MATTHEW 6:1–34

A logical division occurs here in the Sermon. The first section of the Sermon (Matthew 5) has laid down certain theological principles. The Beatitudes describe both the disciples and Jesus himself, into whom they as believers are incorporated. Thus the Beatitudes offer us a Christology with a view to ecclesiology at the very beginning of the Sermon (5:1–12). The parables of the salt and the light focus specifically on these disciples as the agents in whom Jesus now carries out God's salvific work in the world and thus the universal motif is included from the very beginning (5:14–16). Jesus then directs the focus on himself as the fulfillment and subject of the Old Testament. The work of the Messiah means that Jesus ushers in a righteousness different from the morality commonly exhibited by his religious contemporaries (5:17–20). This higher righteousness, which is an extension of God's own righteousness, is characterized by the desire to seek not retaliation but reconciliation (5:21–24). Refusal to seek such reconciliation brings about final, permanent condemnation, from which there is no release (5:25–26). The higher righteousness focuses on God's reconciliation, which is now reflected in the life of the disciple. It presupposes a strict morality, especially as it is applied to man's inner life. Adulterous thoughts are forbidden and the disciple must take all precautions to avoid them (5:17–30). Divorce and calling upon God to act as a security in a future action are forbidden (5:27–33). The focus of the higher righteousness is not its moral implications or even merely the refusal to exercise the right of retaliation against one's enemies. Rather it involves doing good to those who offend the disciple (5:38–48). The disciples are not merely pacifists, peaceful with a peaceful attitude, refraining from belligerent acts, but they work for the good of their enemies. In loving the enemies and praying for the persecutors, the disciples of Jesus demonstrate that God is their Father. With a love that does not discriminate among men, they show glimpses of their Father's perfection. While the first part of the Sermon offers examples of the required perfection, like surrendering the coat and going the extra mile, its chief purpose is not to provide precise examples, but to provide the theology (wider and narrower senses) motivating such action. The first part of the Sermon is in a real sense a theology and not an ethic. This theology is a Christology because it describes what God has already done in Jesus. The next section, beginning with the pericope on the giving of alms or money offerings, has specific directives which are normative for the disciples as they are gathered in the community centering around the words of Jesus. Even these directives are liturgical rubrics and not simply ethical information.

12

THE GIVING OF ALMS—
CHURCH OFFERINGS

MATTHEW 6:1–4

The evangelist records no specific instance of Jesus or the disciples giving alms, although they did submit to paying the temple tax with money miraculously supplied by God in the mouth of a fish (Matthew 17:24–27). Luke (21:1–4) and Mark (12:41–44) contain the pericope of the widow's mite; Matthew does not. Perhaps Matthew wanted to avoid positive references to the temple and its cultus.

While Jesus directs words of rebuke against abuses in the temple in regard to ostentatious giving and the selling of the sacrificial animals (John 2:13–16), there is no indication that he did not submit to the regular temple procedures of sacrifices and offerings. Luke's inclusion of the account of Mary's purification sacrifice (2:22–24) and the visit of the boy Jesus to the temple point to that fact. Throughout his gospel, Luke has taken a more positive attitude to the Jewish sacrificial system. Matthew in the Sermon has chosen to include Jesus' words of rebuke about blowing the trumpet in regard to certain Jewish practices without mentioning Jesus' own participation in the religious system, thus reflecting this evangelist's more negative view of this system. Still, Matthew has included the pericope not chiefly to remind his church that Jesus had condemned certain Jewish practices, but rather to show what type of behavior is required for the higher righteousness.

The RSV translates the Greek word for "righteousness" (*dikaiosynē*) as "piety," though in all other renderings of this word in the gospel it is rendered as "righteousness." The NIV offers "acts of righteousness" and NKJV "charitable deeds." Regardless of the good intentions of the translators in making the meaning more accessible, the reader of these translations would never know that the evangelist by using the word "righteousness" is building upon his previous discussion of the higher righteousness.[1] The higher righteousness, which is the subject of 5:20–48, differs from the

righteousness of the scribes and Pharisees (5:20) precisely in its invisibili-
ty. Instead of the RSV's "Beware of practicing your piety before men," it
might just as easily be rendered "Don't hold forth your righteousness as an
activity before men so that they can see it." So strongly does Jesus feel
about this that he uses the emphatic negative (*mē*) and adds the threat that
if the disciple does his righteousness before men to earn their approval, he
has already forfeited his heavenly reward. In other words, the disciple's display of his righteousness means that God is no longer his Father and the
eschatological reward, which with God is a present reality, is lost.

Matthew 5:21–48, I have suggested, is a commentary on 5:20. The
higher righteousness requires charity. But the giver of the charity must not
be motivated by the desire to make himself known. The higher righteousness cannot be observed in any act which the doer performs for his own
benefit. Specifically condemned are the hypocrites. Jesus here does not
single out the scribes, Pharisees, or any other one group among the Jews.
The evangelist may have chosen the more general word of hypocrites, so
that the reader would know that this word of Jesus was being directed
specifically to him.[2] The word once spoken in history is made contemporary to the situation of the reader. Jesus is not condemning charity, deeds
and gifts of kindness performed for the benefit of the poor (which are
required), but the public manner in which they are done.

Some commentators feel that Jesus' mentioning of the sounding of the
trumpets in the synagogues and streets is simply hyperbole—deliberate
exaggeration—since musical instruments were not used in connection with
the giving of gifts in Jewish worship. Trumpets were used to proclaim fasts,
but there is no knowledge that they were used for bringing gifts to the
temple or synagogue. Blowing the trumpets in the synagogues and streets
is perhaps similar to the phrase "blowing your own horn."[3] Anyone who
announces that he is the giver of the gift has received his reward from the
admiration of the people. His approval comes no longer from God, but
from men. "Men" (*anthrōpoi*) here is used in the characteristic Matthean
sense of those who are opposed to God (16:13). The public givers of charity have aligned themselves with the enemies of God. They have surrendered their right to an eschatological prize in exchange for immediate
gratification. They have their reward!

There is nothing here to suggest that giving alms is forbidden. In fact,
the opposite is required. The Father not only approves of the giving of
alms to the poor, but will reward such giving in the future. The gift given
in secret does not lose its reward, because the Father sees what is done in

secret. In the discussion of anger and adultery, the matter of the internal behavior of the disciple of Jesus has already been brought into the Sermon. The disciple not only refrains from evil outwardly and inwardly, but he actively performs good. The promise of the future reward ushers in the eschatological element, discussed in the judgment scene of Matthew 25, where those on the right hand are rewarded for their acts of charity.[4] The recipients of this charity are the hungry, the thirsty, the stranger, the naked, the sick, and the imprisoned (25:35–36). The givers of the charity are commended for having come to the aid of Jesus, though they are unaware of this (40). Their lack of awareness about the real recipient of their charity (Jesus) may be a commentary on the Sermon's not letting your left hand know what your right hand is doing. The followers of Jesus do not concentrate on their own past acts of charity or the righteousness which motivates them. They become oblivious to what they have done. Their doing good becomes so much a part of their nature that they are unaware of it.

The connection between the higher righteousness of the Sermon and the rewards given the performers of the charity in the judgment scene is drawn closer together when they are identified as the righteous (25:37). They are recognizable to God as the righteous because in their charity they have exemplified God's righteousness, which is his mercy to all people. Matthew's perfect and righteous God is the God of mercy. Though Luther may not have been aware of this constellation of words as they were used in Matthew and Luke, by another route—through Paul's epistles—he concluded that the meaning of God's righteousness was not exhausted by adherence to moral standards, but included the divine forgiveness appearing in Jesus. Righteousness in Matthew, especially the Sermon, while not developed around the Pauline terms of faith and grace, may be understood as the divine merciful relationship of God to the world. On these points Matthew and Paul overlap.

Luke renders Matthew's command to be perfect as the command to be merciful (*oiktirmos*). Matthew sees the internal, higher righteousness of the disciples expressing itself in acts of charity, or more literally, as acts in which mercy is seen (*eleēmosynē*), a word derived from the word for mercy (*eleos*). The Hebrew Old Testament word for "righteousness," *tzedakah*, is translated in the Septuagint, the Greek translation of the Old Testament, by both the words "righteousness" (*dikaiosynē*) and "charity" (*eleēmosynē*). God's righteousness is shown in his mercy for his people. The higher righteousness of the disciples of Jesus is now also shown in their acts of mercy.

So secret is the disciple's giving that the left hand does not know what the right hand is doing. The disciple of Jesus is so generous that he cannot keep account of what he has given. Hands have no cognitive function for the human body. This hyperbole prepares for the conclusion of the judgment scene, where the righteous are unaware that they have come to the aid of Jesus in relieving the distressed (25:37–38). Another possibility is that the left and right hands are parts of the body of Christ, metaphors for members of the community. Matthew 5:29–30 uses similar language in speaking of the removal of the offending hand and foot. The givers of charity in the community are unaware of the extent of the gifts offered by others.[5]

While this is an original word of Jesus spoken within his religious context of Judaism, Jesus in Matthew's gospel does not really show that much concern for the religious rituals, including the procedures for the giving of offerings. His saying in 9:13, quoting from Hosea that God desires mercy and not sacrifice, supports this. In addition, Matthew seems to be negative towards Jerusalem's claim to any permanent religious greatness. Luke is more positive about both Jerusalem and its religious rituals. This is part of Matthew's theme that the gospel originally intended for the Jews is now available for both Jews and Gentiles. Thus it is not improbable that the evangelist has included this pericope with special intent for the collection of offerings in the early church. This would explain why the target of Jesus' ire is the hypocrites without any mention of the Pharisees.[6]

Charitable concern for the poor was an obligation for the entire church. Paul made the impoverished condition of the Jerusalem church the concern of the Corinthians (1 Corinthians 16:3), the Macedonians, and the Achaians (Romans 15:25–26). 1 Corinthians, which speaks of the church as the body (12:31), speaks of charity without love as useless (13:2). One church's assisting another may have been an extension and expansion of the Jerusalem church's custom of holding all things in common for the benefit of the needy (Acts 2:45). There was no question about helping the poor, since through the poor the person of Jesus became visible in the community. Consider the First Beatitude: "Blessed are the poor in spirit," which becomes Luke's "Blessed are the poor." Matthew's application of these words to Christian worship is reinforced by the following pericope with its instructions for prayer and fasting. Making contributions for the support of the poor in the church, praying, and fasting were all components of early worship.

NOTES

1   The problem in interpreting righteousness is seen in that some early manuscripts replace *dikaiosynē* (righteousness) with *eleēmosynē* (alms), probably taken from v. 2, where its inclusion is supported. *Today's English Version* goes to the extreme in rendering "righteousness" as "religious duties," i.e., duties required by one's religion. Where the word "righteousness" is not used in v. 1 and "piety" and "religious duties" are, it gives the false impression that righteousness is a visible phenomenon. Betz offers this acceptable translation: "Be on your guard with respect to your righteousness, not to act before people for the purpose of being seen by them," *Essays on the Sermon on the Mount* (trans. L. L. Welborn; Philadelphia: Fortress, 1985), 329.

2   "Hypocrite" is simply the Greek word for actor; conscious deception may involve self-deception. See Eduard Schweizer, *The Good News According to Matthew* (trans. David E. Green; Atlanta: Knox Press, 1975), 143.

3   What is intended by the blowing of the trumpets at the giving of the alms is uncertain. Gerald Friedlander suggests that Matthew combined two Jewish customs: one, the collecting of the alms for the poor on Friday and the other, the sounding of the trumpet to announce the approaching Sabbath. See his *The Jewish Sources of the Sermon on the Mount* (New York: KTAV, 1969), 98–99. Guelich calls this "a hyperbolic reference to ceremonial fanfare"; *The Sermon on the Mount* (Waco: Word, 1982), 278. Schweizer, *The Good News According to Matthew*, 143, suggests that even though the custom is unknown, it may have been practiced at one time. See also Betz, *Essays on the Sermon on the Mount*, 355–56.

4   Matthew 6:4 is the only place where *o pater sou*, "your [singular] Father," is used in the synoptic gospels and indicates the father-son relationship between God and the follower of Jesus; Guelich, *The Sermon on the Mount*, 280. It also emphasizes the charity of the individual and not that of the collective community.

5   This may be suggested by the singular *sou*, "yours." See note 4, this chapter. For additional suggestions, see Betz, *Essays on the Sermon on the Mount*, 358–59.

6   The Jewish community remains sensitive to Jesus' harsh words against the Pharisees as a sect; see Friedlander, *Jewish Sources*, 99. Others have tried to apply the words of Jesus to one branch of Phariseeism. Today the church's concern can hardly be in resolving the historical question, while failing to see the universal applicability of "hypocrite."

13

THE RUBRIC ON PRAYER

MATTHEW 6:5–15

This pericope on prayer has three parts: a warning, a prayer, and a saying on the necessity of forgiveness. Like the previous pericope on the giving of charitable gifts, a public display of prayer is condemned along with the repetitious pagan prayers of the Gentiles. Jesus then offers his own prayer, the Lord's Prayer. In conclusion, Jesus explains the necessity of forgiveness, if one is to receive God's final forgiveness.[1]

"Whenever you pray" (6:5) uses the plural, but its prohibition speaks not to the issue of public or corporate worship but to the public display of personal piety. The opening words, "whenever you pray," also point to the continual life of prayer and set no minimum or maximum limitations on how often one is to pray. The point is that whenever private prayer is offered, it is to be done in such a way as not to attract public attention. Forbidden is the display of private piety in a public way. Praying and giving charity are required, but may not be done to attract attention. When done this way, it is no longer acceptable to God, but receives its reward from men who admire such actions. The command to avoid open places like street corners and synagogues and to enter a small chamber and lock the door simply means that the suppliant should remain out of sight. What is important is that the one who offers the prayer knows that God, who searches the hearts of men, will know what the prayer is about.

Unexpectedly the evangelist speaks of the Father *seeing*, not *hearing*, the petitioner in secret. God *sees* the petitioner offering up his prayer. It could be that God has already heard the prayer before it is offered and at the moment of the prayer looks upon the inward posture of the one offering the prayer. The suppliant and his prayer remain invisible to all but God. That Matthew is not speaking to the propriety of public worship, but to that of private devotion, is indicated in the switch from the second person plural in v. 5 to the second person singular in v. 6.

The warning that prayers should neither be long nor constantly repeated with the same or similar words seems applicable equally to both the corporate and the private worship life. Matthew shows no hesitancy in preserving a logion of Jesus about Gentiles which casts them in a negative light. Gentiles are held up as examples whose prayer life should not be emulated. Here the word "pagans" rather than "Gentiles" would better carry the sense. Such a caustic reference to the Gentiles would hardly have been preserved unless it had come from Jesus. For this reason alone its authenticity should be above challenge.

Long prayers here are not condemned for their length, but for their repetition. Jesus is described as going away by himself and praying (Matthew 14:23). In the Garden of Gethsemane he offers the same prayer three times to his Father, and it is probable that the evangelist has preserved for us only the first words (Luke 22:44). In the post-ascension church, the disciples of Jesus are described as *always* in the temple praising God (Luke 24:53).

This pericope cannot be taken as an exclusive endorsement for short prayers, though they may indeed be preferable from a practical point of view. The Sermon's warning condemns the view that a prayer's value is determined by the number of words it employs. The length of a prayer does not decide whether it will be answered by God. To think that it does is clearly a pagan view, as it not only attempts to manipulate God but regards him as a remote sovereign and not as Father.

Though some Jewish commentators may tend to be sensitive about the way Jesus or the evangelist speaks of the Jews and their religious leaders, there is nothing to suggest that the evangelist, as he presents Jesus, is being anti-Semitic in the generally accepted sense of the term. An alleged anti-Semitism is sometimes attributed to John. But neither the First nor the Fourth Evangelist is anti-Semitic. The Jews are condemned not because of their race but because they have failed to take advantage of the salvation God was giving the world *through* them. Salvation belongs first to them. They are still called the sons of the kingdom (8:12), and to them the Gospel must go first; Jesus' ministry is exclusively for them (15:24). Matthew intends that his gospel should be read by them. On the other hand the evangelist is equally hard on the Gentiles, a term which might better be translated as "pagans." He uses the Gentiles as examples of those who are excluded from the community of Jesus, and here in the Sermon their type of prayer life, which puts the emphasis on the number of words spoken and on the frequency of repetition, is condemned. The evangelist's condemnations are not in any sense racial, but only a rejection of their religious practices. In this sense both Jew and Gentile fall under

God's condemnation, although for different reasons. Yet both are destined by God to share in salvation. This is virtually the same argument used by Paul in Romans.

Mark's and Luke's toning down or omitting Matthew's derogatory uses of "Gentile" seems to show that as the church began its Gentile mission it was more sensitive about being anti-Gentile than anti-Semitic. Where *ethnos* may be more properly translated as "pagan" in Matthew to catch the negative tone, in Mark and Luke its meaning tends to the more neutral "Gentiles" simply in the sense of non-Jews. Both Mark and especially Luke treat both groups more favorably and tone down Matthew's more negative statements.

The prayers of the Gentiles are unacceptable not only because of their lengthy repetition of words, but also because of wrong goals. Their prayers are replete with requests for *things*. Christians are not to be thus obsessed. Even before the prayer is offered, the Father of the disciples of Jesus already knows what the petitioners need. The prayer of the church presupposes that God is already providing for the common, ordinary things of life, and thus it should move on to the level of the higher righteousness. The Father's awareness of the elementary needs of the community of Jesus is a development of one of the Sermon's basic themes that God sees all things in secret. He not only knows what is in the disciples' hearts, but knows it in such a way that he is already responding to them. His knowledge of all things is not simply a divine omniscience but a fatherly care. The disciples of Jesus live in a close relationship with God as their Father. Since God is already their Father, their prayers do not have to be concerned with the ordinary requests of life. They are to be directed to the higher righteousness which has been revealed in Jesus and which now must come to full expression in their lives. In fact, an excessive concern for *things* indicates that the petitioner is not completely a follower of Jesus. Thus not only does Jesus tell the disciples what forms of prayer are unacceptable, but he delimits the content of the prayer itself by designating improper requests. The follower of Jesus is not only left with a warning against ostentatious prayer, repetitive prayer, and prayer excessively concerned about *things*, but he is given a prayer on which he can rely and which he is to *pray*. This is not an example of how to pray, but the prayer to be prayed. This prayer soon becomes part of the church's regular liturgy.[2]

154 THE SERMON ON THE MOUNT

THE LORD'S PRAYER

Probably no other section of the Bible is so well-known and spoken with such frequency as the Lord's Prayer. It is also known in English as the "Our Father," following the commonly used German *Vaterunser*, the French *Le Notre Pere*, and the Latin *Pater Noster*, translating the prayer's first words according to Matthew's version. The more common title for the prayer in the English-speaking world, "the Lord's Prayer," reflects Luke's version, where the disciples are pictured as coming to Jesus with the request: "Lord, teach us to pray" (11:1). In Latin, the Lord's Prayer is also called the *Oratio Dominica*. Luke's version of the prayer is not contained in his parallel to the Sermon on the Mount but in a section on prayer in general (11:1–13).[3] The occasion in Luke is the coming of the disciples to Jesus while he is in prayer with a request that he should teach them to pray as John had taught his disciples. The Lucan version is somewhat shorter than Matthew's in that it omits "our" and "who art in heaven" in the address and the entire third petition, "Thy will be done." Luke's absence of "our" in "our Father" may point to its use as a private prayer, in distinction to its public, corporate use by Matthew. Matthew's request to God to remove "debts" becomes for Luke "sins." Mark has no version of the prayer at all, and John may at points show traces of it. Luke follows his version of the prayer with several pericopes dealing with the subject of prayer: 1) the man awakened at midnight to handle the requests from his neighbor's sudden need for bread (11:5–8); 2) the assurance that God will certainly answer prayer when asked (11:9–10); 3) evil fathers giving their sons the good things which they ask for (11:11–12); and 4) the Father's giving of the Holy Spirit when asked.

In contrast to Luke's section, which is devoted entirely to the benefits of prayer and to the certainty that it will be answered, Matthew's version of the Lord's Prayer is found between the sections on almsgiving and fasting. Thus Matthew's interest in the prayer is of a general liturgical nature in laying down guidelines of what Christians should do when they worship: give alms, pray, and fast.[4] Its immediate preface is a warning about following the Gentiles who estimated a prayer's value by the number of words and repetitions. Luke has no warning against prayers that are useless because of form and content. On the other hand, Matthew has no specific logion on the effectiveness of prayer. Luke's parable about the man who gets up to answer the request of the neighbor for bread and the Lord's commands to ask and knock, with the promises that those who ask will receive and those who knock will have doors opened to them, is in marked contrast to Matthew's assurance that "your heavenly Father knows that you need them all" (6:32). Luke concludes his pericope on prayer with the assurance that the Holy Spirit, rather than *things*, will be given the petitioner: "If you then, who are evil, know how to give good gifts to your children, how much more will the heavenly Father give the Holy Spirit to those who ask him" (11:13). While Matthew's version of the prayer is to be understood on the level of the higher righteousness which is above and beyond the *things* for which the Gentiles ask, Luke expresses this thought in a positive way, that the heavenly Father will give the Holy Spirit to those who ask him. The question of which version is older or reflects an older tradition is debatable.[5]

One starting point for any consideration of the Lord's Prayer is that it has become the common possession of the Western world in such a way that its origin as a prayer *exclusively* for the church has in some cases been lost.[6] Thus it is not uncommon that the prayer should be used in secular, civil contexts without any specifically clear Christian intention. As God is commonly called Father even outside of a specifically Christian context, the prayer has taken on a certain universal—universalistic—dimension. Yet without the understanding that the prayer is and historically has been seen as the unique possession of the Christian community, its original meaning will remain clouded at best, if not totally lost. There are other indications besides Matthew and Luke that the prayer was in use perhaps as early as the immediate post-resurrection church. Acts 2:42 with its reference to the teaching of the apostles, the Communion, which is the breaking of bread, and *the* prayers, that is, the petitions, may be a specific reference to the use of that version of the Lord's Prayer used by Matthew. The use of the definite article suggests that these prayers tended to be of the more formal rather than informal kind. The order suggests that a definite liturgical ritual was already in place; a recitation of the deeds of Jesus (the oral gospel traditions), the Lord's Supper, the Lord's Prayer.

Later church sources coming from the second century indicate that the Lord's Prayer was communicated to the catechumen shortly before his baptism and that after he was baptized he was given further specific instruction in what the prayer meant.[7] This may provide the clue in understanding that Christians, as sons of God, have received the Spirit of God's Son, who has come so that they can cry "Abba, Father" (Romans 8:14–15). The Spirit who has raised Jesus from the dead has made it possible to call on God as Father (8:11, 15). Already in Rome it may have been the early church custom that only those who were baptized were instructed in the Lord's Prayer and thus only immediately prior to their being baptized were permitted to cry out during the liturgy, "Abba, Father." Though Romans 8:15 would seem to be a reference to the Lucan and not the Matthean version of the prayer, the word "our" in both the Aramaic and the Greek would have followed the word Father and not preceded it. In the Latin *Pater noster* and older, liturgical German *Vater unser*, the biblical order "Father our" is preserved. The use of the word *Abba* points to the prayer's usage in Jerusalem, where Christians may have used this as the ordinary Aramaic word for Father instead of the Greek *pater*. The Aramaic may have been retained outside of Palestine to express the *catholicity* of the church by using a common language in certain parts of the liturgy, very much like the Greek and Hebrew words, *kyrie, alleluia,* and *sabaoth* are still commonly used today. The Lord's Prayer, as the exclusive possession of the Christian community, was placed into the Mass of the Faithful, that part of the service from which all the unbaptized, including the catechumens, those who were being instructed but who had not been baptized, were excluded.[8]

The Matthean version of the Prayer both in context and content is better suited for corporate worship than is the Lucan version. It appears between instructions on how to give alms and fast, both of which had ritualistic meaning for the corporate Christian community. Whereas Luke is more indefinite, without setting down any given command to pray, "Whenever you pray, say…," Matthew has the more definite, "Thus therefore you are to pray." Jesus is commanding the community of his disciples to pray. Though some scholars suggest that Matthew's version is simply a model or guide for all of the church's prayers, it seems that he sets the Prayer down as a ritualistic requirement for his community. His inclusion of the definite pronoun "you," which is grammatically unnecessary as it is already included in the Greek verb, serves to make it more of a direct address to the congregation. In the *Didache* the Lord's Prayer is similar to Matthew's version. It is placed after the instructions for baptizing, thus supporting the view that the Prayer, put forth later in the second century and allowed by Romans 8, was intended exclusively for the ears of the Christian community. The *Didache* also takes Matthew's next section dealing with fasting and combines it together with the Lord's Prayer.

> And let not your fastings be with the hypocrites, for they fast on the second and fifth day of the week; but do you keep your fast the fourth and the preparation [the sixth] day? Neither pray ye as the hypocrites, but as the Lord commanded in his Gospel, *thus pray ye: Our Father,*

which are in heaven, hallowed be Thy name; Thy kingdom come; Thy will be done, as in heaven, also on earth; give us this day our daily bread; and forgive us our debt, as we also forgive our debtors; and lead us not into temptation, but deliver us from the evil one; for thine is the power and the glory for ever and ever. Three times pray ye so.[9]

The section in the *Didache* immediately following the prayer discusses the Eucharist. This further substantiates the prayer's place in the Mass of the Faithful, where the Lord's Supper was celebrated. The English referents "The Lord's Prayer" and "The Lord's Supper" (or "The Lord's Table"; 1 Corinthians 11:20 and 10:21) conveniently suggest that they belong together.

Further grammatical considerations point to Matthew's inclusion of the Prayer for corporate use. In the instructions for praying, the evangelist begins with the second person plural, but quickly switches to the singular form in warning that individual Christians should conduct their prayers in private. In both the Matthean and Lucan versions of the prayer the second person plural is used throughout. Matthew is slightly more pronounced in his use of the plural. Whereas Luke addresses God simply as 'Father,' Matthew uses the more formal and liturgical 'Our Father,' a term which presupposes the worshiping community. Though Paul retains "Father" and "our Father," his sense is clearly corporate in Romans 8:15b–16: "When *we* cry, 'Abba, Father' it is the Spirit himself bearing witness with *our* spirit that *we* are *children* of God." If Paul is making reference to the Lord's Prayer—and I think he is—it is the Spirit who through Baptism gives to Christians the right to call God Father in the Lord's Prayer. The recitation of this prayer is the demonstration that they are God's children, approaching him as their father.[10]

The secularization of the Lord's Prayer among the western Christianized nations has gone hand in hand with a lower form of Christology which stresses Jesus as a man who utilized his innate qualities common to all. Whether this is accidental or a direct cause and effect can be noted but not settled here. Within Christian circles, even those who pride themselves on adhering to a more traditional form of Christianity, the Lord's Prayer is often interpreted in a non-Christian way. Due to its wide use, even those who count themselves as part of more traditional Christianity would have a difficult time trying to find a uniquely Christian meaning in the Prayer. It becomes a prayer as much at home in a Jewish as in a Christian community. The Christian religion has provided the terms for the civil religion in the West, including America, and the Lord's Prayer is part of that civil religion.[11]

Yet apart from the exegetical question of interpreting the Prayer within the perimeters of Matthew's gospel, the Prayer was regarded as one of the sacred treasures of the church. The *Didache* held that it should be prayed three times a day. Tertullian saw in it a summary of the entire Gospel, that is, a statement of faith, and expounded each petition in detail. Origen, independent of Tertullian, held the same view. Cyprian and Tertullian saw its meaning as so sacred that it could only be imparted after the catechumen had been baptized. Augustine claims that the custom of the church was to teach the Creed first during Holy Week and *then* the Lord's Prayer, with Baptism following on the day before Easter. Justin Martyr seems to know of the same tradition, as does the Apostolic Tradition of Hippolytus. The widespread use in the early church and close connections to Matthew's version points to the antiquity and importance of the Lord's Prayer as Matthew recorded it.[12]

If Matthew is given the place of honor among the gospels and the New Testament, and if within Matthew the place of honor is given the Sermon on the Mount as the compendium of Jesus' teaching, then perhaps Tertullian's observation that the Lord's Prayer was compendium of the entire gospel should be reassessed as having value for gospel research.[13] It was not only understood as a prayer of the church but as a confession of its faith. It was treated with higher honor than the Apostles' Creed, as its words were the last to be communicated to the catechumens before their baptism. Not only was it part of the eucharistic worship of the church, but it was included in the canonical hours. Instinctively, later church commentators felt an obligation to expound the Lord's Prayer even if they did not raise the historical questions of its place in the gospel given it by the evangelist.

The Lord's Prayer consists of an address and seven requests or petitions, all in the imperative form. The first three deal with God: the hallowing of his name, the coming of his kingdom, and the performance of his will on earth. The last four requests center on the life of the community of the disciples of Jesus: the giving of bread, the forgiving of debts, the avoidance of temptation, and the deliverance from Satan. Some commentators see only six petitions to form a perfect symmetry of three and three. The petitions on temptation and evil are combined.[14]

"OUR FATHER WHO ART IN HEAVEN"

The Matthean version of the address to God in the Lord's Prayer is more formal than Luke's "Father" and suggests that the prayer was used liturgically, that is, eucharistically, when it was inserted into the gospel.

The Lucan version shows a further development in the expositions following the Prayer, where the Third Evangelist speaks about the heavenly Father giving the Holy Spirit (11:13). Luke developed his setting for the Prayer within a church feeling Paul's influence and thus seems to have Matthew's version or the one which was included in Matthew in view for his own version. With the exception of Mark 11:25 God is never spoken of as "the Father in the heavens" outside of Matthew, where it appears 20 times in slightly varying forms.

Though the English translation places the word "our" as the first word of the Prayer, the Latin with *Pater noster* and the German with *Vater unser* convey the Prayer's original word order, where "Father" comes first.[15] Thus the Prayer opens with a blunt address to God as Father. Only when the Gospel is understood as a totality is the reader able to begin to exhaust what is intended by the word Father in addressing God. Though the concept of God as Father was inherent in Israel's being God's children in a way that the Gentiles were not, the explicit and frequent use of Father in speaking of God in the preaching of Jesus is startlingly unique. This is not to deny that certain highly placed rabbis may have used the word in invoking God, but Jesus used it as part of his common vocabulary in order to express his special relationship with God and he encouraged others to do the same. To those who came to know God through him, he not only gave the invitation but the command to approach God as Father.[16]

This is the only place in Matthew's gospel where God is known as 'our Father,' though the phrase "heavenly Father" and "Father in the heavens" is frequent. Jesus speaks of God as "my Father" and as "your Father," but elsewhere he never places himself with his hearers so that together they speak of God as "our Father." Thus the prayer within the context of Matthew's gospel shows that Jesus has a special messianic consciousness not only about his mission but his person. Though Jesus is the prayer's author, he intends it for the use of his disciples and not for his own. Jesus does use certain petitions for himself. His prayer in Gethsemane (26:42) reflects the Second Petition, "Thy will be done." Where Jesus speaks of God as *his* Father, he refers to his own role as the messianic servant who with total faith and complete trust places his existence in the hands of God (see 26:39, 42). This use points to Jesus' total subservience as God's servant, appointed by him to accomplish salvation. In other places the term "Father" takes on an almost Johannine meaning indicating a supra-earthly relationship with God. The Father and the Son have a complete knowledge of each other in distinction to Christians who can only have a revelation of the Father at the discretionary will of the Son (11:27). The community of the disciples of Jesus are those who not only have been taught all of his teachings but who have been baptized in the name of the Father and of the Son and of the Holy Spirit (28:20).[17]

The coming of Jesus means that his disciples now know the Father of Jesus as their own Father. The Sermon has already introduced the concept of God's fatherhood in the Sixth Beatitude, where the peacemakers will be called God's sons (5:9). They alone have the right to call him Father (5:9). In serving as the lights in the world, his followers fulfill the purpose of their existence when they bring others to recognize God as their Father. The community of the followers of Jesus shows that God is their Father precisely in that they pray for their persecutors and become perfect, that is, conciliatory, in their attitude to all men. They count no men as their enemies. Since God is their Father, their good works have value because they reflect the special relationship that they have with God. He is aware of them. Those works lose their value when they are done from a motive of personal glory to gain the attention of others (6:2).

Matthew's gospel develops another dimension of God's relationship to the community of Jesus as sons of the Father when Jesus identifies the eleven disciples as his brothers in the post-Resurrection narrative. "Go tell my brothers to go to Galilee, and there they will see me" (28:10). Since God has become their father, they have entered into a relationship with each other as brothers. The Lord's Prayer has become the prayer of the post-Resurrection community.

Thus the Prayer's address to God as Father is appropriate only in the mouths of the community of those who have been reconciled to God by Jesus and live lives committed to reconciliation. Equally important, they work for the reconciliation of all men to God and to each other through the preaching of Jesus and his message. Not only is prayer to God as Father now made permissible through Jesus, but it becomes necessary for those who have become members of the community of Jesus. The Prayer's introduction in Matthew, "Thus therefore you shall pray," makes the Prayer to the Father a self-understood prerequisite.

As mentioned, the Lucan version omits "our" from the phrase "our Father." Matthew's inclusion of "our" has literary, theological, and liturgical significance. Matthew's gospel in intent, form, and content is for the church. He is the only evangelist who uses "church," though it seems unlikely the others did not know the word. Theologically, it indicates that the followers of Jesus should not adopt an individualistic attitude to salvation. God's righteousness (grace) is to all men and the community as community reflects God's concern for the whole. The Son of Man gives his life for the community, the New Israel, and the Eleven, who constitute this New Israel. They are to carry this message to all nations. Those who have come to see that God is working in Jesus reflect their relation to God by calling him Father and their relationship to each other as brothers when they speak of God as "our" Father.

The use of the word "our" also indicates that at the time of the Prayer's inclusion into the Sermon and the gospel, it was part of the liturgical worship of the early Christian community. The *Didache*, coming at the close of the apostolic age, commands that it be prayed three times a day.[18] At least one of these was probably in corporate worship. In the earliest communities, especially in the urban areas where the church first settled, the Christians gathered together each day and there the Prayer would be offered. This was happening in Jerusalem and was followed in other places. Whether they *gathered* three times a day is not necessarily the required interpretation of the *Didache*. The Prayer's corporate use soon passed over into private use. Even when the Prayer was used in private devotion, it was always in the context of the corporate life of the community of the followers of Jesus.[19] Luke's exclusion of "our" in the address had led some commentators to point to his version as earlier than Matthew's. Just the reverse seems the case. Luke also understands that the Prayer is for the benefit of the entire community, as the plural is consistently used throughout his version of the Prayer; however, in the first of the explanatory expositions that follow, he singles out the community members individually: "which one of you…" (11:5). Luke is addressing the personal prayer life of the church members. Though the Prayer was first intended for the corporate worship of the community of Jesus, it quickly came into use in the less formal and private settings. Still, its private use always reflected its public use.

With the one exception in Mark (11:25–26), the phrase "who art in the heavens" is characteristically and uniquely Matthean.[20] Not only is God acknowledged as the Father of those who have gathered themselves into the community of the followers of Jesus, but he is "placed" in the heavens. The reason for including "who are in the heavens" after "Father" may have been the common Jewish practice of using "father" to speak of Abraham. God is Father in a much different way. According to the Fourth Gospel, Jesus questions the Jews whether Abraham is really their father (8:39–40) and the rich man in hell cries out to his father Abraham (Luke 16:24, 30). Both Paul (Romans 4:1, 12) and James (2:21) can speak of Abraham as the father of Christians. Matthew seems to reserve the term "Father" for God. The Baptist warns the Jews against presuming on their relationship to Abraham as their father (3:9). The real Father, for whom Matthew reserves the title, is God: "And call no man your father on earth, for you have one Father who is in heaven" (23:9).

The phrase "who art in the heavens" does not point to the location of God as if he were in heaven but not on earth, but rather to God's transcendence as the Creator over his creation; it refers to his majesty, his glory. Unlike other gods or human fathers, including Abraham and the patriarchs, he is not placed under the limitations of ordinary existence. This is the God who knows all the things done in secret, including the thoughts of the heart (6:4; 5:28), simply because he is above all things. "Who art in the heavens" is characteristically Hebrew and would explain Luke's omission of the phrase. He approximates it once as "the Father from heaven" (11:13). For Luke's predominantly Gentile and formerly pagan audience the phrase might have indicated that God was like the gods of the Greek and Roman world that lived somewhere beyond the clouds or in the skies. This is not what Matthew intends with "who art in the heavens." The word "heavenly" in today's English has become so inexact at times, meaning simply "exquisite;" retaining Matthew's original "who art in the heavens" may present less problems. Heavens should be understood simply as the rule of God in Jesus without reference to specific location.[21]

"HALLOWED BE THY NAME"

In Old Testament thought God's name is virtually equivalent with himself. The holiness of the name meant the holiness of God. Since the phrase "who art in the heavens" refers to God's transcendence above human limitations, the First Petition, that his name be kept holy, is only a commentary on the address "Our Father." Both the address and the First Petition speak of his transcendent nature. One commentator notes that the passive and not the active voice is used to avoid the idea that God should come with fierce vengeance to impose his holiness upon his people. The passive form of the third person imperative is also used in the next two petitions. This form, which does not exist in English, prevents the petitioner from addressing a direct command to God to inform him on what he should do. By the use of the aorist passive imperative in the first three petitions, the force of a command to God is muted.[22]

The hallowing of his name, the coming of his kingdom, and the performing of his will on earth are not to be superimposed by a brute display of omnipotence, but by the gentle leading of God, who is now known as Father. The use of the passive does, however, refer to the hallowing of God's name as his activity alone, and not a human action, even by those who are gathered in the community of the followers of Jesus. In the Old Testament God glorifies his own name; he is implored to save his people for the glory of his name. While the holiness of God's name further explicates his transcendental existence, it is also a word that explains his relationship to the world in the redemptive work of Jesus and in the community gathered around him. They share in his holiness. The prayer for the hallowing of God's name means that the God whom the disciples of Jesus now worship as Father is above all things and they can put themselves into his arms with total trust. This petition, "Hallowed (holy) be Thy name," places the disciples of Jesus together with the angels in singing, "Holy, holy, holy is the Lord of hosts" (Isaiah 6:3).[23]

While the chief and uniquely new factor in the preaching of Jesus is reconciliation, the holiness of God calls attention to the total lack of human moral perfection, which necessitates such reconciliation. Not only is God transcendental to human beings as the Creator is to the creature, but he stands apart from his creatures as pure holiness stands apart from human depravity. Some commentators call attention to the fact that the use of the aorist passive voice reflects the eschatological character of the Prayer. This means that the first three Petitions, all of which use the aorist passive, point to that time when God's name will be holy, his kingdom will come, and his will be done. His work has already begun but will not be fully realized until the final appearing of Jesus, the Son of Man, as judge.[24]

"THY KINGDOM COME"

The Second Petition must be understood in relation to Matthew's description of Jesus as one who preaches the kingdom and as a summary of Matthew's entire gospel. "Kingdom" for Matthew can only be understood in the sense that Jesus is the king. The royal genealogy, the conception, the birth in Bethlehem, the triumphal entry into Jerusalem, and his death all are part of Matthew's presentation of Jesus as king. Behind this lies the Old Testament office of king, which reached its fullest expression in the reigns of David and Solomon, upon both of whom the evangelist relies in presenting Jesus as king. The term "kingdom" for the evangelist does not in any way take on a political hue. In John this is made explicit when Jesus responds to Pilate that his kingdom is not of this world (18:36). The Synoptics agree in seeing Jesus confess to Pilate that he is a king, but his kingship is of such a religious, otherworldly character that even the Roman procurator understands it in a nonthreatening sense without any political implications. He finds Jesus innocent, but the Jews insist that the kingship of Jesus means political insurrection against Rome (27:11, 24). For Matthew Jesus stands aloof from civil and political affairs.

The word "kingdom" focuses not on God as the Creator King, but on God's work in Jesus, whom he has designated to construct himself a kingdom.[25] Both the Baptist and Jesus come preaching that the kingdom is near. The parables (Chapters 13, 24, 25) are also descriptions of the Kingdom; their central content is Jesus. "Thy kingdom come" is thus the prayer that God would conclude his work of salvation in Jesus. This work reaches its point of culmination in the crucifixion and the resurrection, but it will become visible to all when the Son of Man reveals himself as the king on the Last Day (25:41).

Those who pray "Thy kingdom come" must ask the question whether the kingdom appeared totally in Jesus or whether it still remains to be completed as a future event. Both the Baptist and Jesus are definite in saying that while the kingdom is near, it has not yet fully arrived. It has arrived in the sense that Jesus as King is working among his people (12:28). The crucifixion and resurrection mean that the anticipatory waiting for the coming of the kingdom has been resolved. The resurrection indicates that in the crucifixion Jesus has been recognized as qualified to be God's King and enthroned. But still another question remains: If the Kingdom has *already* appeared in what Jesus has done, how can the Prayer be offered in the post-resurrection church?

This petition does have its focus particularly on Jesus and what he accomplishes for God and for the benefit of many; nevertheless, his work in bringing together all the people of God has not been completed. The kingdom parables of Matthew 13 understand the work of Jesus and the church as being cut from one cloth. The work of Jesus becomes the work of the church. The Beatitudes prepare the reader for this corporate relationship between Jesus and his followers. In Matthew 13 the parables of the treasure in the field and the pearl (44–46) are atonement parables focusing on how much God personally sacrificed of himself for the redemption of the world. God's kingdom is his redemptive activity in Jesus, but it extends itself in the preaching of its redemption. The kingdom thus is described as distributing the seed of the word until the final close of the age when the good and the evil shall be revealed. The prayer for the coming of the Kingdom in the post-resurrection church does not ask God to finish his work of atonement, but that the benefits of the atonement through preaching reach the widest number of people. In Matthew the petition would have specific reference to the final work of Jesus as king when all nations shall appear before him and acknowledge who he is (25:31–46). Then all will call him "Lord."

While Luke has the petition "Thy kingdom come," he does not have the next one, "Thy will be done." One plausible explanation for this omission is that for Luke the kingdom does not refer exclusively to what God *has done* in Jesus but also to what God *is doing* through the community of the followers of Jesus. Matthew's two petitions "Thy kingdom come" and "Thy will be done" become for Luke one, "Thy kingdom come." The kingdom for Luke is not exclusively christological, but it is also ecclesiological.

For Matthew, "kingdom" includes God's opposition to Satan's kingdom. The coming of Jesus means that God's rule in him makes inroads into Satan's rule in the lives of people (12:26, 28). This provides another eschatological dimension to this petition. The church prays that when Jesus is revealed as Lord (5:41), Satan's defeat will be exhibited before all men.[26] "Thy kingdom come" embraces everything that God does for man in Jesus; Matthew's gospel is the account of the coming of this kingdom. Thus this petition could serve as a summary title of the gospel.

"THY WILL BE DONE"

If the Second Petition, "Thy kingdom come," speaks specifically to what God has done (Matthew) and is doing (Matthew and Luke) in Jesus, the Third Petition for Matthew speaks of what God is accomplishing among men as a response to his kingdom. "Thy will be done" presupposes "Thy kingdom come" and is a consequence of it. The community of Jesus' followers prays that God may work *among* them, as he has already worked *in* Jesus. As mentioned, Luke sees the kingdom and the will of God being accomplished as one work and thus omits this petition. For Matthew these two activities are distinguished from each other. For Matthew the Father's will is the divine desire to save all people: Jesus "will save his people from their sins" (Matthew 1:21). The performance of the Father's will in the church is the certain mark that it belongs to Jesus. Thus in the pericope of the children, it is the Father's will that none of these little ones should be lost (18:14). Matthew's church is baptizing children (28:19, 20). Even Jesus' submission to the Father's will is in the context of whether another plan of salvation for the world is possible (26:42). Jesus thus understands himself as the one through whom God's will is being accomplished.[27] The person who survives the judgment of the Last Day is not merely the one who recognizes Jesus as Lord but the one who does the Father's will, that is, he spreads the message of salvation.

The temptation is to understand performing the will of God in a moral or ethical sense as the fulfillment of divine legal demands. This interpretation fails on several counts. The Prayer is addressed not to God as Lawgiver but to the God who has become Father in Jesus and on account of him has established a new redemptive relationship with men. God's will is that the redemption effected in Jesus becomes operative in the world through the community gathered around him.[28] What God has begun in Jesus is now brought to final completion in and through the church, the followers of Jesus. God's will is that all may recognize him as Father and that they in turn be recognized as his sons by their offering up this prayer: "Our Father." For where this prayer is truly prayed, God's will has been realized. In the parable of the two sons who are asked to work the vineyard, the son who refuses and then does the father's will is compared to the tax collectors and prostitutes who believed the message of John (21:28–32).

In the context of the Gospel, performing the will of God involves being baptized. John's message necessarily involved being baptized (3:1–6). Doing the will of God is believing. Refusing the will of God is not repenting and believing. Jerusalem is condemned because the will of its inhabitants has thwarted the will of God for their salvation. In 12:50 Jesus says that his disciples are his mother, sisters, and brothers because they have done the will of his Father.[29] This serves as a commentary on and elaboration of this petition in the Lord's Prayer. Those who pray it have become the family of Jesus and thus are recognized as qualified to pray "Our Father."

Some in the early church understood the petition for the coming of the kingdom as a prayer for the Holy Spirit. Gregory of Nyssa understood the coming of God's kingdom as the coming of the Holy Spirit. "Thy will be done" was thus seen as a request for the Holy Spirit. This understanding is not without support either in the church tradition or the New Testament itself.[30] The coming of the kingdom through the preaching of the Gospel has been ascribed in the Christian tradition to the Holy Spirit. This follows Paul, who attributed the making of a confession in Jesus to the Holy Spirit (1 Corinthians 23:3). In Acts, Luke sees the Holy Spirit as the instigator of the church's growth and missionary endeavors. Moreover, Luke has included as a commentary to his version of the Lord's Prayer these words: "...how much more will the Father from heaven give the Holy Spirit to those who ask him!" (11:13). In his version of the Prayer Luke has no specific request for the Spirit, but in his explanation of the Prayer he interprets Matthew's "the good things" as the Holy Spirit. The post-apostolic church in interpreting the first three (Luke: two) petitions clearly followed Luke's lead. The "good things" or the Holy Spirit, while possibly applicable to everything requested in the prayer, has its real center point in the request for the coming of the kingdom or the doing of God's will. In Matthew too the doing of God's will is made possible by the Holy Spirit. Jesus goes into the wilderness to perform the Father's will with the assistance of the Spirit (4:1), and in the hour of persecution it is the Spirit who testifies to Jesus through the apostles (10:20).

"ON EARTH AS IT IS IN HEAVEN"

This phrase reflects Genesis 1:1, where heaven and earth refer to the totality of God's creation. But the phrase presupposes that the earth is still estranged from heaven. Some commentators see in the structure of the Prayer that the words "on earth as it is in heaven" apply not only to the petition "Thy will be done" but also to the previous two, "Hallowed be Thy name" and "Thy kingdom come."[31] In Greek, each of the three petitions begins with the verb, includes the noun, and concludes with "thy" or "of you." Though this cannot be duplicated with precision in English, it would come close to looking like this:

Our Father who art in heaven,
> Holy be the name of you.
> Come the kingdom of you.
> Do the will of you,
>> On earth as it is in heaven.[32]

The first half of the Lord's Prayer is easily recognized as a composite unit, grammatically focusing the content on God. In contrast, the second half has to do more specifically with requests from, for, and about the community. One commentator finds that the requests of these first three petitions are so similar that the petitions for the coming of the kingdom and the performing of the divine will are simply further explications of the hallowing of the divine name.[33] The coming of the kingdom and the doing of God's will are in effect the actualizing of making God's name holy. The first three petitions are then taken as explanations of the address: "Our Father who art in heaven." Yet this is not a mere address, but the confession that, in Jesus, God has become the Father. The first three petitions develop different aspects of this confession. The name of God becomes holy when others through the revelation made in Jesus learn to know him as Father. This is Luther's intent in the Small Catechism where he explains that his will is done among us by the pure preaching of the Word. The Kingdom is the accomplishment of the Father's plan in Jesus. The doing of God's will is the Spirit's activity in bringing people to recognize that in Jesus God has become their Father.

The church since Matthew has distinguished between prayer and creed. For many Christians it is one thing to *pray* the Lord's Prayer and another to *say* the Creed. The early church, however, saw the Prayer as a creed and prayed it in a Trinitarian sense. Praying was confessing faith in the Father of Jesus.[34] The Lord's Prayer anticipated the Apostles' Creed. In post-Enlightenment Christianity, God has been understood generally in a unitarian sense, with the role of Jesus limited to that of a revealer. Of all the evangelists Matthew has the most explicit Trinitarian theology, as exhibited in the last verses with the command to make disciples by baptizing them in the name of the Father and of the Son and of the Holy Spirit. Thus Matthew's Gospel is marked by the tension of an advanced theology while still dependent on the Old Testament for its content and structure.[35]

In his baptism Jesus receives the Father's approval in the voice from heaven (3:17) and sees the Spirit of God (3:16), who directs him in his messianic ministry (4:1). The "our" of the "Our Father" is spoken by those who have been given faith to recognize who Jesus really is and have been gathered together by the Spirit in a community to commemorate and celebrate what God has done through him. The words of the "Our Father" are made known only to those who have been joined to the community of Jesus by Baptism and the working of the Spirit. In Luke's gospel the prayer for the kingdom was understood as one for the continual working of the Holy Spirit in their midst. Thus it would seem that, from its inclusion in Matthew's gospel, the Lord's Prayer was understood in a "Christianized" sense and not simply as a near-random selection of sayings taken over from Judaism with meanings hardly different from what rabbis had seen in them. The Lord's Prayer was first of all a confession of what God had done in Jesus and was still doing through the Holy Spirit in the church. It was also a prayer that God would be gracious to his children as the community of the followers of Jesus and that he would come to their assistance.

THE LORD'S PRAYER IN ITS CONCERN FOR THE CHURCH

The second half of the Lord's Prayer, with its picture of the church in the need caused by its suffering and persecution, stands in sharp contrast

to God's majestic work in the first three petitions. The aorist passives of
the first three petitions, suggesting the sublime majestic working of God
pursuing his goals according to his own nature, are replaced by active
aorist imperatives, suggesting an urgency in a race with an impending
peril.[36] These are direct, undisguised commands. From God's point of
view, which is the perspective of the first three petitions, all he desires will
inevitably take place. Since God is God, all that takes place in heaven will
finally, eschatologically, take place on earth. This is what it means when
the Prayer's first part concludes with "on earth as it is in heaven." Here
there is divine certainty. The church can possess this certainty as she prays
the Lord's Prayer. From the view of earth, however, the ultimate victory of
God over his enemies (who have now also become the church's enemies)
does not seem as certain. In fact just the opposite is so. God's cause is suffering. Hence the near-desperate cries of the last four petitions.

In the English language the imperative is in the active voice—giving a
command directly to another person. The English language has difficulty
expressing an imperative in the passive voice. The passive imperatives in
Greek, all in the aorist tense in the first three petitions, suggest the certainty with which God will bring about the hallowing of his name, the
coming of his kingdom, and the doing of his will. The *active* imperative in
the aorist tense in the second part of the Prayer carries with it an immedi-
acy: "Do it right now." Thus the Fourth Petition is not simply a request to
keep giving us bread, but rather "Give us the bread right away." By itself
it would appear that the concluding four petitions have a note of rudeness
or coarseness to them. They are unconditional. They are demanding.
They ask for immediate resolution of the problems.[37] The last four petitions reflect and anticipate the terror of the disciples in the storm (8:28),
of the sinking Peter (8:30), and the desperation of the Canaanite woman
(15:22). Like the Prayer's last petitions, these requests for immediate help
use the aorist imperative.

The demand for immediate relief in the final four petitions is understandable in that as the church prays she is aware that her existence is
threatened by Satan. If the phrase "on earth as it is in heaven" gives meaning to all of the first three petitions, "Deliver us from the Evil One
(Satan)," the final one, gives meaning to the last four. The church's prayer
for bread, forgiveness, avoidance of temptation is made under the real
threat that Satan wants to deprive the church of her life's sustenance.
Unless the church's requests are answered right away, she will be destroyed

by Satan. The church exists under the threat that she will be eschatologically removed from God's presence.

In other parts of the Sermon the Satanic threat to the church is developed. God and mammon cannot be served at the same time (6:24). In the chapter on the parables Satan is held responsible for unbelief and for unbelievers masquerading as members of the community of Jesus (13:19, 25). The church's real life as part of God's kingdom is hid with God where ultimate victory is assured; however, the church's life in the world, the life which is seen, is continually threatened by Satanic forces which appear eminently successful. In the face of this threat her cries expressed in the last four petitions are uttered out of sheer desperation.

The urgency of the last four petitions can also be understood as a mark of the community's hope for itself. Those who offer them up to God are those who have come to know him as Father in Jesus. There is no need for formality, lengthy ritual, and repetition. The community of God's children has every right to expect the best possible treatment from him whom they know as Father. Serpents are not given in the place of fish or stones in the place of bread (7:9–12). The prayer of desperate urgency asking for immediate resolution does not point to the church's unbelief but to its faith even in the hour of her trial.

"GIVE US THIS DAY OUR DAILY BREAD" (THE EUCHARISTIC PETITION)

No other article in the Lord's Prayer has given scholars as much cause for debate as this one, having left them with many unanswered questions. Controversy centers around the meaning of the Greek words for "bread" and "daily." The Greek word *epiousion*, which is rendered in English as "daily," is found for certain in ancient literature only in the Matthean and Lucan versions of the Lord's Prayer. Some scholars claim that the word has been identified in the Egyptian papyri, but it is not completely spelled out and thus the evidence is at this time inconclusive. The word has been connected to two different verbs, one of which means "to be" and the other "to come." Thus attached to the word "bread" *epiousios* would have either of these two meanings: the bread which we need for our existence (our being), or the bread which we need for tomorrow. Thus the petition in the Lord's Prayer would read: "Give us today the bread which we need to live" or "Give us today enough bread for tomorrow." The first meaning may be reflected in the common translation "daily bread." The second one, "bread for the future," has growing support, as scholars note the strong eschatological thrust of the Prayer.[38] Though this meaning is not absolutely certain, it is an attractive solution that fits the eschatological thrust of the Prayer and the entire gospel. When bread is taken literally, it means that God should attend to our earthly needs; but instead of giving us an overabundance, he should give us just enough to see us through one day at a time, since the end is impending. Bread taken in a literal sense in both understandings, necessary bread or bread for the future, would mean ordinary food; in Luther's words, "all that we need to support this body and life." Though many prominent scholars today see here a reference to the ordinary food of life, it is doubtful that it was taken this way in the early post-apostolic church.[39] This petition was understood first sacramentally as a prayer for Jesus himself, the Bread of Life. Commonly called the spiritual view, the Fourth Petition would then mean that the church prayed that in the Lord's Supper it would feed on Jesus. The Catholic tradition following the spiritual view continued the ancient church understanding. Protestant scholars tended in the opposite direction. This may be a clear case where the predisposition of the interpreters on the importance of the Sacrament determined their conclusions.[40]

In Gerhardsson's view, nothing new or significant on the meaning of *epiousios* has been offered in the last 50 years.[41] If the matter cannot be resolved by designating a commonly agreed-upon meaning for the word itself, since it is used only in the Lord's Prayer, then the meaning must come from the possibilities allowed by the gospel itself and early interpretations. In other words, it had a definite meaning for those who first heard the Gospel read in its entirety. The two interpretations of seeing it as the bread we need for our existence today or for tomorrow are not mutually exclusive, so we are not completely at sea in locating a meaning. Though the phrase "daily bread" is part of our regular religious vocabulary, it does not convey the full sense. The word "daily" does not violate the meaning of *epiousios*, but it hardly does it justice. "Daily," the usual English translation, is redundant, since the last word of the petition, "today" (of which there is no doubt in its meaning), carries with it the same idea as does "daily." Such a redundancy in a short prayer is hard to explain and not necessary for its meaning. Nothing is lost by trying to find another meaning. Since the word *epiousios* may have more than one translation, other approaches must be sought to determine the meaning of the Fourth Petition.[42]

Several things can be noted about the petition "Give us this day our daily bread." First of all, among the seven petitions it is placed fourth and thus is directly in the middle of the seven petitions of the Lord's Prayer. If

172 THE SERMON ON THE MOUNT

only six petitions are acknowledged, it still occupies the first position in the
"we" petitions, those requests in the Prayer by which the church prays for
its own benefit. The first three deal with what God does for himself: the
hallowing of his name, the coming of his kingdom, and the performance
of his will on earth.[43] Unique to the Fourth Petition is that it is the only
one in which the thing asked for is mentioned first. All the others place the
thing requested after the verb. For example, the Fifth Petition has the
same order as the Greek, "Forgive us our trespasses." The order of the
Fourth Petition is, "The bread of us which we need (for tomorrow) give to
us today." Our common English rendering reverses the word order to
"Give us this day our daily bread," and thus the emphasis on bread is lost.
The Greek version calls attention to the desperate cry of the petitioner for
bread, an agony lost in the English translation.

Common is the interpretation that this petition is a request for earthly food, as a prerequisite necessary for the disciples to accomplish the work
of Jesus in this world. Without ordinary sustenance they could not live and
effectively carry out the work which has been entrusted to them; "Even
when the reign of God has drawn nigh, the people of God need daily
food."[44] Other commentators suggest that as God supplies enough food for
tomorrow, the disciple of Jesus does not need to be burdened down with
concerns.[45] Such interpretations are not without merit but seem to be
motivated more by a growing consciousness of overpopulation with its
increased demand on the sources of food production than the first-century church's real life around the Eucharist, which nourishes her.

Other considerations point strongly toward the eucharistic interpretation of the bread petition. Perhaps the choice between the earthly and the
heavenly bread is artificial and "bread" could be taken first as a reference
to earthly food and then in a second sense to a higher level and understood
in a sacramental sense as a reference to Jesus, the bread from heaven. Such
a double interpretation was offered by some Western fathers, including
Tertullian, Cyprian, and Augustine. Thus the petition for bread is our asking God to provide both for our earthly and our spiritual, heavenly sustenance. For the Christian the earthly eating cannot be divorced from the
heavenly one. Even if the request for daily bread is taken over from the
Eighteen Benedictions—there seems no reason to deny at least an influence—the disciples of Jesus in the post-resurrection church recognized
that these words had a more profound meaning.

The first objection raised against a eucharistic understanding of this
petition is that the Lord's Supper was instituted after the Lord's Prayer.

Such an objection fails to realize that Matthew has intended his gospel not as a chronological account of the life of Jesus but rather as a theological compendium of his life and message. It also does not take into account that the first hearers (readers) of this gospel already knew what it contained. For these very first Christians bread was associated with Jesus and the Supper that commemorated his death for them. It is unlikely that they would have thought of anything else. At least at the second hearing, the eucharistic interpretations become obvious. Those who find a eucharistic meaning for bread impossible because they regard the Gospel as a chronological record instead of a theological discourse should logically be compelled to conclude that the Lord's Prayer's request for the forgiveness of sins has nothing to do with the death of Jesus, because it had not happened and he had not discussed it with his disciples. Luke, for example, connects the Prayer's petition on forgiveness with the death of Jesus by showing that he forgave his enemies from the cross (23:34). Both Matthew and Luke presuppose that the reader knows of Jesus' death and resurrection and his institution of Baptism and the Supper. Though Matthew in his gospel brings together various logia, he intends them to be taken as a totality, with one section shedding light on the other. An *a priori* exclusion of the possibility that the Fourth Petition is a reference to the Lord's Supper fails to take into consideration that Matthew intended his gospel as catechesis or instruction for new Christians and addressed chronology only in such matters as the birth and resurrection. The order of his gospel is topically arranged for a church that was already preaching Jesus as crucified and resurrected, requiring Baptism, and celebrating the Lord's Supper.[46]

Thus if the question is asked, "What did the original hearers of Jesus understand by the word 'bread?'," a second question has to be asked at the same time: "What did Matthew want the original hearers of his gospel to understand when they heard these words?" The gospel, as we have it, was written for Matthew's church. A related matter is the meaning of "bread" in the post-resurrection community, where it has a decisively sacramental meaning. How could it be otherwise? Ultimately everything in the gospels had to be understood in a post-resurrection sense. The resurrection is the interpretative event, bestowing on the words and acts of Jesus a fullness of meaning that was not self-evident to those who heard and saw them before the crucifixion. Matthew pictures the original hearers of his Sermon not as the crowds whose response is astonishment, but as the disciples, to whom Jesus directs the instruction.[47] In recording the Sermon, Matthew is instructing his hearers.

An allowance for a further interpretation of the words of Jesus must be made for those who did not know his words before the crucifixion and only came to learn them as candidates for Baptism in the post-resurrection church. The crowds too, who hear the Sermon but do not fully understand, would have had at least a minimal sacramental understanding of bread, as it had a ritual and redemptive significance from its use in the Old Testament.[48] For the Jews bread was not simply food, but the means through which God nourished Israel as his own people. The manna of the wilderness clearly had a sacramental significance, as the Father, not Moses, fed the people. Manna, though inferior to Jesus, was nevertheless the bread from heaven (John 6:31, 32). The place of the petition for bread in the Prayer itself gives it such a pivotal role in the structure that it is almost impossible not to see that here is a request for something extraordinary. Not only is the word "bread" placed first in the petition, in a way which is totally unlike the other six, but the following petition, "And forgive us our debts," is connected with it with the conjunction *kai*. Some scholars see no connection between God's granting forgiveness and providing ordinary bread for daily living.[49] Just the opposite can well be true. Excessive concern for earthly food destroys faith (6:25–33); lack of food can also undermine faith (Proverbs 30:8-9). In John's gospel, forgiveness is attached to the sacramental eating of the bread which is Jesus' body (John 6:51). In Matthew's gospel, the forgiveness of sins ("sins" is Luke's substitute for Matthew's "debts") is specifically attached to the drinking cup of the blood of Jesus (26:28) and not to the sacramental bread. (The Supper, however, could be referred to in the early church by any of its parts: bread, cup, body, blood.) Luke complements Matthew by saying that both the body (bread) and blood of Jesus (cup) are given for the church's benefit (22:19–20). There is little doubt that Matthew saw both sacramental elements and not only the cup as salvifically beneficial. In fact Luke's specific attachment of salvific benefit to the sacramental bread may have been intended to overcome any misunderstanding that both elements were vehicles of salvation for the church.

Perhaps most problematic for interpreting "bread" as ordinary food is the negative attitude taken to it not only in the Sermon but in Matthew's gospel. In 6:25–34, which closely follow the Lord's Prayer, Jesus explicitly and at length forbids concern about earthly bread.[50] Gentiles, that is, pagans, are the ones who pray about things, and their preoccupation with tomorrow is forbidden (6:32, 34). Concern for food is placed right after the warning against serving mammon. Perhaps even more striking is a following pericope on fasting (6:16–18). The Lord's Prayer is followed first by a theological explanation of the petition on the necessity of forgiving one's offenders (14–15). This then is followed by some verses on fasting. How can it be explained that after a petition for ordinary food the evangelist offers a pericope on the proper way in which one should abstain from food by fasting? The earthly food, requested in the Lord's Prayer and then presumably granted, is then refused through fasting. How could the evangelist permit such a glaring contradiction to stand, if indeed the Fourth Petition is a prayer for ordinary bread? The ordinances for fasting in the Sermon must have their prime reference to the post-resurrection church, that time when Jesus would be visibly absent from his church (9:15). Matthew does picture Jesus as fasting in preparation for his temptation (4:2); but rather than being given to abstinence he was in contrast to the Baptist known as a glutton and a winebibber (11:18–19).

The petition for bread in the Lord's Prayer is thus likely a request for *the* bread and food needed for the kingdom that is coming. This bread is a *viaticum*, a food that nourishes the believers for the coming kingdom. Even if it cannot be known for certain what the Greek word *epiousios* means, the entire thrust of the Lord's Prayer is eschatological, that is, it concentrates on what God is *going* to do in Jesus here on earth for the church. The petition has to do with the food which is necessary for existence in the kingdom now on earth. The nature of this bread is best described as an everlasting bread, as coming from God, identified with Jesus (15:26–27), and necessary for the Christian's existence.[51]

The coming of the kingdom means negatively a lack of concern for one's own life and positively a concern for those things that make life possible in the new world. Fasting does not have its value in that man is deprived of food, but rather it anticipates the next life, in which man is fed by God. He lives a life which is no longer dependent on ordinary food. In his fast in the desert Jesus refuses to turn stones into bread because even in this world man is nourished not "by bread alone, but by every word that proceeds from the mouth of God" (4:4). God's Word is bread and food for those who live in his presence. No dichotomy exists between the redemptive Word and Jesus. For the church that Word must not only come from Jesus, but must be Jesus himself. Moses does without food and drink for 40 days in Sinai because his existence is determined by God (Exodus 34:28). The two pericopes of the miraculous feedings (Matthew 14:13–21; 15:32–39) share the purpose not only of showing the compassion of Jesus but of showing that the disciples of Jesus are not to be concerned for food,

even if it is given in a miraculous way. The divine providing of food for the
crowds does not generate faith in them or in the disciples, who twice ask
the question of how they will be fed. In spite of the first divine feeding, the
disciples remain concerned about their being fed.[52]

Matthew coordinates his picture of the eschatological eating of the
next world with his condemnation for concern and anxiety about the
earthly bread. The first statement of Jesus that the Gentiles shall be saved
is made in the context of their sitting at a banquet with the patriarchs in
the kingdom of the heavens (8:11). This heavenly eating in Matthew is
eschatological, as it comes to its fullest expression in the appearance of
Jesus on the Last Day. This is also taught in the parable of the wedding
feast. The filling of the wedding hall with guests is a picture of that eschatological banquet (22:1–10).[53] Luke's version of the parable begins with
"Blessed is he who shall eat bread in the kingdom of God" (14:15). The
Lucan beatitude is descriptive of Matthew 8:11, where the Gentiles join
the patriarchs in banqueting.

The eschatological eating, which will accompany the final appearing
of Jesus, is joined by Matthew as promise to the institution of the Last
Supper. "I tell you I shall not drink again of this fruit of the vine until
that day when I drink it new with you in the Father's kingdom" (26:29).
The Supper gives not only the bread as the body of Jesus which forgives
sins, but it is already a participation in the heavenly banquet, that is, an
unveiling of what God will do continually for the followers of Jesus in
the new kingdom. The petition for bread is a request not only for divine
help in God's kingdom now present in the Lord's Supper but for participation in the final supper.[54] It is the bread of the morrow, of God's
revealed kingdom.

Thus the bread of the Fourth Petition can hardly refer to the earthly
food, since concern for the earthly bread means that the disciple of Jesus
is no longer understanding God as his heavenly Father who provides for
all his needs and even those of unbelievers and the brute creation
(Matthew 6:25, 32). It refers best to the bread that belongs uniquely to the
entire community. The concept of the community appears twice in the
petition: "Give *us* this day *our* daily bread." The prayer is not "Give *me*
this day *my* daily bread." This is the bread which is not given to satisfy
the needs of individuals but the needs of the community of the followers
of Jesus.[55]

Without this bread they cannot exist before God in the trials and persecutions of today and they cannot persevere until the final revealing of

that kingdom on the Day of Judgment. This bread provides sustenance as the church suffers and at the same time anticipates the final manifestation of Jesus as king. Already in the apostolic church, bread became synonymous with that sacramental meal commemorating the death of Jesus. The eating of the bread was proclamation of the Lord's death (1 Corinthians 11:26). Luke, as mentioned, attaches a sacramental benefit to both the bread and the cup, though it can hardly be argued that Matthew's attachment of this benefit to the cup alone was intended to exclude the bread from offering any salvific benefit. The Fifth Petition does in fact attach forgiveness to the bread in the Fourth Petition by the word "and." In the Lucan post-resurrection appearances the Third Evangelist uses "bread" within the context of obvious sacramental significance.

In Luke 24:30 Jesus' eating of the bread with the disciples in Emmaus is freighted with eucharistic language. "When he was at table with them, he took (*labōn*) the bread (*ton arton*) and blessed (*eulogēsen*), and broke (*klasas*) it, and gave (*epedidou*) it to them." All five of the indicated Greek words are used in each of the synoptic accounts of the Lord's Supper (Matthew 26:26; Luke 22:19; Mark 14:22) in the same order: taking bread, blessing it, breaking it, giving it. Matthew's version reads, "Now as they were eating, Jesus took (*labōn*) bread (*arton*), and blessed (*eulogēsas*) and broke it (*eklasen*), and gave (*dous*) it to his disciples." The eucharistic action in the synoptic gospels included taking, blessing, breaking, and giving the bread, the same order used at Emmaus.[56] The intention of the Lucan pericope is that the resurrected Lord will maintain his presence in the church through "the breaking of the bread," the Eucharist; as Luke writes, "he was known to them in the breaking of the bread" (24:35). The Supper was the moment of the revelation of the resurrected Lord. Luke also sees the Eucharist, here called "the bread," as one of the marks of the early Jerusalem congregation: "And they devoted themselves to the apostles' teaching [*didachē tōn apostolōn*]: a possible reference to the gospel of Matthew and especially the Sermon on the Mount] and fellowship [*koinōnia*: the Communion], to the breaking of bread [*klasei tou artou*] and the prayers" [the petitions of the Lord's Prayer]" (Acts 2:42). This passage resembles Paul's description of the Lord's Supper in 1 Corinthians 10:16: "The bread [*ton arton*] which we break [*klōmen*], is it not a participation [*koinōnia*] in the body of Christ?" The Acts passage, written after 1 Corinthians, would have been understood by its first readers as referring to the eucharistic eating in the post-ascension church. The Communion or the participation (*koinōnia*) was the breaking of bread, as these two acts stand in apposition.[57] It is not certain whether

Acts 2:46 is inexact when it seems to refer to the eucharistic action as a daily affair: "And day by day, attending the temple together and *breaking bread* in their homes [church houses], they partook of food [possibly the heavenly food] with glad and generous hearts." It is also unclear whether "day by day" refers to their temple prayers only or also to their eucharistic celebration.

The custom of a daily sacramental celebration is required by the Roman Catholic Church of its priests, who under ordinary circumstances are to offer up one Mass each day. A daily celebration might have originated with the interpretation that the early Christians celebrated the sacrament daily. There is equally persuasive evidence that it was a weekly event commemorating Sunday as the day of the resurrection. The "today" in "Give us this day our daily bread" could be and indeed has been taken as a command for a daily celebration of the Lord's Supper.[58] Though the Lord's Prayer served as *the* prayer of the Christian community, it was prayed also privately, but not individualistically. Yet the one who prayed privately did so in the context of the Christian community. It may be that the practice of a daily Eucharist was not uniform in all the apostolic churches. At Troas a weekly celebration on the first day of the week may have been the more usual custom: "On the first day of the week [literally: "on the day after the Sabbath," that is, Sunday], when we were gathered together to break bread [*klasai arton*], Paul..." (Acts 20:7). Two things can be noted about the church in Troas. The term "on the first day after the Sabbath" may be a deliberate attempt on Luke's part to refer to the Sunday celebration of the Lord's Supper as taking place in commemoration of Easter, which Matthew also describes as taking place on the first day of the Sabbath (28:1). Second, the breaking of the bread is part of the terminology used in the Pauline epistles for the sacramental eating (1 Corinthians 10:16).[59]

A long-standing and perhaps irresolvable debate is whether John 6 is eucharistic. If it is, then the testimony of the Fourth Gospel could be added to Luke-Acts and Paul in understanding bread as eucharistic. The Lutheran tradition generally opposed a eucharistic interpretation. Historically, Luther's opponent Zwingli had used the passage "the flesh profits nothing" (6:63) as evidence against understanding the bread as Christ's body. The solution was for Luther to remove John 6 from eucharistic discussion. Luther's encounter with Zwingli still accounts for a widespread Lutheran reluctance to understand John 6 as eucharistic.

Church tradition, however, from the very earliest times right up to the Reformation saw eucharistic significance in John 6, and even the

Lutherans incorporated its language into public expressions of their sacramental piety. On the superficial level, it would be hard to deny that the
Johannine language is sacramental. Such phrases as "the true bread,"
"bread of God," and "Bread of Life" point to something beyond ordinary
bodily nourishment. The person who eats this bread never dies. It is further described as the flesh of Jesus given for the world's life. The one eating the flesh and blood will be raised up on the Last Day (33, 34, 35,
48–54). Even John's substitute of flesh (*sarx*) for body (*sōma*) is understandable from his opposition to any spiritualizing of Christianity. What presented a problem in accepting a eucharistic understanding was taking the
eating of the flesh and the blood as an absolute requirement (53). It was
argued that since some people are saved without receiving the Sacrament,
this absolute requirement would have to be understood in a figurative and
not real sense. The only requirement for salvation is faith. Thus the eating and drinking of Jesus was interpreted as faith. Such a sense was, however, condemned by the Lutherans when the Reformed applied it to the
eucharistic words in the synoptic gospels and Paul. A eucharistic interpretation of John 6, however, could be seen as no more an obstacle than the
necessity attached to Baptism in John 3:5, for which the church has always
made exceptions. Reserving Baptisms for the Easter vigil indicated that in
these cases its absence was not salvifically threatening. John 6:53 stresses
the refusal to eat the flesh and blood of Jesus as the cause for damnation.
· Eating the flesh of Jesus is no more or no less an absolute requirement
than Baptism. Space does not permit a detailed study of John 6 with all of
its implications, but there are certain indications that this chapter was
intended by the Fourth Evangelist to provide a commentary in some sense
on the Fourth Petition of the Lord's Prayer, "Give us this day our daily
bread," whether he knew it from the common possession of the church or
from Matthew.[60]

The argument that Jesus had not yet instituted the Lord's Supper at
the time the Lord's Prayer was given is the same kind of argument raised
against any eucharistic understanding of John 6. Both arguments do not
take into account that the gospels were written for post-Easter Christian
communities who were already instructed, baptized, and were gathering
regularly for sacramental worship. The gospels were written for liturgical
use, as they were to be read at the weekly Eucharist.[61] This is even more
obvious in John's community than it was in Matthew's. The Fourth Gospel
must in some sense presuppose information about Jesus which only
Matthew and Luke preserve, as John does not have birth narratives and the

institution of Baptism and the Lord's Supper. He does, however, provide theological commentary on events known to us only through the Synoptics, so John 6 serves as a theological commentary on the Lord's Supper, as John 3 with the Nicodemus account serves as one on Baptism.

John uses eucharistic language to portray the feeding of the five thousand, an account found in all three synoptic gospels. That all four gospels should report one event from Jesus' ministry prior to his suffering is remarkable. Whereas John uses the feeding of the five thousand to introduce a eucharistic discussion, Matthew's feeding of the five thousand is followed by that of the four thousand. Whatever the intent of the first miraculous feeding was, it is enforced by a second one. Then comes the warning against the leaven of the Pharisees and Sadducees. All four gospels agree in that although the miraculous feedings reveal that God is active in Jesus in a special way, such earthly feedings should not be understood as ultimate. Jesus' warning, "Do not labor for the food which perishes" (John 6:27) serves as parallel to the warning to beware of the leaven of the Pharisees and Sadducees (Matthew 16:11, 12). John's understanding of "bread" as Jesus himself is similar to Matthew's, yet John makes that meaning more explicit. For example, in the warning against the leaven of the Pharisees and Sadducees (16:6) the reference to bread is clearly implied; unless the bread is in view, the explicit reference to leaven cannot be clearly understood. Leaven is identified as their teachings, which corrupt the true teachings of Jesus (16:11, 12). The teachings of Jesus are the bread that the leaven of the Pharisees may corrupt. Between the two Matthean miraculous feedings comes the account of the Canaanite woman, who when refused bread, insists on having the crumbs. Jesus introduces the concept of bread as what seems to be an obvious self-reference in his role as the Redeemer of Israel. "I was only sent to the lost sheep of the house of Israel" (15:24; cf. 1:21, "he shall save *his* people from their sins.") The bread that Jesus refuses her is himself in his redemptive (and healing) work. The language of the crumbs falling from the tables of their masters is the same as Paul's eucharistic language in 1 Corinthians 10:21: "you cannot partake of the table of the Lord." In the pericope of the Canaanite woman the evangelist may have deliberately employed what had already become eucharistic language in the church, not only to point to Jesus as the Bread but to the availability of this Bread at the church's table, which had become known as the table of the Lord (1 Corinthians 10:21). At this table participants as members of the kingdom had become lords (*kyrioi:* Jesus is *kyrios,* the Lord) (Matthew 15:27). Matthew places the pericope of the Canaanite woman between two miraculous feedings to identify Jesus as the true Bread. The crowds seek an earthly bread like the manna that is destined for corruption. The woman seeks the heavenly Bread that lasts forever. The crowds along with the disciples experience and benefit from the wondrous feeding, but they do not believe or really comprehend. The woman sees no miracle, is rejected by Jesus, and still insists that she is entitled to receive the crumbs from the Bread which is Jesus. Matthew does not have John's "I am the Bread," but he nevertheless makes the identification between the bread and Jesus.[62]

Also remarkable is that in both miraculous feeding accounts (the five thousand and four thousand), Matthew makes use of language which he will employ in the institution of the Eucharist (26:26–27). In the first account there is a blessing (*eulogeō*), a breaking of the bread, and distribution to the disciples, who in turn distribute it to the crowds (14:19). In the second feeding there is a thanking (*eucharistō*), a breaking of bread, and a distribution to the disciples, and again they give it to the crowds (15:36). In the institution of the Supper, there is a blessing (*eulogeō*), a breaking of the bread, and a distribution to the disciples. Use of identical language is hardly coincidental, but rather a deliberate attempt on the part of the Evangelist to connect these three events. With the cup there is a thanksgiving (*eucharisto*).[63] John 6:11 also initiates the miracle with the same eucharistic language; Jesus takes bread, gives thanks, and distributes. For Matthew Jesus as the real Bread is implicit. For John, as befits a theological commentator, Jesus as the real Bread is explicit, as is characteristic of his discourses. Both Matthew and John agree in finding the earthly bread inadequate for the life of God now being revealed in Jesus. For this new life Jesus is the true Bread. Where John concentrates on the person of Jesus, Matthew seems to expand this to include Jesus with his message. Common to both Matthew and John is that Jesus is *the* Bread.

In John, after Jesus speaks about a bread superior to the one given in the wilderness, the Jews ask Jesus, "Lord, give us this bread always" (6:34). The phrase is strikingly similar to the Fourth Petition. In both, the thing asked for (the bread) and the verb (give) are the same. The aorist tense carries with it an urgency. Matthew's "each day" becomes John's "always," but both stress that this bread is necessary each day. "Always" has the same meaning as "each day." Both stress the community aspect with "us." John pictures the Jews refusing to believe and murmuring as did their forefathers in the desert (6:43). Their behavior resembles that of those who refuse the king's invitation to his son's wedding in the Matthean parable

(22:5-7). *Whether John intended it or not, his handling of the bread as the flesh of Jesus given for the life of the world (6:51) serves as an interpretative reflection on the synoptic-Pauline tradition which directly identifies the sacramental elements as Jesus in his salvific work: body given and blood shed.*

The social consciousness of Christian churches today has been raised to such a high level that few churches would understand their mission without some sort of commitment to relieve world hunger. Matthew 25 makes this a constituting element on the Day of Judgment. This heightened contemporary concern to feed the hungry has had an adverse affect and presented an obstacle to understanding "Give us this day our daily bread" as a request for the heavenly bread, the bread of the other world and the world to come.

The church fathers of whom we have the earliest records understood the bread of the Lord's Prayer as the eucharistic food: Origen (233), Cyril of Jerusalem (350), and Marius Victorinus (359).[64] Later the material view was fostered by the Antioch school, Basil of Caesarea (365), Gregory of Nyssa (395), and John Chrysostom (395). Some saw both a material and spiritual sense in the petition. At the time of the Reformation the material view of "daily bread" prevailed and Luther put this into his catechisms. This view, of course, has been very influential for the Lutheran catechetical tradition ever since. The Reformed tradition with its symbolic interpretation of the Supper followed the material understanding.[65]

Though the Lord's Prayer is used in a variety of settings, its original place in the liturgy was in connection with the Lord's Supper, the Mass of the Faithful. It was prayed just before the distribution of the elements. The question could be raised whether its place in the liturgy in connection with the Eucharist was responsible for the words being understood eucharistically. The evidence, I believe, points in the opposite direction. Since the words were already eucharistic, they were necessarily and naturally included in the service with the distribution of the bread. The inclusion of the prayer in the Eucharist occurred before the gospels were written. Matthew is not an innovator, but one who preserves the words of Jesus and the church's teaching. Acts 2:42 may indicate that the Supper and the Prayer were placed side by side in the very earliest Jerusalem communities. If the Sermon on the Mount was used in a eucharistic connection, then the early church as disclosed in Acts is only following the pattern which emerged in Matthew.

Perhaps a middle ground for "bread" is most satisfactory, as indicated at the beginning of this discussion. Some early fathers understood bread in the literal sense as earthly good and in the metaphorical sense as a reference to Christ in the Sacrament. Tertullian (200), Cyprian (250), and Cyril of Alexandria (429–444), to cite just a few, see in this petition a reference first to Christ, the bread of heaven and second to the bread which we need in order to live in this world. Theologically there is much to commend such a view, even though the earliest Eastern fathers exclusively favored the spiritual, eucharistic view. The one who feeds the spiritual life with his flesh as the Bread is the same one who feeds the physical life with earthly bread. The earthly bread is made possible by the heavenly Bread. He feeds all (Matthew 5:45), so that all may be led to know that he is the real Bread (Matthew 15:26), 27) which gives life to the world (John 6:33).[66]

Thus the first community of Jesus and his followers today have not understood the physical eating of food and the spiritual eating of the Sacrament as opposed to one another. The physical eating derives its meaning from the spiritual eating. In an extended sense, all ordinary eating becomes eucharistic for the followers of Jesus because the God who provides Jesus as the true Bread also provides the bread (6:31, 7:9) needed to pass through this life to its consummation. The prayer, known as the common table prayer, used in many Christian households is clearly eucharistic, though few are aware of it: "Come, Lord Jesus. Be our Guest. And let these (thy) gifts to us be blessed." If such a prayer had been used in the early church, the presence of Jesus and the blessing of the good would have been understood in the church eucharistically, even with an eschatological note included in the address, "Come, Lord Jesus." The address "Come, Lord Jesus" is both Pauline and Johannine. The Fourth Petition, "Give us this day our daily bread," places the Eucharist squarely not only in the middle of the Lord's Prayer but in the middle of the life of the community of Jesus and the lives of all members of that community.[67]

The prayer for bread is not simply a prayer for bread or food in general, but *the* Bread (*ho artos*), which is Jesus. Thus the first petition in which the church asks the Father to satisfy her needs is first and finally a prayer for Jesus himself.[68] Faith not only believes in Jesus, but its first request is for him. The next petition, of forgiving trespasses, serves only to reinforce the eucharistic understanding of "bread" in the Prayer.[69]

"AND FORGIVE US OUR DEBTS [TRESPASSES], AS WE FORGIVE OUR DEBTORS [THOSE WHO TRESPASS AGAINST US]"

In the Western church the reception of the Lord's Supper was contingent on having received absolution from the priest or pastor. In the Roman

Catholic Church annual confession before the priests is required. In Lutheran congregations Luther's instructions for saying confession before the pastor are now only rarely, if ever, observed. Most liturgies, Catholic or Protestant, contain a general confession, recited by all, and an assurance from the minister that sins have been forgiven by God is put in the place of a specific absolution for the individual. This was hardly early church practice, and the reasons for this development cannot be discussed here, as they involve the understanding of the role of sin, the clergy, forgiveness, and confession and absolution. Still there remains a fundamental connection between a confession of sins and the Lord's Supper. It is still generally practiced that without prior confession and absolution the Supper may not be received. This fundamental connection between absolution and the Lord's Supper may also be found in the Lord's Prayer.

The Matthean version speaks of release from debts owed to God and seems to be more original than its more theologically interpretative Lucan parallel: "And forgive us our sins, for we ourselves forgive everyone who is indebted to us" (11:4). Whereas both Matthew and Luke use the word "debt" to express the wrongs others have done to us, only Matthew uses it to express our offenses against God. Luke introduces the more strictly theological term "sins:" "Forgive us our sins."[70] This serves to distinguish the wrongs done against God as a higher or different kind than those done against others. Matthew knows the word "sins" for wrongs done in the Christian community, but these refer to violations which result in removal of the offender from the community (18:15–20). The *Didache* follows Matthew's "debts" and not Luke's "sins."

The Matthean version of the Prayer does not suggest that God's forgiving us is caused by our forgiving others; the word "as" is used, not "because." "As" means "like" or "similar." We ask that God would forgive us *as*, not *because* we forgive others. Some hold the view that our forgiving precedes God's, but this is done more from a theological and not a grammatical consideration.[71] Matthew's "debts" is more theologically graphic than Luke's "sins." Humans are somehow in debt to God. They owe God something so large and beyond possibility of repayment that their only recourse is to ask that the debt be forgiven. This petition of the Lord's Prayer with its request for God to forgive our debts owed him has the unique distinction of having a commentary about it placed immediately after the prayer: "For if you forgive men their trespasses…" (6:14–15). This short commentary goes to the heart of describing God's activity with man as one of reconciliation and forgiveness. Matthew has already placed the topic of reconciliation before the Prayer (5:38–48) and now he comments on it immediately following the Prayer. The teacher who errs in one point will at least be included in the kingdom, but the one who fails to be reconciled demonstrates in his failure to be reconciled that he does not know God as reconciliatory Father and is excluded.[72] The attention given by the evangelist to this petition on the necessity of forgiveness, not only in the Sermon but in other places in the gospel, points to it as central for his understanding of the message and mission of Jesus.

Matthew's "debts" prepare for the concept of payment as the self-description of Jesus' death as a ransom (*lytron*) for many (20:28). The language here is monetary; Matthew remains the tax collector! Both the Greek word and its Hebrew antecedents in the Old Testament, when used both of God and man, refer to repurchasing a person, sometimes in the sense of making a sacrifice. God has purchased Israel (Old Testament) and the church, the New Israel (New Testament), as his own. This petition is further explicated in the parable of the unmerciful servant (18:23–35). Here God's relationship to man, the redemption motif, is expressed in monetary terms. Thus it resembles the Fifth Petition's request to forgive debts. The servant of the parable is not imprisoned for the enormity of his debt but for failure to act generously and mercifully to his debtor. "And should you not have had mercy on your fellow servant, as I had mercy on you?" (18:33). The parable concludes with, "So also my heavenly Father will do to every one of you, if you do not forgive your brother from the heart" (35), a clear parallel to 6:15: "neither will your Father forgive your trespasses." Though all offenses or debts to God are forgiven, for the failure to be reconciled and to forgive there is no divine mercy.

While our releasing others from their obligations to us cannot be understood as the cause, reason, or basis of God's gracious attitude to us in a Pelagian sense, our failure to forgive others is a certain sign that God is no longer our Father, since he is known for having forgiven us and all people. The unforgiving person is no longer recognized as a member of the community of the followers of Jesus in praying "Our Father."[73]

In both the Matthean and Lucan versions of the Prayer, the verb "forgive" is an aorist, so that it has this force: "Release us right away from the burden of our debts or sins." The present tense would suggest that we should be forgiven every time we sin. The petitioner has so committed himself to God that even the thought of future sin becomes impossible for him. He asks for immediate release from an intolerable burden. He cannot continue doing what threatens his life before God. Here the church stands not only as the community of the followers of Jesus, but also for those who can claim no moral advantage with God. Even their participation in the community of Jesus does not in any way lessen their moral culpability before God. He is the only deliverer, the Redeemer.

Though some of our manuscripts and the *Didache* have "as we forgive" (present tense) and "our debtors" (those who trespass against us), other manuscripts favored by scholars render it "as we *have* forgiven [perfect tense] our debtors" (those who trespass against us). In Matthew the past sense of the perfect tense is favored, and it is probably original; in Luke the perfect was replaced by the present. The perfect tense may have suggested that God's forgiving us was dependent in a causal sense on our having first forgiven others. The *Didache*, though largely following Matthew, has Luke's present tense, indicating that some in the early church may have been aware of the theological problems connected with Matthew's perfect tense. Only a Pelagian would suggest that God acted for man's redemption only after men had shown mercy to one another. God's saving action in Jesus must take precedence over any human response. The reasons for the textual changes in some early manuscripts where "as we forgive" (present tense) were substituted for "as we *have* forgiven" (perfect tense) were theological, as the past sense of the perfect presents problems. Though the perfect tense with its past sense presents problems, it appears to be the more authentic and is the preferred reading.

Theological problems aside, the use of the perfect tense seems to be preferred not only on textual grounds but from the Lord's Prayer's place in the liturgical setting as preliminary to the Eucharist in the early church. The phrase "as we have forgiven our debtors" points to the act of reconciliation practiced in the early church *before* the Lord's Prayer and the eucharistic action.[74] The grammar of the Fourth and Fifth Petitions thus reflects an early liturgical usage of the prayer. The Lord's Prayer with the phrases "Give us this day our daily bread" and "forgive us our trespasses" pointed forward to the specific eucharistic action, and with the phrase "as we *have* forgiven our debtors" looked backward to the reconciliatory action as having just taken place between individual members of the community. The perfect tense refers to an action not in the distant past, but just recently completed. This recently completed action was reconciliation among the members of the eucharistic community. It was not a matter of confessing secret sins against God, but real and presumably known offenses against other members of the community. This individual accountability and reconciliation has been regrettably lost and most likely cannot be restored within a modern liturgical framework.

The first word of the petition, "And," specifically attaches God's forgiveness to the sacramental or eucharistic eating in the Fourth Petition and joins the request for bread to the forgiveness. It did not seem strange to Matthew's church to understand forgiveness as the unique function or purpose of the bread (Sacrament), as the same connection is made in the Words of Institution themselves: "...My blood of the covenant, which is poured out for many for the forgiveness of sins" (26:28). Today's church may not be aware of all the connections that Matthew makes between the Sermon on the Mount and the other parts of his gospel, but it is aware that the celebration of the Supper presupposes harmony among its members. Matthew's church knew of this as an explicit prerequisite, but not in the sense of legal requirement. Such harmony was the necessary reflection of God's generous attitude to all men.

"And Lead Us Not into Temptation"

It was never the intention of this petition to suggest that God causes anyone to sin. It is fundamental to the Old Testament that God is not only without sin, but that his nature is completely opposed to it and works to eradicate it. Satan is by nature God's enemy, and human beings are caught in the middle. They struggle with supra-cosmic forces. The Sermon will soon speak of the impossibility of serving two masters, good and evil, God and Satan (6:24).

The Epistle of James speaks of temptations in two ways. The first type is the temptation not to confess the faith and even to deny it. James says this type of temptation is a blessing, since it gives faith an opportunity to exercise itself by overcoming the temptation and making a confession (1:2–4, 12). About this James writes: "Blessed is the man who endures trial, for when he has stood the test, he will receive the crown of life which God has promised to those who love him" (1:12). The second type comes from the heart and lures into sin. About this James says: "But each person is tempted when he is lured and enticed by his own desire. Then desire when it has conceived gives birth to sin; and sin when it is full-grown brings forth death" (1:14–15). It could be that, even though his epistle probably precedes the writing down of the Lord's Prayer in Matthew's gospel, James is offering a commentary to correct any possible confusion about the phrase "And lead us not into temptation."[75] The Prayer was probably in use in the earliest post-resurrection period, before it was written down.

James 1:13 gives a clear reference: "Let no one say when he is tempted, 'I am tempted by God;' for God cannot be tempted with evil and he himself tempts no one."

This petition, along with the next and last with its request for deliverance from evil, describes the community of Jesus not from the viewpoint of God's greater reality as fed and forgiven by God, but from the earthly, worldly reality of being beset with struggles. Luke omits the petition requesting deliverance from evil and thus combines its thought with this one on temptation.[76] Though the petition to forgive is so structured as to indicate that the petitioner has no intention of further sinning, the plea not to be led into temptation reflects the earthly life of the disciple of Jesus whose weaknesses become evident as he is beset with difficulties that can cause him to renounce his faith. Though he knows that God will stand by him, he is so beset by frailty that he prays he may never encounter the temptation.[77]

Temptation is a prominent motif in Matthew's understanding of the person of Jesus. After his baptism, he is led by the Spirit to be tempted by Satan (4:1, 2). His temptations are intended to entice him away from the work God has given him by substituting other apparently satisfactory alternatives. Instead of nourishing the inner life with God's Word, Jesus is tempted to use his authority to feed the physical life (4:3–4). He is tempted to inaugurate his messianic reign not through suffering but by a public display of the miraculous (4:5–6). Last of all, he is tempted to accomplish the glorification of the Messiah as the ruler of all things not through the Father's exaltation of his servant, but through worship of Satan (4:8–10). These temptations provide motifs that the evangelist weaves into other parts of the gospel: the feeding of the crowds and their admiration of him, the temptation of Peter to turn Jesus away from death, the entry into Jerusalem on Palm Sunday, the Garden of Gethsemane, and the call to come down from the cross. The evangelist pictures Jesus as the one who is obedient to the Father's will for the world's salvation. By not succumbing to these temptations, he prays this petition for himself and so provides a model for others who now pray the Lord's Prayer.

Matthew's church is already suffering persecution—just like Jesus— but the persecution was becoming an occasion to suppress or even to denounce allegiance to Jesus. Prominent in the synoptic gospels is Peter's denial, the disciple who is typical of all the disciples in their failing to confess Jesus in the hour of his trial. "You will all fall away because of me this night" (Matthew 26:31). Mark generalizes this for his church by omitting "this night" (14:27). "Pray that you will not enter into temptation" (Matthew 26:41) is in fact an admonition to pray the Sixth Petition.[78] The greatest danger for the early community of the disciples of Jesus was apostasy, and this prayer must be seen as a plea for divine assistance not to bring the followers of Jesus into any situation where they would renounce their allegiance to him. Before them they had the positive example of Jesus, who overcame the temptation to misuse and renounce his messianic mission and the negative examples of Peter and the other disciples who were ashamed of Jesus.

The petition "And lead us not into temptation" also contains as a subsidiary but essential ingredient the plea that God would rescue the followers of Jesus from being submerged and drowned in their own sins. The Sermon requires and presupposes moral behavior, but makes its demands more acute by placing the inner life of the believer in an intimate relationship with God. Confronted with the burden of God's demands, the follower of Jesus knows that only God can deliver him from sin. The community offers up this prayer from an awareness of its own weakness when left alone and connects it with the next petition, "But deliver us from evil." Temptations, not overcome with divine aid, bring about destruction.

"BUT DELIVER US FROM EVIL"

This verse is omitted from the Lucan version and suggests that Luke understood the sense of it as already present in the previous petition, "And lead us not into temptation." Luke's version suggests that here and in the petition on God's will the previous petitions are sufficient to carry the meaning. God's keeping us from a position where we would lose our faith would on the other side of the coin mean that we are to be kept out of Satan's grasp. The Greek word for "evil" (ponēros) can be understood as either neuter or masculine, "the evil thing" or "the evil one." English translations cannot indicate the grammatical choice here. By translating it "evil," they favor the neuter idea of deliverance from an evil thing instead of from the Evil One, i.e., Satan.

But the word for "evil" in Matthew and the entire New Testament makes specific reference to Satan. He is the Evil One (ponēros) and those individuals and angels who are in league with him are the evil ones (ponēroi). The use of the singular here suggests that the masculine would be appropriate and that this petition should be rendered as "But deliver us from the Evil One," that is, Satan. If evil in a general sense is favored, the meaning would not

be essentially altered. Thus the sense would be, "Deliver us from evil motivated by Satan."[79]

Satan's opposition to God's work in Jesus comes to expression in theological shorthand in the *Christus Victor* motif, where the work of Jesus is
understood not only as performed before God (atonement) and for the
community of his followers (forgiveness), but also over against Satan. The
petition goes beyond asking that sins be forgiven to one that asks for deliverance from Satan at the Last Judgment. As mentioned, more recent commentators on the Lord's Prayer have noted the strong eschatological tone
throughout the Lord's Prayer. This last petition brings this to final, clear
expression. Falling under God's condemnation on the Last Day can
become a present reality *now*! No one is immune to Satan's influence. The
Last Petition expresses both pessimism and hope. The human condition is
so desperate that only God can aid it, and he does!

AN EARLY ADDITION: "FOR THINE IS THE KINGDOM AND THE POWER AND THE GLORY, FOREVER. AMEN."

The prayer's ending used to be a pointless cause of discussion
between Protestants and Catholics (whose liturgies omitted it). From a
purely textual perspective, most manuscripts omit the ending from the
original version of the prayer as it was included in both Matthew and
Luke. Yet it was added early and the disciples themselves may have used
it. Jesus himself may have used it on one of several occasions in which
he discoursed on the Prayer or used it as an ending in other prayers. Of
course, this cannot be definitely proven, but it is not unlikely since this
ending was commonly used among the Jews at the time of Jesus and may
be derived originally from 1 Chronicles 29:11. Its omission from Luke
is not conclusive in answering whether or not Jesus or the apostles knew
its use for two reasons: the Third Gospel does not reflect liturgical
usage to the extent that Matthew does; and Luke omits parts of
Matthew's prayer. The ending is found in the *Didache* at the end of the
first century, and thus it is not unlikely that it was in regular use
throughout the church before some of the books now constituting our
New Testament canon were completed.[80] We must take into account
that the Lord's Prayer was probably prayed many times by the disciples
of Jesus before his death. We must leave the question open as to whether
Jesus was responsible for the ending, though it seems to be more defensible that his disciples may have added it when they prayed it among
themselves. The matter cannot be simply resolved by manuscript evi-

dence alone. As it is a decisively Jewish ending, it seems that it was added before the Gentile period of the church.[81]

When this ending was attached to the Prayer, these words were understood from the context of Matthew's gospel; "kingdom," "power," and "glory" are all Matthean words, though he did not pen them. While in Jewish thought of that day "kingdom" referred to God's reign and sovereignty over the world,[82] in Matthew the word refers specifically to God's work accomplished in the suffering of Jesus and his final appearing. "Glory" applies to the majesty of God, but Matthew uses the term to describe the coming of Jesus as the judge who has assumed God's majesty (19:28; 25:31). In 24:30 glory and power are used together also in an eschatological sense of the coming of the Son of Man. Kingdom, power, and glory are used in Matthew's gospel not to offer an abstract picture of a sovereign God, but as descriptions of what God is doing now in Jesus (kingdom) and what he will do (kingdom, power, and glory).

The problem in interpreting the ending comes in whether the church today can take the doxology, originally Jewish, and understand it in the sense given to it in Matthew's gospel, where these terms have no meaning apart from what God is doing in Jesus. "For Thine is the kingdom and the power and the glory forever" may actually cause the petitioner to think of abstract divine attributes as Judaism did in Jesus' day and thus fail to see the Lord's Prayer as uniquely and characteristically *Christian*, deriving its meaning from God's work in Jesus. The doxology, regardless of its origin in Judaism, must be understood within the revelation of God's Messiah.

THE SERMON'S EXPOSITION OF THE PRAYER

The importance of forgiveness within the community and the necessity of reconciliation with all men has been presented in several forms already in the Sermon and is the topic of the Fifth Petition on forgiving debts. Matthew now substitutes the word "trespasses" (*paraptōmata*) for the Prayer's "debts" (*opheilēmata*). The word "debts" in the Prayer prepares for the parable of the unmerciful servant and outside of Matthew is not used in a strictly theological sense. In Romans 4:4 it is used as illustration where the worker receives his wages, the amount due him. In five Pauline epistles "trespasses," like the words for "sins," is strictly a theological term and is used as a synonym for sins. As the logion on trespasses appears immediately after the Sermon, it points to the Fifth Petition as being most crucial for the community of the followers of Jesus. Failure not only to understand what it means but also to carry it out results in the Father's displeasure on the day of judgment.[83]

With this pericope the evangelist presupposes that the Lord's Prayer has been prayed. The "our Father" of the Prayer here becomes "your Father." This is thus a homiletical exposition on what has been prayed. The concept of "debts" is now replaced by the more inclusive "trespasses." Luke in his version of the Lord's Prayer uses the even clearer "sins," but he has no parallel to Matthew's exposition. Luke's substitute "sins" is self-interpreting. The evangelist Matthew requires that sins be forgiven not just to members of the community but to all people. This is consistent with the logia on loving the enemy and greeting those outside of the community (5:43–47). Forgiveness is an indiscriminate act that asks no question about the identity of the offender, whether or not he belongs to the community of the followers of Jesus. The Christian's indiscriminate forgiveness reflects the universal forgiveness of the God who has revealed himself as Father in Jesus.[84] The divine quality that uniquely identifies God is the readiness not to condemn but to forgive. Because of his new relationship with God as Father, the follower of Jesus begins *now* to resemble God in forgiving others.

The eschatological element, so characteristic of the Sermon to this point, is brought forward again as the evangelist says that the Father *will* forgive or *will* not forgive. Jesus is not speaking to the matter of forgiveness as present reality, as Paul does in asking how he can know whether he *now* stands as justified before God. The believer is placed within the eschatological reality of the day of judgment. On that day those who belong to God as his children will be recognized by their having forgiven all those who have offended them. Refusal to forgive one's offenders shows that such a person does not really know God as Father and is excluded from his fellowship. The chief and unique character of the religion of Jesus is God's reconciliation with all people. For this reason he has pinpointed it as the major feature of the Lord's Prayer, which he intends not only as a confession of the community of Jesus but as a summary of his entire Gospel. Without the awareness and practice of this reconciliation, the follower of Jesus forfeits his right to the Father's forgiveness. For this fault the evangelist allows no possibility of relief. Matthew's Gospel was intended to regulate church life in a sense that the other Gospels did not. Though the Gospels resemble one another and in some sense depend on one another, they do not have to have the exact same purpose.

NOTES

1   These words of Jesus obviously reflect the original setting in which his teaching stood at variance with the scribes and Pharisees who are challenging his authority from God, but it is evident in the sections on charity, prayer, and fasting that Matthew intends these words for his readers in the early Christian community. William Farmer, "The Sermon on the Mount: A Form-Critical and Redactional Analysis of Matthew 5:1–7:29," *SBL Seminar Papers* 25 (Atlanta: Scholars Press, 1986), 68. The instruction on almsgiving, prayer, and fasting finds no parallel in Mark and Luke. This may indicate that they do not share Matthew's liturgical interest, at least to the same extent. Betz recognizes these instructions as rubrics; *Essays on the Sermon on the Mount* (trans. L. L. Welborn; Philadelphia: Fortress, 1985), 330–31.

2   Guelich makes the point that in contrast to the Gentiles who do not have the confidence that God will answer their prayers, those who are his children can come to him as their Father. See his *The Sermon on the Mount* (Waco: Word, 1982), 283.

3   By far the most comprehensive research done on the Lords' Prayer is Jean Carmignac, *Recherches sur le "Notre Perè"* (Paris: Letouzey and Ane, 1969). For a discussion of the relationship between Matthew and Luke, see pages 18–28. Recognizing the liturgical style of Matthew's version of the Lords' Prayer are Gundry, *Matthew: A Commentary on his Literary and Theological Art* (Grand Rapids: Eerdmans, 1982), 104–5, and Willy Rordorf, "Lord's Prayer in the Light of its Liturgical Use in the Early Church," *Studia Liturgica*, 14 (No. 1), 1–19 (1980–1981). While Guelich acknowledges that Matthew's form of the prayer is more liturgical than Luke's, it is for him a model rather than a prescription; see his *The Sermon on the Mount* (Waco: Word, 1982), 284. See also D. A. Carson, *The Sermon on the Mount* (Grand Rapids: Baker, 1978), 61. See also Frederick Dale Bruner, *The Christ Book: A Historical/Theological Commentary, Matthew 1–12* (Waco: Word, 1987), 238. Reformed and Neo-Evangelical scholars tend to see the Lord's Prayer as a model prayer rather than a liturgical prescription. In the *Didache* the Lord's Prayer is prescribed. Assigning to the Lord's Prayer a liturgical rote in the early church may for some cast doubt on its being attributed to Jesus. Betz, who sees the Lord's Prayer as part of the liturgy of Matthew's church, attributes it to Jesus and recognizes it as the oldest piece of the Sermon; *Essays on the Sermon on the Mount*, 349.

4   Davies also recognizes the connection between these activities as belonging to "the piety of the new community." Thus the evangelist is thinking "'institutionally,'" i.e., this is the prayer to be used by the New Israel. See *The Setting of the Sermon on the Mount* (Atlanta: Scholars, 1989), 310.

5   Guelich, *The Sermon on the Mount*, 285, comes to no firm conclusion in its meaning. He notes that since the oft-debated *epiousion* ("daily") is found in both Matthew and Luke, the prayer was translated from its supposed original Hebrew or Aramaic at a very early stage. Davies affirms that the prayer goes back to Jesus because there is a mark of conflict between the Christian and Jewish communities (*The Setting of the Sermon on the Mount*, 311–12). Schweizer, like Guelich, notes that since both versions contain the problematical *epiousion* that both are dependent on an older version. *The Good News According to Matthew* (trans. David E. Green; Atlanta: Knox Press, 1975), 147. Ernst Lohmeyer agrees with Guelich and Schweizer in seeing one earlier version behind each. *The Lord's Prayer* (trans. John Bowden; London: Collins, 1965), 28–29. For the most detailed study of the prob-

lem see Carmignac, *Recherches sur le "Notre Pere,"* 18–28. Here are four solutions.
  1) the Lord's Prayer was given in two different forms;
  2) Luke more faithfully reproduces the words of Jesus;
  3) Matthew preserves the original words of Jesus; and
  4) Matthew and Luke faithfully reproduce it for two different communities.

6 Gerald Friedlander finds nothing original in the Lord's Prayer and finds its expression in pre-Christian literature; see his *The Jewish Sources of the Sermon on the Mount* (New York: KTAV, 1969), 163. Without debating that its words and phrases are found in other religious literature, especially the Old Testament and Judaism, its uniqueness rests not in a unique vocabulary but in the meaning given to its words within the context of Matthew's Gospel. Also strikingly different is its brevity. Schweizer, *The Good News According to Matthew*, 146–59) shows the parallels between the prayer and the Shemoneh Esreh, the Eighteen Benedictions of Judaism. Davies leans in the direction of seeing Matthew's version of the Lord's Prayer as his equivalent to the Abbreviated Eighteen, a shortened form of the much longer Shemoneh Esreh.

7 Rordorf, "Lord's Prayer," 2–3. Augustine says that it is the custom of the church that during Holy Week first the words of the Creed and then those of the Lord's Prayer are conveyed to the catechumens. Rordorf believes that traces of this custom are as early as Justin, the *Apostolic Tradition*, and the *Didache*. Supporting an early liturgical usage of the prayer is a Latin translation probably from the first century, see Carmignac, *Recherches*, 446–50. See also Schweizer, *The Good News According to Matthew*, 149.

8 Rordorf, "Lord's Prayer," 4, argues convincingly that the "Our Father" presupposes that the one offering the prayer is baptized and regenerated by the Holy Spirit. Only through regeneration does God become their Father. For other New Testament references to the Lord's Prayer, see C. W. F. Smith, "The Lord's Prayer," *The Interpreter's Dictionary of the Bible* (ed. George A. Buttrick, et al.; New York: Abingdon, 1962), III, 154.

9 *Didache* 8:2. Davies, *The Setting of the Sermon on the Mount*, 309, holds that "Nevertheless, the Matthean form of the Lord's Prayer occurs in the context of a Christian community set over against Phariseeism." He disputes that the Lucan version was prepared for the community.

10 Joachim Jeremias, "Abba," in *The Prayers of Jesus* (Napierville: A. R. Allenson, 1967), 11–66. Betz takes exception to the idea of an Aramaic version of the Lord's Prayer. *Essays on the Sermon on the Mount*, 388. We are then left without an explanation of why Christians in Rome were praying to God with the Aramaic "Abba."

11 A debate over the use of the Lord's Prayer in San Francisco public schools broke out in 1975. Objecting to its use was Abram S. Isaacs who recognized "its rabbinical spirit in every line," but opposed its recitation because it had become a distinctively Christian prayer. See Abram S. Isaacs, "What shall the Public Schools Teach," in *A Documentary History of Religion in America* Vol. 2 since 1865 (ed. Edwin S. Gaustad; Grand Rapids: Eerdmans, 1983), 53–54. Its Christian character may not be as obvious to others. Betz holds that Jesus and his disciples had no unique relationship to God and so the Lord's Prayer can express the longing of all humanity. *Essays on the Sermon on the Mount*, 388–89.

12 Jeremias, *The Prayers of Jesus*, 91, holds that though Luke is original in regard to length, Matthew is the more original in regard to wording.

13 Rordorf, "Lord's Prayer," 2–3. Tertullian's *De oratione* 1:6, "breviarium totius evangelii."

14 On the structure of the Lord's Prayer see Birger Gerhardsson, "The Matthaean Version of the Lord's Prayer (Matthew 6:9b–13): Some Observations," in *The New Testament Age* (ed. William C. Weinrich; Macon, Ga.: Mercer, 1984), I, 207–20.

15 Gundry holds that the "our" was added to the prayer in a liturgical setting before the evangelist included the prayer in the gospel; see his *Matthew: A Commentary*, 104–5. He also claims the Kaddish, used in the synagogue, provided Jesus with the basis for the prayer. "Exalted and *hallowed be his* great *name* in the world which he created according to *his will. May he let his kingdom rule.*" Italics indicate parallels with the Lord's Prayer.

16 Ernst Lohmeyer, *"Our Father." An Introduction to the Lord's Prayer* (trans. John Bowden; New York: Harper and Row, 1965), 39–41.

17 For a discussion on Matthew's use of "Father," see Guelich, *The Sermon on the Mount*, 285–89. A more detailed discussion is put forth by Carmignac, *Recherches*, 55–69, who draws the analogy between the Christian as God's child and the Trinity.

18 *Didache* 8:3.

19 So Davies, who notes that the communal nature of the Prayer does not negate its individual use. Rather the individual is united with the community in offering this prayer, *The Setting of the Sermon on the Mount*, 311. Also Rordorf, "Lord's Prayer," 1–2.

20 This phrase is not found in the major manuscripts and is an example according to C. S. Mann of the way in which assimilation between the gospels took place. This assimilation is not difficult to explain, as Mark 11:25 with the request that the followers of Jesus should forgive one another "is certainly an echo of the similar petition in the Lord's Prayer (Matt 6:12, Luke 11:3–4) and is wholly in line not only with Matt 5:23–24 but also with the teaching on forgiveness in Paul and the rest of the New Testament. The Greek of *your Father ... forgive the wrongs you have done* in this verse is verbally identical with Matt 6:14. This is significant, for only here does Mark use *your Father* (*pater hymōn*) and only here does he use *paratoma* for *wrongs*. This would support Mark's dependence on Matthew." C. S. Mann, *Mark*, Anchor Bible (Garden City, N.Y.: Doubleday, 1986), 454. It may also indicate that in spite of the omission of the Prayer in Mark, it was being used by his church. If Mark did not have the Prayer in view, the manuscript copyists did.

21 "Heavens" may not simply be Matthew's circumlocution of the divine name, as is often claimed. Matthew is not hesitant about its use in other places. According to Guelich, *The Sermon on the Mount*, 287–88, the heavens are for Matthew God's point of departure in bringing about redemption on earth. Betz notes that in the *epiklesis* God as the Father is addressed as dwelling in the "heavens" (plural), but in the phrase concluding the first half of the Lord's Prayer, heaven is singular: "on earth as it is in heaven." He explains that in the address the plural "heavens" refers to the higher realm of God and that the singular refers to the stars as part of the created cosmos. God's will is done in the celestial regions, but not on earth among men (378). The phrase "on earth as it is in heaven" reflects Gen 1:1 (LXX): "In the beginning God created the heavens and the earth" (*en archē epoiēsen ho theos ton ouranon kai tēn gēn*). The Latin Vulgate has *in principio creavit Deus caelum et terram*. Though the plural form *heavens* is used in Gen 1:1 in Hebrew (*hashamayim*), the plural is the ordinary form; it appeared in Greek in the singular.

22 Gerhardsson, "The Matthean Version," 212–23. "One must not adopt the role of God's counselor."

23 Carmignac, *Recherches*, 88.

24 See Guelich, *The Sermon on the Mount*, 210. Also Schweizer, *The Good News According to Matthew*, 151. "It is God himself, therefore, who honors his name. The Lord's Prayer also expresses this notion indirectly by its use of the passive. The Greek verb form implies an action that takes place only once; the petition therefore looks for a final fulfillment in which God will be all in all (1 Corinthians 15:28), and in which every knee will bow in honor of God the Father in heaven, on earth, and under the earth, and every tongue confess that Jesus Christ is Lord (Philippians 2:10–11)."

25 Schweizer, *The Good News According to Matthew*, 152. "Thus whoever prays for the coming of this kingdom, prays also for the establishment of Jesus' authority, which is at work in the words and deeds of his disciples and is already causing 'Satan (to) fall like lightning from heaven' (Luke 10:17–18)."

26 Guelich, *The Sermon on the Mount*, 260, points out that the aorist points to the "once-for-all character" of the coming of the kingdom as an eschatological motif, but it cannot be so stressed to exclude the present activity of the kingdom which, it is true, is pushing towards the final consummation. The strength of this petition is not that God will come with vengeance upon his enemies.

27 The prayer of Jesus in Gethsemane, "Thy will be done," is identical with the Third Petition. This lends credence to the view that the evangelists see the Lord's Prayer not as a random selection of petitions, but as petitions which find their focus in the rest of the Gospel.

28 Schweizer, *The Good News According to Matthew*, 152.

29 Gundry, *Matthew: A Commentary*, 106, points out that the will of God is a favorite theme in Matthew. For an extended discussion on the will of God in Matthew, see Carmignac, *Recherches*, 102–7.

30 *Synopsis Quattuor Evangeliorum.* 9th ed. rev. (ed. Kurt Aland; Stuttgart: Deutsche Bibelstiftung, 1976), 288. The phrase "Let your Holy Spirit come upon us and cleanse us," was found in some manuscripts for Luke's "Thy kingdom come" (11:2). Gregory of Nyssa followed this reading. Schweizer, *The Good News According to Matthew*, 148, notes that a prayer for the Spirit was sometimes substituted for the First Petition. He surmises that these were originally baptismal prayers and that they were read back into the Lord's Prayer. As Luke has two petitions for Matthew's three, it seems that very early in the church the first part of the Lord's Prayer, the "Thou-Petitions," were understood as prayers for the Holy Spirit.

31 E.g., Rordorf, "Lord's Prayer."

32 Anthony Charles Dean sees the prayer organized like this:
  "Our Father in heaven!
  As in heaven, so on earth
  Thy name reverenced,
  Thy Kingdom come,
  Thy will be done."
  Taken from *Our Father: A Study of the Lord's Prayer* (London: Hodder and Stoughton, 1926), 117.

33 Gerhardsson, "Matthean Version," 213.

34 Carmignac, *Recherches*, 60–62, 68–69.

35 Brevard S. Childs, *The New Testament as Canon* (Philadelphia: Fortress, 1984), 68–71.

36 The division between the "Thou-Petitions" and the "We-Petitions" is based on both content and grammatical style. Guelich, *The Sermon on the Mount*, 118–221.

37 Davies, *The Setting of the Sermon on the Mount*, 310, notes that the transition in the Lord's Prayer and the Shemoneh Esreh, the Eighteen Benedictions, occurs with the request for bread. With the former it concludes the first part and with the latter it begins the second.

38 Lohmeyer, "Our Father," 155–57. Such was also a view of the Lutheran dogmatician Abram Calov in 1676. See also Carmignac, *Recherches*, 132–33, for a listing of those who held the futuristic view. Gundry, *Matthew: A Commentary*, 107, is so certain of this position that he holds the matter closed.

39 Carmignac, *Recherches*, 177–79, with his list shows that Protestant scholars are more likely to support the position of the material understanding of bread. Rordorf (page 7) states quite emphatically that "earliest patristic exegesis of the Our Father almost exclusively follows a spiritual line of interpretation of this petition." Carmignac, *Recherches*, 144–55, provides a listing of the early church fathers and their respective positions. Early church fathers understood the Fourth Petition with its request for bread eucharistically. Within the context of the Sermon on the Mount, a reference to the Lord's Supper may not be as evident as it would be within the context of the entire gospel. The Sermon on the Mount is intended by the evangelist to be heard within one reading of the entire gospel and not as a collection of disparate verses or even discourses, so that each has its own autonomous existence. In light of a eucharistic interpretation of the Fourth Petition, the question might be asked whether the first three petitions might have any sacramental significance. Charles Gieschen has argued that "the name of Jesus" is that of Father-Son-Holy Spirit which God reveals in Baptism (Matt 28:19). So in each case or at least the majority of cases, the phrase "the name of Jesus" has a Triune reference. See his *Angelomorphic Christology: Antecedents and Early Evidence* (Leiden: E. J. Brill, 1998), 70–80. By praying to God as Father, Jesus begins this Trinitarian revelation which will come to a conclusion at the gospel's end in connection with Baptism. This leads to the suggestion that "thy kingdom come" not only refers to what Jesus will do for mankind by his death, but also to the participation of the ones who pray the Lord's Prayer in the Lord's Supper. Here the evidence may be just as persuasive. The Prayer specifically asks for the the coming of the Father's kingdom and not the kingdom of God or of the heavens, both of which have a slightly different meaning than "the Father's kingdom." In 13:43, the only other use outside of the Lord's Prayer and the institution of the Eucharist, it refers to completed salvation. Noteworthy is its inclusion in 26:29 with the promise of Jesus to participate in the Eucharist with his disciples in his Father's kingdom. The phrase is strongly reminiscent of the Second Petition of the Lord's Prayer. The Third Petition, that God's will would be done on earth, sets down what he intends to do in the first two petitions through Baptism and the Lord's Supper. One could hardly argue against the idea that participating with Christ in the fruit of the vine in his Father's kingdom is not in some sense a fulfillment of the petition "thy kingdom come."

40 Luther, as the preeminent Protestant reformer, moved from a spiritual to a material understanding of bread, but perhaps without completely surrendering the former. His Small Catechism and Large Catechism, both from 1529, offer the material view. In his other writings Luther did understand it eucharistically, that is, in a

spiritual sense. Carmignac, *Recherches*, 166–70, traces the Reformer's thought through 21 writings. Luther may very well approach a eucharistic interpretation of bread in his Easter hymn (1525) "Christ lag in Todesbanden" ("Christ Jesus Lay in Death's Strong Bands") in the final stanza: "Then let us feast this Easter Day on Christ the Bread of heaven." Luther's aversion to Zwingli's use of John 6 denying the Real Presence is the most adequate explanation for his reluctance to locate references to the Sacrament any place else than in the Words of Institution.

41 Gerhardsson, "Matthaean Version," 215, n. 18, makes this comment in regard to a survey made by Anton Fridrichsen published in 1930.

42 A useful and readable survey of the problem is provided by Geoffrey Wainwright, *Eucharist and Eschatology*, 2nd ed. (London: Epworth, 1978; New York: Oxford University, 1981), 30–34.

43 Concerning the Fourth Petition, Guelich, *The Sermon on the Mount*, 291, notes that it "turns the focus of the following petitions from God (*your*) to the petitioners (*us/we*) and serves formally as the pivot for the Prayer."

44 Gerhardsson, "Matthean Version," 215.

45 Gundry, *Matthew: A Commentary*, 107. See also Lohmeyer, "Our Father," 156–57.

46 Carmignac, *Recherches*, 186–88, lists and rebuts nine sets of arguments, including the one based on order of time against a eucharistic interpretation of the Fourth Petition.

47 This should not be stated too sharply, as the evangelists by recording these words of Jesus intends them as authoritative for the churches which are instructed in the teaching of the apostles. See Childs, *The New Testament as Canon*, 74, "The Sermon of Jesus was not preserved by the evangelists apart from his concern that the words of Jesus function kerygmatically for succeeding generations of readers."

48 Carmignac, *Recherches*, 192–98.

49 Guelich, *The Sermon on the Mount*, 293–94, makes no reference to the "and" at the beginning of the Fifth Petition and thus obviates the need for any gramatical discussion. He favors the material interpretation of bread. Gundry, *Matthew: A Commentary*, 108, sees a parallelism between the Fourth and Fifth Petitions, with the former asking for physical bread and the latter for spiritual forgiveness. Schweizer, *The Good News According to Matthew*, 153–54, holds a view similar to Guelich.

50 Even the Jewish scholar Friedlander, *The Jewish Sources of the Sermon on the Mount*, 154–55), who is unaware of a eucharistic or spiritual interpretation of bread, notes that the physical interpretation contradicts 6:34 with its admonition against anxiety. The Neo-Evangelical scholar Donald A. Carson makes no allusion to the spiritual or sacramental understanding of this petition; see his *The Sermon on the Mount* (Grand Rapids: Baker, 1978), 68–69. His warning against our ingratitude to God in the midst of drought in various parts of the world hardly does justice to the universal applicability of this petition.

51 The word supersubstantial comes from Jerome's Vulgate, the Latin translation of the Bible. By this word he intended to convey the meaning that this bread was above every substance, that is, it is the divine bread of the Eucharist and the miraculous feedings. See Wainwright, *Eucharist and Eschatology*, 34–37.

52 See the disciples' responses in Matt 15:33 and 16:7.

53 Schweizer, *The Good News According to Matthew*, 153–54, who holds to the material interpretation of bread, nevertheless understands the earthly Jesus' table fellow-

ship as anticipatory of the eschatological eating. He does not, however, recognize that the Fourth Petition has such eschatological overtones. Lohmeyer, "Our Father," 157, also similarly recognizes the eschatological but not sacramental import of this petition.

54 Wainwright, *Eucharist and Eschatology*, 37–41.

55 Gerhardsson, "Matthaean Version," 216, who favors the material understanding of bread, notes that the prayer is for the spiritual and material health not only of the congregation but of the individual. This is not to deny the importance of the individual, but this petition speaks of the bread as belonging to the entire community. The concept of community is reinforced by the "to us" and "our bread." This bread belongs to them collectively and they receive it collectively. It is prayed for by the community and is also given to them within the context of the community.

56 For a discussion of the eucharistic language see Wainwright, *Eucharist and Eschatology*, 35–38, 169–72, fn. 125–41.

57 Wainwright, *Eucharist and Eschatology*, 57; Rordorf, "Lord's Prayer," 6. Joachim Jeremias says that the breaking of bread was not the Jewish term for a full meal. Wainwright, *Eucharist and Eschatology*, 170, n. 131, asserts on the basis of this that the phrase is a *terminus technicus* for the Sacrament.

58 Wainwright offers convincing evidence that the Eucharist was celebrated only once a week to commemorate Easter and even the Ascension was adjusted to fall on Sunday. The *Didache* (14:1) also speaks of a weekly Eucharist: "And on the Lord's own day gather yourselves together and break bread and give thanks." Rordorf, "Lord's Prayer," 8, suggests that the eucharistic use of the Lord's Prayer with its "this day" may have been a motive for daily celebration in the early church.

59 Wainwright, *Eucharist and Eschatology*, 170.

60 William O. Walker, Jr. suggests a literary dependency of John on Matthew including John's dependency for his eucharistic language on the Fourth Petition of the Lord's Prayer. "The Lord's Prayer in Matthew and in John," *New Testament Studies* 28, No. 2 (April 1982), 243–45. For a discussion of the Sermon's relationship to the Johannine writings see W. H. Davies, *The Setting of the Sermon on the Mount* (Atlanta: Scholars, 1989), 405–14.

61 Martin Hengel, "Probleme des Markusevangeliums" in *Das Evangelium und die Evangelien: Vorträge vom Tuebinger Symposium 1982* (ed. Peter Stuhlmacher; *Wissenschaftliche Untersuchungen zum Neuen Testament*, vol. 28. (ed. Martin Hengel and Otfried Hofius; Tübingen: J. C. B. Mohr, 1983), 256, 264. Hengel understands that the synoptic gospels were composed for liturgical usage. He understands 1 Timothy 4:13 and Revelation 1:3 as references to such liturgical readings. Readings from the Torah had to be initiated in the Gentile churches as soon as they were established, otherwise Paul's arguments in his epistles would have been lost to his readers. John, presumably coming somewhat later than the Synoptics, would have found an already established and waiting niche in the eucharistic services. This, of course, is an unsettled issue.

62 Wainwright, *Eucharist and Eschatology*, 28–29, notes the eucharistic language of this pericope and raises the question of why the early church found no use for it, 161, n. 73. In its use of Matthew 7:6 with its demand that the holy not be given to the dogs, the church found support for not giving the Eucharist to the unbaptized and heretics. This writer is not aware that the pericope of the Canaanite woman found a eucharistic place. It may indicate that Matthew's language influenced the

church's liturgy rather than the reverse.

63 For a discussion of the eucharistic language in the feeding accounts of all four gospels see Wainwright, *Eucharist and Eschatology*, 35–36. The comparison is also made with 1 Corinthians 11.

64 Carmignac, *Recherches*, 144–91.

65 Rordorf "Lord's Prayer," 16, n. 25, calls attention to the word "Lord" in the early church: "It is interesting to note that the adjective 'dominicus,' originally attached to 'the Lord's Supper,' could equally well be applied to 'the Lord's day,' and then to 'the Lord's house' (the church) and finally to 'the Lord's Prayer' (which first occurs in St. Cyprian)."

66 Carmignac, *Recherches*, 156–60.

67 Rordorf, "Lord's Prayer," 6, who favors a sacramental interpretation of the Fourth Petition as its original sense, offers a cautious warning, 17, n. 43: "At this juncture I must observe that I am not ruling out a literal interpretation of the Fourth Petition of the Lord's Prayer, or saying that it does not permit us to ask for ordinary bread; but we must not lose sight of the fact that this petition is concerned *above all with eschatological and sacramental bread,*" "Lord's Prayer," 16–17, n. 30.

68 Wainwright, *Eucharist and Eschatology*, 30, 161–62, n. 80, along with other scholars, observes that the Lord's Prayer's most usual place in the liturgy, before the Communion, was due to the petition for bread. Whether it was used as a consecratory prayer is found by him to be improbable. Before the question of whether or not the Lord's Prayer is "a eucharistic consecration prayer," the prior question of the nature of such a prayer has to be addressed. Minimally, the Lord's Prayer was used eucharistically in the church from the earliest times until the present. The connection between the Fourth Petition and the Lord's Supper probably is lost to the consciousness of most worshipers.

69 Rordorf, "Lord's Prayer," notes that the similarities between the Lord's Prayer and the eucharistic prayer of the *Didache* (10) are too numerous to list. Such parallelisms indicate that this eucharistic prayer was a reconstruction of the Lord's Prayer. What would be worthy of note is that the eucharistic prayer of the *Didache* (10:3) refers both to the material and spiritual bread: "Thou, Almighty master, didst create all things for thy name's sake, and didst give food and drink unto men for enjoyment, that they might render thanks to thee; but didst bestow upon us spiritual food and drink and eternal life through Thy Son."

70 Guelich, *The Sermon on the Mount*, 293–94, notes that Matthew's "debts" translates the Aramaic word which is used for sins. Carmignac, *Recherches*, 22, also finds Matthew the older, as its parallelism is not found in Luke.

71 Carmignac, *Recherches*, 232–35, discusses the Pelagian understandings of the Fifth Petition.

72 Similar is the comment of Guelich, *The Sermon on the Mount*, 375. "Therefore, to stand in judgment over another means that we ourselves have yet to experience God's forgiving mercy and cannot expect to receive it at the judgment."

73 Though the Lord's Prayer is seen as having many parallels with the Eighteen Benedictions, which were recited three times a day in Judaism, there is no corresponding petition to "as we have forgiven our debtors." The closest comes in: "Forgive us, our Father, for we have sinned; pardon us; our King, for we have offended; you are pleased to forgive and to pardon." Quoted from Schweizer, *The*

Good News According to Matthew, 155–56.

74 For a discussion of the differences in Matthew and Luke and the variants see Rordorf, "Lord's Prayer," 9–14.

75 David P. Scaer, *James The Apostle of Faith* (St. Louis: Concordia, 1983), 42–45, 52–55. See also Guelich, *The Sermon on the Mount*, 295).

76 Schweizer, *The Good News According to Matthew*, 156, understands the deliverance from evil as part of the Sixth Petition. Also Gerhardsson, "Matthean Version," 217.

77 Schweizer, *The Good News According to Matthew*, 156. "Whoever prays the Lord's Prayer is not outstandingly pious, not a religious superstar; he does not ask God for the opportunity to prove his faith, but asks not be put to the test." Also Gerhardsson, "Matthean Version," 217.

78 Gundry, *Matthew: A Commentary*, 109. Unlike Schweizer, Gundry does not see this petition as a request to be kept from all temptations, but for assistance in overcoming them. Perhaps Schweizer is right in saying that the Christian should fear the temptations, but Gundry catches James' spirit in that temptation is an occasion for joy.

79 Gerhardsson, "Matthaean Version," 217, says correctly that the choice is of little significance.

80 *Didache*. At the end of the prayer, it has "for Thine is the power and the glory for ever and ever" (8:2). In the eucharistic prayer this phrase is found twice: "Thine is the glory for ever and ever" (10:2, 5). The doxology—in one form or another—is commonly used in the majority of Christian traditions.

81 Davies, *The Setting of the Sermon on the Mount*, 451–53, details his own conversion to the view that it was known and used by Jesus since it is unlikely that Jesus would have ended a prayer without a doxology. This simply was the custom of the day. Against the argument that the first Christian synagogues were untutored, he notes that Matthew was not untutored but articulate and liturgically conscious.

82 The Jewish concept of the kingdom as the messianic age was expressed in near-millennialistic language and admittedly seemed unlike the one preached by Jesus. See Friedlander, *The Jewish Sources of the Sermon on the Mount*, 137–47.

83 See note 72 above.

84 Schweizer, *The Good News According to Matthew*, 154–55.

14

A BRIEF TREATISE ON FASTING

MATTHEW 6:16–18

Fasting was part of ordinary Jewish piety in Jesus' day and was derived from Old Testament rituals attached to such days as the Atonement and New Year's. Not only was fasting associated with national calamities, but individuals also fasted at personal tragedies. David fasts when his first son by Bathsheba is dying (2 Samuel 12:16), and Esther fasts before she confronts her husband, the king (Esther 4:15–16). Both public and private fasting reflected the sense of mortification and helplessness before God.[1]

The sayings on fasting were included by the evangelist not merely to inform the reader of Jesus' disapproval of the ostentatious, visible piety of his contemporaries. The charges of gluttony against Jesus should not be interpreted to mean that he and his disciples exempted themselves from the national fast days of the Jews. Unlike his ostentatious contemporaries, Jesus did not announce to others when he was fasting.[2] Rather than dispense with fasting, the early Christian community retained the practice. Matthew intends to address these words of Jesus to his church, for whom fasting was in vogue. This instruction assumes that people are fasting, and Jesus' words provide guidelines on how it is to be carried out. Davies notes that the Jewish and Christian communities were aware of and influenced by the other's custom of fasting.[3]

At first glance, Matthew 9:14–17 indicates a problem in that Jesus and the disciples, in contrast to the disciples of John the Baptist and the Pharisees, do not fast. Some might be compelled to point out a contradiction that the evangelist permitted to stand. Why include rules on fasting, since Jesus and his followers were not known for practicing it as a display of personal piety? The Sermon's instruction about fasting hardly seems appropriate when compared with the words of Jesus that fasting is inappropriate while the Bridegroom is present (9:15). This pericope, along with 11:18 where John is described as abstaining from food and Jesus as eating and drinking, has been used to show that fasting was appropriate in the religion of the old covenant but has no real place in Christianity. One commentator remarks that the community of the followers of Jesus is marked not by fasting but by participation in the meal.[4] Negative views on the religious value of fasting are reinforced by Luke's story of the publican and the Pharisee where the latter boasts that he fasts twice in the week and in comparison with the publican remains unjustified (18:12, 14). The question remains as to why the evangelist let the regulation on fasting stand, since neither Mark nor Luke has any regulation on fasting. While it may be concluded that their churches do not know of the custom, it should be pointed out that neither do they know of Matthew's triad of worship involving almsgiving, prayer, and fasting. The fasting pericope is not a random logion in Matthew, but it rather belongs to a constellation of important sayings of the Lord.

Though the eucharistic feasting is anticipatory participation in the eschatological banqueting, fasting for Matthew remains appropriate for the followers of Jesus. Fasting played an integral part in early church worship. The selection of Barnabas and Paul at Antioch for the Asian mission was made while the clergy there were worshiping and fasting (Acts 13:2), activities that parallel the praying and fasting of the Matthean liturgical triad. Jesus himself fasted (Matthew 4:2). In response to the question of why the disciples of John fast and Jesus' do not, he answers that they will fast when the bridegroom is taken away from them (Matthew 9:15), most probably a reference to his death. The Old Testament prophets fasted as they waited for deliverance. The church adopts the same posture as it awaits the final parousia. Jesus' strictures against fasting make it no more inherently wrong than praying and giving alms, against which he also directed strictures concerning the manner in which they were done. Both fasting and praying are common religious phenomena and expressions of piety; they were practices for the community of the followers of Jesus as well as for the Pharisees and the disciples of John. The example of the Lucan Pharisee can no more be used as evidence against fasting than it can be used as evidence against praying. The *Didache* requires fasting on the fourth and sixth days, and forbids it on the second and the fifth days as do the "hypocrites" (Pharisees).[5] The *Didache* handles fasting in its discussion of the Lord's Prayer, right after Baptism and just before the Lord's Supper. Fasting in connection with the Lord's Supper has a long church tradition, and the reference in the *Didache* indicates that it was already in place by the end of the first century, if not before. Taking the evidence of the *Didache* it might be argued that the fasting and the worship of the "teachers and elders" in the church at Antioch (Acts 13:2) was in fact a eucharistic service.

The place of fasting in the Sermon, in such close proximity to the Lord's Prayer (so prominent in the early eucharistic liturgy), may suggest that the evangelist intended his fasting instructions as preparation for eucharistic participation. Such a view is not without problems, as there are many indications that the early church's eucharistic celebration was done in the context of an ordinary meal, following the example of Jesus, who instituted the Supper during the eating of a meal. This is not an insurmountable problem, as the fasting could have taken place before the eucharistic meal. In what sense the final supper of Jesus was a Passover meal is debatable, but the language of the Passover and the Exodus surrounds it. Paul enjoins the Corinthians to do their eating and drinking at home before they come together for the eucharistic meal (1 Corinthians 11:20–22). Fasting was not in vogue there, and the absence of this custom may have been the source of one of its problems. Paul's instructions to the Corinthians may have been the origin of the eucharistic celebration as separate from ordinary eating, the now nearly universally observed custom everywhere in Christendom. The understanding that the Eucharist was performed in the context of an ordinary meal is perpetuated in calling Christmas, Easter, and Pentecost *feast* days. This was done with good reason. The church in her eucharistic celebrations anticipates and participates in the banquet of the Lamb, and expressions of unrestrained joy are not inappropriate. This still does not negate the theological significance of fasting for Matthew's church. The feasting associated with the Eucharist might have been heightened by fasting. If the Lord's Supper was seen as a *parousia*, a coming of the Lord, fasting before its celebration would have been as appropriate for it as it was for John and his disciples before the coming of Jesus. Fasting on Wednesdays and Fridays may have been directly connected with the weekly Sunday Eucharist, since the Christian community focused all its activity on that one event. This does not rule out a shorter fast preceding the Eucharist. The *Didache* reinforces this view, as fasting is required before Baptism and the regulation for fasting precedes the Lord's Prayer and the eucharistic prayer.[6]

Matthew 6 begins with a warning of practicing, or better, exercising your righteousness before people (1). The clear implication is that it should be done before God. The evangelist then records three examples of how this righteousness is to be done and not done: 1) "when you give alms"; 2) "when you pray" (5); and now finally 3) "when you fast" (16). All three sections begin with the same Greek word for "when" (*hotan*) and all are instructions. Between the instructions on praying and fasting comes the Lord's Prayer, introduced by the indicative, "Thus you therefore are to pray." Matthew also includes the theological explanation of the necessity of forgiveness. Like the instructions on giving alms and prayer, it is to be done not before people but before God, who sees in secret. Those who do all these things publicly have their reward from people and lose their reward from God. Thus we have three integral parts of early church piety: giving to the poor, praying, and fasting. Regardless of the abuses, fasting in Matthew's church was as much a part of the Christian life of piety as was giving to the poor and praying.[7]

Since fasting has value with God and not before men, the member of the community of Jesus should so freshen up his appearance that no one has any idea that he is fasting. The *Didache* announces the days on which the fasting is taking place, but like the directive in the Sermon notes that the act of fasting is to be covered up. How one covers up his fasting, whether it is washing the face or use of special ointments, is not as important as the fact that he is fasting.

With the contemporary generation's concern for diet and proper nutrition, it is not uncommon to understand the biblical fasting as having a physical benefit for the body. Fasting is said to purge the body and be an aid to weight control. Lenten fasting is used to foster weight loss. Such physical advantages are certainly desirable, but fasting is prized in the Sermon for its salvific and not physical benefit. The fasting of the disciple of Jesus will be rewarded by the Father on the Last Day, as long as that fasting is done in secret (6:18).

Fasting in the Old Testament was done as a sign of a penitent, contrite heart before God, as it brought the person to an awareness of his own frailty. Without common food his life was in danger of perishing. Ultimately he was made aware of his frailty and dependence on God. In a more positive vein, fasting anticipated the new life of the Christian community that was being fed on the supernatural food. Jesus responds to Satan that man does not live by bread alone, and the church is fed on the supernatural eucharistic food offered in Jesus, who is the real bread from heaven, a theme which appears in the pericope of the Canaanite woman who, when she is refused bread, is satisfied with crumbs.

The question of how Moses on Sinai and Jesus in the wilderness survived without food or drink is not to be answered by what is physiologically possible or demonstrable. In the life lived directly before God ordinary food is no longer necessary, since God himself becomes their supplier and food. Both Moses and Jesus in their fasting moved into a new dimension and higher level of reality.

Fasting serves as a confession that the newer and higher level of reality has taken hold in the life of the disciple. Paul's discussion on the importance of certain foods may be related to fasting: "Food will not commend us to God. We are no worse off if we do not eat, and no better off if we do" (1 Corinthians 8:8). Similarly the stomach, which is meant for food, will be destroyed (1 Corinthians 6:13). With fasting one says that the reality of this world will be replaced by that of the next. The food of the next world, sacramentally present now, is Jesus, the Bread of Life. Since nothing should interfere with the food of immortality, Christians fasted before the eucharistic eating. This fasting was already in place for Matthew's church. "The days will come, when the Bridegroom is taken away from them, *and then they will fast*" (9:15). Since within the community of the followers of Jesus there is a constant or continual coming of Jesus in the supper, the fasting pericope remains valid.

NOTES

1   Robert A. Guelich, *The Sermon on the Mount* (Waco: Word, 1982), 298–99.

2   Eduard Schweizer, *The Good News According to Matthew* (trans. David E. Green; Atlanta: Knox, 1975), 227. Davies asserts that Jesus himself did not fast, but that the discussion of Mark 2:18–20 "is aimed at justifying the practice in the church;" see his *The Setting of the Sermon on the Mount* (Atlanta: Scholars, 1989), 283. Somehow this assertion has to be squared with all three synoptic accounts of Jesus' temptation that he did fast.

3   William Farmer, "The Sermon on the Mount: A Form-Critical and Redactional Analysis of Matthew 5:1–7:29," *SBL Seminar Papers* 25 (Atlanta: Scholars Press, 1986), 68. Davies, *Setting of the Sermon*, 314–15, notes that while the Judaism of the end of the first century was concerned about excessive fasting, Matthew's "was most concerned with the avoidance of hypocrisy."

4   Guelich, *Sermon on the Mount*, 299–300.

5   *Didache* 8:1. The regulations about fasting suggest that the *Didache* had to be written very early, even before the end of the first century, when the Jewish custom of fasting on Mondays and Thursdays was still a concern to it. See Davies, *Setting of the Sermon*, 315, who uses the similarities of fasting customs between the Jewish and Christian communities to see Matthew as an answer to Jamnia, an argument for a dating around 100 A.D. Betz notes that "hypocrites" in the *Didache* are reference to the Jews; *Essays on the Sermon on the Mount* (trans. L. L. Welborn; Philadelphia: Fortress, 1985), 419. In an overwhelming number of cases, "hypocrites" is used in Matthew, but sparingly in Mark and Luke and never in the epistles. This suggests that the *Didache* came from a community similar to Matthew's and that both writings are very early. Paul, for all his favoring of the Gentiles, never resorts to calling Jews "hypocrites." This use fell into disfavor because it may have been counterproductive

in winning the Jews for Christianity. Jesus' use of the term in Matthew had religious and not ethnic implications.

6 *Didache* 8:9.

7 Schweizer, *Good News According to Matthew*, 159, notes, probably correctly, that the tripartite schema of almsgiving, prayer, and fasting was taken over from the Judaism of Jesus' day and was practiced in Matthew's church.

15

THE TREASURES IN HEAVEN

MATTHEW 6:19–21

While the positive command to put "treasures in heaven" may not be immediately intelligible to the modern ear, the negative command of this pericope to avoid accumulation of earthly wealth is immediately understandable in spite of the fact that the language comes from the world of first-century Palestine. Everything in this world eventually decays; hence nothing earthly is worthy of ultimate concern. By itself this pessimistic philosophy would hardly be uniquely Christian. Stoicism and Epicureanism took different attitudes to life but held to the same transitory view of reality. The evangelist here again divides his universe into two spheres: heaven, where God reigns, and earth, where sin has sway.[1] This division reflects the Lord's Prayer with its request that the making holy of his name, the coming of his kingdom, and the performance of his will be done "on earth as it is in heaven" (6:10). On earth all things are subject to change and destruction. In heaven they are not.

One commentator finds that for Matthew the "treasures in heaven" is simply the kingdom of heaven;[2] another concludes the phrase is indefinite.[3] Still another suggests the treasures are lavished upon the disciples in the consummated kingdom.[4] No unanimity of scholarly opinion must be overcome in suggesting another view.

The "treasures on earth" seem to be fine clothing subject to destruction by moths or larvae and precious metals that will eventually rust. These "treasures" can also be stolen. Thievery in Palestine was done by digging beneath the walls of the earthen structures, a picturesque architectural detail not suggested in the English phrase "break in and steal."[5] But what are the treasures in heaven and how does one lay or store them up?

If we take the view that Matthew is putting together disconnected logia without a logical pattern, we are destined to remain uncertain. But Matthew, like a skilled, careful literary theologian, has developed his ecclesiology within the framework of a specific Christology. His views of the church are an extension of what he thinks about Jesus. The word "treasures" by itself is indefinite, but in the context of this section it has two definite meanings. The "treasures on earth" refer to monetary wealth of some sort; those things valued by the person are different for each person. The "treasures in heaven" refer to wealth of a different type. Matthew's main theme in the Sermon up to this point is reconciliation as a mark of the community of the followers of Jesus. The petition dealing with forgiveness is the only one explicated in the Sermon, and this is placed immediately after the Lord's Prayer. The phrase "treasure for yourselves treasures in heaven" (a literal translation) refers to the reconciling work of the community of Jesus. The members of this community are reconciled among themselves and preach God's reconciliation in Jesus to all people. As they live their lives and preach this message, reconciliation takes place, people are joined to this community, and thereby treasures are laid up in heaven. This is the work of God in and through the community of Jesus, since the clear message of the Sermon is that God's work, especially that of reconciliation, has become the identifying mark of the community. The controlling phrase of the first part of the Lord's Prayer is "on earth as it is in heaven." God's work of reconciliation must become the distinguishing characteristic of the followers of Jesus. Reconciling with each other is the work of the community because God has already been reconciled with them. What is done in the community for the benefit of others lasts. More simply put, the "treasures in heaven" are the church.

In some places in Matthew "treasures" should be taken literally, things of great monetary worth, as in the account of the Magi (2:11) and the treasures that are doomed for corruption in this pericope. It can also refer to the heart. The good and evil treasures in Matthew 12:35 are interpreted by Luke as the heart, the moral nature (6:45). In the parable of the treasure in the field, the treasure refers not to something in a man but outside of him. The man who buys the field after he has sold all things (13:44) may refer to God's purchase of the church. The treasure is what God wants: *he wants the church*. Here the idea of atonement is implicit.

The church is also designated in Matthew 13 as the wheat and the good fish. Especially informative in determining what the Sermon means here by treasures is the pericope of the rich young man. Jesus says, "If you would be perfect (*teleios*), go, sell what you possess and give to the poor, and you will have treasure in heaven" (Matthew 19:21). Not the selling of his wealth but the giving to the poor assures him of treasure in heaven. Second, giving to the poor and having treasure in heaven resemble the last words of the Sermon's pericope: "For where your treasure is, there will your heart be also" (6:21). The promise of Jesus that the young man will be perfect when he sells and gives to the poor is similar to the Sermon's "You therefore must be perfect, as your heavenly Father is perfect" (5:48). Perfection here is not a life free of moral blemishes but consists of having a reconciling attitude to all people in all things. It relieves those who are in debt to the disciple of Jesus in all matters and it relieves the poor of their poverty as an imitation of God's generous treatment of all people (5:45).

Not only does the pericope of the rich young man provide Jesus' own commentary on the Sermon's treasures, both James and Luke have similar understandings. James has this logion: "Come now, you rich, weep and howl for the miseries that are coming upon you. Your riches have rotted and your garments are moth-eaten. Your gold and silver have rusted, and their rust will be evidence against you and will eat your flesh like fire. You have laid up treasure for the last days" (James 5:1–3). As the Sermon looks forward to the destruction of treasures laid up on earth, James looks back on those in the church who already have ignored this warning and have in fact laid up treasures on earth. Both James and the Sermon are eschatological, but James adds the final condemnation. The warning in the Sermon is matched by a condemning verdict in James. The rust which destroys the precious metals (Matthew 6:19) is now destroying the rich (James 5:3).[6] James has developed an original word of Jesus for his homiletical purposes. Since the Epistle of James seems to be a mosaic of the Sermon on the Mount (probably written before the gospel of Matthew), it may indicate that Jesus' Sermon was used regularly, in essentially the form we have it now, in the church even before its inscription by Matthew.[7]

Luke's closest parallel to this section is found not in his version of the Sermon but in a section on the Father's giving the kingdom to the church, on selling one's possessions, giving alms (or performing deeds of mercy), and acquiring purses that do not grow old (12:32–34). These purses are further described as unfailing treasures in the heavens, safe from moth and thief. Luke's conclusion (34) is nearly identical with Matthew's (6:21): "For where your treasure is, there will your heart be also."[8] Luke substitutes deeds of mercy for Matthew's helping the poor. In both cases treasure is secured in heaven. Luke may also be providing additional commentary material on the meaning of treasures in stories found only in his gospel: the rich fool (12:16–21), who in the end loses all; and Lazarus and the rich man (16:19–31), who ignored poor Lazarus and was at last doomed. The true treasures are those who need the help of the church.

The understanding of the true treasures may be explained by a story from the church in the third century. The deacon and later martyr St. Lawrence was asked by the Roman imperial authorities to show them the church's treasures. Lawrence gathered together and presented to the authorities the poor, for which impudence he was put to death. Such an account by itself is not valid exegetical evidence, but it does vividly demonstrate that the treasures are people in need. We cannot rule out the possibility that the Sermon's words about treasures were at the core of this story. The Sermon's pericope on laying up treasures in heaven and avoiding the pursuits of this world as one's ultimate concern anticipates the next three pericopes, where total allegiance to the kingdom's purposes are required.

NOTES

1 Robert A. Guelich, *Sermon on the Mount* (Waco: Word, 1982), 326.

2 Eduard Schweizer, *The Good News According to Matthew* (trans. David E. Green; Atlanta: Knox Press, 1975), 163.

3 Guelich, *Sermon on the Mount*, 327.

4 So Donald A. Carson, *The Sermon on the Mount: An Evangelical Exposition* (Grand Rapids: Baker, 1978), 76.

5 Guelich, *Sermon on the Mount*, 327.

6 David P. Scaer, *James: The Apostle of Faith* (St. Louis: Concordia, 1983), 120–21.

7 This is hardly the only place where James makes a homiletical application of logia later included in the Sermon for his purposes. See Frederick Henry Chase, *The Lord's Prayer in the Early Church* (vol. 1, no. 3 of *Texts and Studies: Contributions to Biblical and Patristic Literature*; gen. ed. J. A. Robinson; Cambridge: Cambridge University Press, 1891), 48.

8 Matthew's singular *you* is paralleled by Luke's plural *you*, a point not detectable in English.

16

THE TOTAL ALLEGIANCE

MATTHEW 6:22–24

One commentator has remarked that this is one of the most difficult sections of the Sermon on the Mount.[1] Perhaps the imagery here is the same as Paul's description of the church as the body of Christ. The eye would be the leader of the church who fails to understand the message of Jesus and brings in a darkness that leads to the church's destruction. A previous pericope in the Sermon uses the body imagery (5:29–30). Such a Pauline interpretation fits only awkwardly here, though, since the previous and the next pericopes seem to be describing the singleness of mind and purpose necessary for the community of the followers of Jesus. Nevertheless such an interpretation is not impossible when compared to Luke's parallel 11:34–36 with its warning not to let the light in the body become darkness. Luke introduces his parallel to Matthew 5:15 in another form: "No one after lighting a lamp puts it in a cellar or under a bushel, but on a stand, that those who enter may see the light" (6:33). In both the Matthean and Lucan versions of the Sermon this pericope speaks about the community's responsibility to the world as the bearer of the Gospel. Thus it seems best to take it as a reference to individual commitment among the members of the community.

This commitment means total resolve to store treasures in heaven, that is, to bring about reconciliation. Perhaps the Matthean pericope is troublesome only because the evangelist shifts the meaning of the words so slightly. The first use of "eye" refers to the physical eye, and second the use to the spiritual function of seeing the things of God. The eye as the "lamp of the body" simply describes the eye as an organ of seeing—physical, not spiritual seeing.[2] When it fails to function, the person is blind. The last part of the pericope, "If then the light in you is darkness, how great is the darkness!" is speaking not of physical but of spiritual darkness. The eye metaphorically becomes the means through which the message of Jesus is received. Light and darkness take on a theological meaning,[3] not only representing good and evil, but the realms of God and Satan.

This subtle shift from a discussion of the physical body to the spiritual life is signaled by the use of "evil" (*ponēros*; 23) to describe the eye. The Greek is far stronger than the RSV's "not sound," the eye is not even called bad, but evil. Faith has been effectively assaulted by the Evil One (*ponēros*), Satan, and the victim's entire being is thrown into darkness. The pericope is the same type of warning found in the parable of the sower, where Satan snatches away faith (13:19). In the Sermon it immediately precedes the section on the impossibility of serving two masters. It is connected both in substance and vocabulary with the saying that the followers of Jesus are the light of the world (5:14–16). Where light has been replaced by darkness in the follower of Jesus, he is no longer the light of the world, but lives in an impenetrable darkness.

This saying on two masters (6:24) summarizes the Sermon's concern about the impossibility of being a disciple of Jesus with less than full commitment. The antagonism is between God and mammon, the Aramaic word for possessions.[4] The concept that divided loyalties are impossible is true in any situation or culture. It is as true for the slave of the ancient world with two owners as it is for anyone else. The impossibility of divided loyalties is taken up in a slightly different form in the logion of a house divided against itself (Matthew 12:25). The impossibility of divided loyalty or serving two masters finds its most acute expression in serving God and possessions.

The word "serve" suggests slavery, total devotion to the master. The word "masters" (*kyrioi*) was used in Matthew's church in its singular form (*kyrios*) as a reference to Jesus as the eschatological judge (7:21, 22; 25:37). The use of the plural here suggests a rivalry for the devotion of worship.[5] The words "love" and "devoted to" suggest the posture of faith, and the words "hate" and "despise" suggest unbelief.

While "mammon" is the word for things, it is virtually personified here as Satan. Satan incarnates himself as mammon, possessions. Mammon and Satan, seemingly independent, demand of their devotees the same allegiance that is offered in faith to God. Satan, in wealth, appears as a lord and demands the same commitment as does Jesus. This is not an essentially new thought introduced here by the evangelist, as it has been offered in the pericope of the treasures in heaven. But here wealth not only rusts away but demands divine worship. While the connection between Satan and possessions may not be so evident in the Sermon, it has already been introduced in the third temptation of Jesus, where Satan promises all the kingdoms of the world if Jesus worships him

(4:8–9). Riches are Satan's surrogates, and through them he draws people away from God. Yet the person who pursues the simple means of sustenance can also be tempted to do this with such avidity that he effectively begins to call Satan lord and no longer accords Jesus that honor, regardless of how often he uses the title of him.

Matthew's warning against serving two masters (lords) finds its parallel in Luke after the story of the unjust steward, who changes the ledgers of his master's debtors (16:1–13). In Luke it is given a slightly advanced meaning. Luke agrees with Matthew that riches are not to be used as an object of devotion, but adds that mammon or riches can be the means to further one's standing in the kingdom. Luke's concern that money not become an object of one's devotion is made clear in his comment about Jesus' hearers: "The Pharisees, who were lovers of money, heard all this, and they scoffed at him" (16:14). Perhaps Matthew's condemnation of the deification of wealth as a personification of Satan was taken by some in the early church as requiring renunciation of personal property. The pericope of the rich young man could also be taken to support self-imposed poverty. Luke does not allow for any such misinterpretation by saying that wealth is not only an object of worship but it may also be used for the benefit of the kingdom and of others. Matthew's warning about serving two masters is directed not primarily against the accumulation of wealth, but more against undue concern about the ordinary things needed to maintain life. His gospel, as is evidenced in the next pericope centering on cares and anxieties, cannot be used as a manifesto against wealth and a statement of commendation for those less than wealthy and poor.

NOTES

1   Robert A. Guelich, *The Sermon on the Mount* (Waco: Word, 1982), 239. So also W. D. Davies, *The Setting of the Sermon on the Mount* (Atlanta: Scholars, 1989), 384.

2   Schweizer admits this pericope is ambiguous as to the question of whether the eye is functioning to bring light into the body or revealing what is in the body. He favors the former interpretation, but takes it as reference to a spiritual seeing. See his *The Good News According to Matthew* (trans. David E. Green; Atlanta: Knox Press, 1975), 163.

3   The preaching of Jesus in Galilee is the light shining in darkness and over those who sit in death's shadow (4:16). See the discussion in Guelich, *Sermon on the Mount*, 332.

4   Guelich, *Sermon on the Mount*, 334, provides an extensive discussion on "mammon," a word with Semitic roots meaning property and material possessions, not simply money.

5 Gerald Friedlander finds a parallel in the *Testaments of the Twelve Patriarchs, The Testimony of Judah* XVIII, 6: "He who serves two opposite passions cannot serve God, for the passions blind his soul and he goes about by day as though it were night." See his *The Jewish Sources of the Sermon on the Mount* (New York: KTAV, 1969), 185. This is only an approximate parallel, as it makes the division between opposing passions and not between God and the passions.

17

THE LITTLE SERMON
WITHIN THE SERMON

MATTHEW 6:25–34

Jesus' "sermon" in the Sermon on the Mount has more the quality of pastoral preaching than it does that of doctrinal teaching. Its homiletical style provides a gentle leading of the congregation. Nothing essentially new is added, as the previous section of the Sermon is presupposed. Typical of the Sermon up to this point is its high christological goals matched with threats for those who do not emulate them. This section, however, is more realistic and speaks to the followers of Jesus within the reality of this world *as they are and not as they should be*. The Sermon's characteristic eschatological possibilities are replaced by the realities of the present world. There are no threats here. The followers of Jesus are not provided with specific instructions on how they should confront the practical problems of ordinary existence. Its homiletical tone is built on the previous more doctrinal parts of the Sermon, but along with the Beatitudes and the Lord's Prayer, it is one of the most beautiful and well-known parts of the Sermon.[1] It is a sweet preaching of the gospel.[2]

The first words, "Therefore I tell you" (or "On account of what I have just said, I say to you"), join this section not only to the previous pericope on the impossibility of serving both God and mammon but to everything that has preceded in the Sermon. These are not words addressed to people who are uncertain about their religious allegiance, but to those who have by God's power been led to see and receive the invitation of Jesus with all of its demands for complete loyalty to God, along with the renunciation of the world with its wealth. Here are not the calamitous thunderings against the accumulation of money, but gentle guidings on how the followers of Jesus should face this world.

The pericope revolves around two points: food and clothing. The disciple of Jesus who is overly concerned about how he will be nourished and clothed shows that God is not his Father. The admonition of Jesus against concern about food and clothing cannot, however, be taken as an excuse for profligate living and idleness. Forbidden here is making something temporal—even the ordinary means of life—the prime reason for one's existence. Thus here in the Sermon the meaning is not that the disciple should not engage in the ordinary pursuits of the world, but that such pursuits should not be the main reason for his existence. They do not provide the ultimate goal for the follower of Jesus.

The Greek word for "life" ("do not be anxious about your *psychē*") can also be translated "soul." Jesus is not speaking about the soul in an isolated sense, but he is speaking about the soul which, instead of focusing upon God as Father, is so absorbed with this world that it only focuses on the needs of the body. In the New Testament the soul is also called the spirit (*pneuma*), as it reflects upon God. It is called the soul (*psychē*), as it is introverted within itself and becomes concerned about how it will survive and thrive in the world.[3] Paul uses a cognate word (*psychikos*) to describe the man who is incapable of receiving the Holy Spirit (1 Corinthians 2:14). Such a person is so preoccupied with himself and the world that he does not allow himself to think about the things of God.

The command not to be concerned about what shall be eaten and drunk complements the Fourth Beatitude: "Blessed are those who hunger and thirst for righteousness, for they shall be filled" (5:6). The one desiring the higher food of God's righteousness revealed in Jesus can no longer be overly concerned or anxious about how he will be fed. Food, drink, and clothing are references to the necessities of life. The person who hungers after ordinary things is still living the ordinary life and not the life now made possible by the coming of God's kingdom in Jesus.

Having stated the basic premise that the disciple's undue concern for his earthly existence is improper in the kingdom, an expository defense of this position is presented. Why should the follower of Jesus be unconcerned about what he will eat and drink or how he will clothe his body?

First of all, Jesus uses an argument from the greater to the lesser.[4] Life itself is more important than food, and the body more than clothing. The existence of life and the body is not a cause for concern. Yet they are more difficult to produce than food and clothing. If the disciple has no concern about why and how the life and body came into existence, he should be concerned even less about how they will be maintained through food and protected by clothing. The God who creates life will also preserve it.

Second, Jesus now reverses the argument, going from the lesser to the greater. If God cares for such insignificant creatures as birds which, of course, engage in no commercial occupation, he will certainly provide for human beings. Here Jesus is speaking about the entire agricultural enterprise, from the sowing of the seed to the storing of the harvest. Luke shows a few differences in his parallel. The word "God" replaces Matthew's "heavenly Father" and "ravens" replaces "birds" (12:34).[5]

The third argument against concern is its futility. The older translation spoke of the impossibility of making oneself taller by a cubit. The newer translations catch an alternative, preferred, and perhaps more reasonable meaning by referring to the impossibility of lengthening one's life. It is not within man's power to lengthen his life even by a "cubit" of time, that is, about an hour.[6]

Fourth, the Sermon holds up the examples of the "lilies of the earth" (or "of the field"). They do neither the hard fieldwork nor the more delicate work of the artisan in his home. Thus Jesus has embraced the ordinary occupations engaged in the production of goods in the ancient world. Ordinary people worked as artisans at home or in the fields. This is not a suggestion that one give up gainful employment. Jesus was a carpenter by trade (Mark 6:3). In a sense the birds and the lilies carry out the assignments given them by God. They are productive in ways determined for them by God. The point is that humans, who play a much more important role in the world for God and who accomplish great things, should have complete confidence that God will care for them. They should be free from anxiety about the ordinary things in life. After all, God does provide for comparatively insignificant creatures. The insignificant flowers, clothed by God, are even more magnificent than Solomon, Israel's most splendid king, renowned for his fabulous wealth.

Jesus may introduce a messianic theme in mentioning Solomon. Matthew uses Solomon as a messianic referent in other places in his gospel. Solomon's name appears twice in connection with the genealogy (1:6, 7). The bringing of gifts by the Magi to the infant Jesus recaptures Solomon's receiving of the Gentile kings. Finally, in a comparison with Solomon, Jesus describes the kingly nature of his own office, "behold, something greater than Solomon is here" (12:42). While David more than any other king personified the messianic qualities, Solomon was seen as the highest expression of that messianic office. The Sermon with its description of Solomon "in all his glory" (6:29) uses language generally appropriate for God (cf. Matthew 25:31, where "the Son of Man comes in his glory").

The fifth and final argument in this series is a reference to the grass, which in spite of its magnificence quickly fades away and is burned. This

argument builds upon the previous one. The grass not only has an insignificant existence in comparison with man, but its short life finally meets its
end by burning. Humankind, of course, is a much more significant creature than grass. The burning of the grass and the flower was taken over
from Isaiah 40 into the New Testament in James 1:9–11 and was used there
as an eschatological threat. Rich men are like flowers that in spite of their
beauty are doomed. Although the Sermon mentions the short life of the
flowers, there is here no thought of doom; rather it gently lifts up the trou-
bled follower of Jesus by asking him to ponder how God provides for those
things which are considered less important.

The little sermon of 6:25–34 concludes with a summary. The prohibitions against concern for eating, drinking, and clothing are repeated. The
"therefore" means that those in the community should heed these arguments and not ask what they will eat, drink, or wear (31). These are matters over which the unconverted Gentiles, that is, the heathen, worry.[7] The
disciples of Jesus know that God as Father will provide even before being
asked. God is aware of his children's needs and has already provided for
them. Prayer is not the cause of God's giving. In his Small Catechism
Luther says, "God gives daily bread indeed without our prayer, also to all
the wicked; but we pray … that he would lead us … to receive our daily
bread with thanksgiving." Praying with long requests in a public way is
forbidden (6:7). Now prayers with undue concern for material things are
also forbidden; such prayers are like heathen requests. The true God does
not value the prayers of his children because of the number of words.

Luke includes his parallel not in his Sermon on the Plain (6:17–49),
but as an appendix to the parable of the rich fool (12:16–21), where its
meaning is more obvious than in Matthew. Matthew argues that if you
serve God and not mammon, you will not have anxieties. He does not
argue from the foolishness of wealth, as Luke does. Luke is more direct
with his story of the rich fool who dies before he can enjoy his wealth.
Thus he teaches how empty the accumulation of wealth is. Death brings
everything to nothing. Matthew handles this thought with the corruption
brought on by moth and rust (6:19). Luke's parable of the rich fool presents the same basic principle as Matthew but graphically, simply, and to
the point. Luke joins his parable of the rich fool to his admonition against
anxiety with the word "barns." The barns torn down and rebuilt by the
rich man provide the connecting link with the barns into which birds do
not gather (12:18, 24).

Matthew takes up the same concern about anxiety in the parable of the sower, where the seeds that fell among the thorns are those who are concerned about this world or age (13:22). They hear the Word and intellectually comprehend its message, but no change in their lives is effected. They live anxiously as if there were no God.

In his final argument against worrying, Jesus concludes by addressing his disciples as "men of little faith" (*oligopistoi*; v. 30). According to the canonical arrangement, Matthew is the first gospel. The reader of the canonical Scriptures encounters at this juncture the first instance of the word "faith," which is so essential for New Testament Christianity. A number of things can be noted about its appearance here. This form of address limits the audience to the followers of Jesus and excludes the crowds who also hear the Sermon but whose final reaction is amazement (7:28). The phrase "men of little faith" allows us to ask about the relationship of Matthew and Paul. The word is not used by Paul, who uses "faith" but not "little faith." Still, Matthew's use of it presupposes a congregation that has already been instructed on the meaning of the term "faith." Like Paul's connection between faith and righteousness, Matthew follows his "men of little faith" (30) with the command to pursue righteousness (33). The Matthean equivalent of the Pauline "believing" or "having faith" is "Repent, for the kingdom of heaven is at hand" (4:17), and "Seek ... his kingdom," the phrase used in the Sermon (6:33). Whether the stress in the compound Greek word "those of little faith" is on "faith" or "little" is debatable. I think the emphasis is on faith.[8] Even people with the smallest amount of faith should have no anxieties about having enough to survive. Thus the word is in no sense an admonishment to have more faith—as if this were possible—but an invitation to use what is already there. Faith as small as a mustard seed is still able to move a mountain (Matthew 17:20). "Faith" in the Sermon describes the relationship of the followers of Jesus not simply to the message, but the speaker of the Sermon. Belief in Jesus' message about God's kingdom, now coming in him, necessarily means that his followers will not be distressed with concern for the ordinary things in this life.

The little sermon (6:25–34) seems to be an exposition in reverse of the Fourth Petition, the one obligating the community of Jesus to ask for him who is the Bread of Life. Jesus is the Bread we need for our existence before God or the bread we need for the coming age, the age in which the Kingdom is completely manifested. Since God provides the food for the new age, he certainly will provide the lesser food for this age. Anxiety over bread has no place as it indicates lack of faith.

The exposition on anxieties is not only a comparatively long one, but virtually prohibits the prayers of the Gentiles who seek all these things, that is, food, drink, and clothing (32). The religious life of the heathen finds its center not in God but in satisfying of the ordinary necessities of life. So firm is this pericope in its condemnation of the Gentiles in their asking for things, that in retrospect it is almost impossible to understand the bread of the Lord's Prayer as referring to earthly food.[9] Such a contradiction would have been obvious to the evangelist who is meticulous in laying out his argument. The disciple of Jesus thanks God as his Father. The Father gives because he already knows our needs, and not only ours but the needs of those who do not acknowledge him as Father. He only desires that all may come to know him as their provider.

The final verses of this pericope, 6:33–34, are an invitation to faith and to put behind all concerns about this world. In verse 33, a number of interesting textual variants are evident, all of which may have been theologically motivated. The RSV reflects a common choice and has "But seek first *his* kingdom and his righteousness." Other scholars favor an original reading that would translate the text "But seek first the kingdom *of God* and his righteousness." Another variant reads "But seek first *the* Kingdom and his righteousness."[10] The latter is the most difficult reading, since "kingdom" in Greek is a feminine noun and is followed by "his," a masculine possessive adjective, which is seemingly without a referent. As a rule the more difficult reading is preferred. There is a theological issue at stake here. Is the "righteousness" of this verse the righteousness revealed in Jesus, in whom God's kingdom has come?[11] This may be the best explanation. Paul's unique theological perspective may not be foreign to Matthew's congregations; for both, righteousness is to be understood as coming with the kingdom.

Several explanations can account for the early Christian scribes changing the manuscripts. It was grammatically awkward to have "his righteousness," when the only antecedent for "his" was a feminine noun, "kingdom." By adding "of God" to "kingdom," they were identifying this righteousness as God's own. "His" now referred to "God." Adding "of God" also provided a theological interpretation. However, there are several reasons for favoring, "But seek first the kingdom (feminine) and his (masculine) righteousness." One very good reason for not including the phrase "of God" after "kingdom" is that its use is generally uncharacteristic of Matthew.[12] The evangelist's usual phrase is "the kingdom of the heavens," which is consistently and without exception replaced by Mark and Luke with "the kingdom of God." When Matthew uses "the kingdom of God," he uses it to describe salvation as a completed reality, not as God's present redemptive activity in Jesus. Prostitutes enter the kingdom of God and the kingdom of God is taken away from God's ancient people (21:31, 43). For Matthew "the kingdom of the heavens" is used to designate God's present redemptive activity in Jesus, especially his death and resurrection, but also his return. This may be the reason Matthew summarizes the messages of both John and Jesus as a coming near of "the kingdom of the heavens" rather than "the kingdom of God." Mark and Luke may have substituted "kingdom of God" not only because it was perhaps more intelligible to their audiences than "the kingdom of the heavens," but because they looked upon what God has done in Jesus as accomplished past reality. By keeping "the kingdom of the heavens" Matthew may be preserving the original forward thrust found in the preaching of John and Jesus. "The kingdom of God" would be less usual for Matthew, as would be "his—the Father's—kingdom," since he uses both this phrase to designate what God *has* already accomplished and not what he *is* doing.

Some of the early church fathers (e.g., Clement, Augustine, Cyril, and Justin) caught Matthew's sense by adding the words "of the heavens." Jesus is described as preaching the coming of the kingdom of the heavens, and the Sermon *is* that preaching. "Seek the kingdom" means, therefore, to pay attention to what Jesus has said about the kingdom of the heavens *in the Sermon.*

Righteousness must be understood in the christological sense; otherwise, an unhealthy triumphalism results, sometimes expressing itself in political activism and other times in millennialism, two sides of one coin.

"First" is attached not only to "the kingdom" but to "his righteousness." The disciple is to seek the kingdom and the righteousness that the Kingdom necessarily brings with it. Jesus puts before the community of his followers one goal, not two. Luke has simplified Matthew's "kingdom and his righteousness" by having only the abridged "his kingdom" (12:31), suggesting that the terms have an overlapping if not synonymous meaning. For Luke the kingdom is God's righteousness, so he omits the word "righteousness" entirely: "Seek his kingdom." Luke may also have feared that in the Gentile world righteousness would be interpreted in the sense of the ethical, civil righteousness of Roman society.

The real problem in the phrase "the kingdom and his righteousness" is finding an antecedent for the word "his." The solution lies perhaps in the fact that the kingdom of the heavens is itself the manifestation of God's work in Jesus. In the first and final sense, *he* is both kingdom and righteousness. Israel's God was Israel's righteousness. Even when others enter the kingdom, Jesus fills all of it and remains its focal point. The Eighth and Ninth Beatitudes might help provide the link. "Blessed are those who are persecuted for righteousness' sake, for theirs is the kingdom of heaven" (5:10) is the last of the eight which are all characterized by the indefinite third person plural, "Blessed are those." The Ninth Beatitude is different, as it uses the second person plural. "Blessed *are you,* when men revile you and persecute you ... on account of me." The persecution for the sake of righteousness is followed by the persecution for the sake of Jesus. *They are persecuted not for two different causes—righteousness and Jesus—but one: the righteousness that God reveals in Jesus.* This righteousness is the chief content of the Sermon.

The command to seek righteousness brackets the section on the "higher righteousness," which begins with 5:21 by forbidding anger with the brother and requiring reconciliation, since God is currently showing by what he does in nature that he is beneficent to all men. Retaliation is impossible, since God has put aside his right to retaliation and demonstrated his love for all people. This righteousness is also summarized in the Fifth Petition of the Lord's Prayer, "And forgive us our debts, as we also have forgiven our debtors."

The follower of Jesus not only makes this righteousness the beginning of his life with God, but its entire content. The command to seek this righteousness means seeking what God has righteously done in Jesus. In the Christian community, prayers for wealth and for ordinary, necessary things are to be replaced with prayers asking for God's righteousness of love and reconciliation. The person who prays for this righteousness need not pray for anything else, as all these things will be given to him.

The disciple of Jesus who has sought the kingdom is not rewarded with things. There is nothing here to suggest a cause-and-effect reaction. God does not continue to give him all things because he continues to seek the kingdom. Neither does God's providing for him cease because he refuses to seek the kingdom or renounces it. God does not retaliate against the offender by depriving him of his necessities or even his luxuries. Also there is no suggestion that after we have sought the kingdom we are allowed to seek other things.[13] All things have come to the follower of Jesus incidentally, by God's grace, but not as a reward for what he has done. Often Christianity has deteriorated into luring people into church on the promise of future wealth. The reasoning goes like this: If they want all things, they should first seek God. This is not only a falsification of the purposes of Christianity in its classical form, but a flagrant violation of the obvious and clearly intended message of the Sermon. Religion used to further one's goals, especially financial, is not that of the Sermon.

The "little sermon" concludes with a gentle, anticlimactic warning, missing from Luke,[14] to avoid concern about the future. "Therefore do not be anxious about tomorrow, for tomorrow will be anxious for itself. Let the day's own trouble be sufficient for the day" (6:34). The disciple is not promised freedom from misfortune in his life. The word here for "trouble" (*kakia*) is not the same one used for Satan as the Evil One (*ponēros*). Here it means the bad things. Satan will not determine the fate of the follower of Jesus; nevertheless trials will enter his life. These words of Jesus do not hold before the Christian a high, unobtainable goal. Troubles, what Matthew calls the bad things, are part of the Christian's lot as long as he is part of this world. Ideally there should be none, since the kingdom has come. Realistically they are the bane of life as he awaits the final manifestation of the kingdom. Limit them to the present day. They are so burdensome that no one can handle more than a day's share. Here is Jesus, the *Seelsorger*, the physician of the soul, who takes the disciple as he is, and not as he will be or should be, and accepts him.

This section has set forth for the disciple practical directives that are derived from the Sermon's theme of God's reconciling righteousness revealed in Jesus. It concludes the first part of the Sermon and makes it a complete theological unit. The next section is more loosely constructed and handles different aspects within the community of the followers of Jesus (7:1–14). Then the Sermon's last section focuses on the last times (7:15–27).

NOTES

1   Luke has a parallel section in 12:22–32, following the parable of the rich fool (16–21). It is not included in his version of the Sermon. In Luke this pericope accentuates the meaninglessness of accumulated wealth. This practical motive is the reason the follower of Jesus should really have no cares about the things of this world. In Matthew the basis for having no cares is the impossibility of serving two masters. Robert H. Gundry, *Matthew: A Commentary on his Literary and Theological Art* (Grand Rapids: Eerdmans, 1982), 115.

2   Robert A. Guelich treats this as a unified section; see his *The Sermon on the Mount* (Waco: Word, 1982), 334–35. Guelich does not believe that it was originally part of the Sermon on the Mount (115). Though the tone of this section is noticeably different from the previous material, this can be explained by its serving as a commentary on what has preceded. The condemnation of the Gentiles (6:32) is characteristic of Matthew and of his version of the Sermon, where their praying is criticized (6:7). Luke 12:30 is similar to Matthew 6:32, but seems less than fully

integrated in Luke. This might be the only place in Luke where Gentiles are used negatively in the sense of unbelieving pagans, a use common in Matthew. W. D. Davies
also notes the style of this section of the Sermon in Matthew and its parallel in Luke
are not what "we usually associate with catechetical instruction and exhortation, of the
kind of prudential maxims we find in the book of Proverbs"; see his *The Setting of the
Sermon on the Mount* (Atlanta: Scholars, 1989), 369.

3 Guelich, *Sermon on the Mount*, 336, notes that the use of *psychē* is not in opposition to
   sōma, the body, but is parallel.

4 Eduard Schweizer, *The Good News According to Matthew* (trans. David E. Greene;
   Atlanta: Knox Press, 1975), 164. See also Guelich, *Sermon on the Mount*, 337.

5 Guelich, *Sermon on the Mount*, 337, suggests that Matthew substituted "birds" for
   "ravens" because of the unclean nature of that bird. He also points out, however, that
   "birds of the heaven" (Genesis 1:26) is a familiar Old Testament expression.

6 Guelich, *Sermon on the Mount*, 338; Davies, *Setting of the Sermon*, 458. "And which of
   you by being anxious can add a cubit to his span of life?"

7 The parable of the rich fool in Luke 12:16–21 seems to be a commentary by way of an
   illustration on the command of Jesus not to be concerned about eating and drinking
   (Luke 12:29 and Matthew 6:32). Whether the rich fool is a Gentile or a Jew is insignificant; he acted like an unbelieving pagan. What is noteworthy about Luke's handling of
   the issues is that the illustration precedes the command.

8 Guelich, *Sermon on the Mount*, 340, says that the phrase stresses not the absence of
   faith, but its weakness. The use of the term "little faith" strengthens the view that the
   major stress of the Sermon up to this point is not on Law but on Gospel, an implicit
   proclamation of Christ.

9 Guelich, *Sermon on the Mount*, 341, lays the groundwork for eliminating understanding
   the Fourth Petition as a request for earthly goods: "the Father's knowledge of one's
   needs in this context precludes undue concern for life's necessities...." But Guelich still
   holds to a material interpretation of the Fourth Petition.

10 So Guelich, *Sermon on the Mount*, 347. "To *seek righteousness*, to set one's efforts in pursuit of
   conduct corresponding to the Father's will is not merely the prelude to the entrance requirement of the *Kingdom*. It is concomitant of the presence of the *Kingdom*."

11 Gundry, *Matthew: A Commentary*, 118–19, understands that God's righteousness will
   vindicate his disciples with vengeance. Thus the disciples should look forward to God's
   final rule of the world. Gundry is right in saying that God will bring his own righteousness, but something is lacking in understanding divine righteousness as wrath.
   Schweizer, *Good News According to Matthew*, 166, holds a similar view.

12 So Gundry, *Matthew: A Commentary*, 119. Betz also notes that "of God" must be an
   addition, since the Sermon consistently speaks of "the kingdom of the heavens," however, the same idea is implied. It contains the ideas of the sum total of the disciple's
   duties to God. *Essays on the Sermon on the Mount* (trans. L. L. Welborn; Philadelphia:
   Fortress, 1985), 481–85.

13 Guelich, *Sermon on the Mount*, 347–48, says that "our needs are not eclipsed by our
   commitment to the Father; they are simply placed in perspective." Since this life is
   transitory in comparison with the coming one, its needs are largely eclipsed.

14 Gundry, *Matthew: A Commentary*, 119, holds that Matthew added it as his own editorial
   comment. It might be argued the other way around: Luke omitted it, as he does many
   of Matthew's sayings, simply because its surface meaning is not that apparent. Davies,
   Setting of the Sermon, 300, notes the admonition to take no care for the future would
   have struck the community of Jamnia as irresponsible.

PART 3

OTHER MATTERS
OF
CHURCH CONCERN

MATTHEW 7:1–12

18

LIFE IN THE CHURCH

MATTHEW 7:1–5

The final chapter of the Sermon continues the homiletical style begun in 6:25–34. The evangelist again provides an exposition of sayings made previously. The prohibition against judgment is set within the eschatological framework characterizing the Sermon. The coming of the kingdom of God in Jesus means not only persecution for Jesus and his followers, but also that in him God will judge the world. The person who utters a condemning word against his brother has assumed the role of Jesus as judge (7:23). Yet there is an even more fundamental truth in the saying. "Judge not, that you be not judged" puts forth as a negative command the Sermon's positive demand for forgiveness. "Forgive us our trespasses, as we forgive those who trespass against us" is, in a sense, the other side of the one coin stamped reconciliation.[1]

"For with the judgment you pronounce you will be judged" is similar to the exposition following the Lord's Prayer, where God forgives only those who forgive and does not forgive those who refuse to forgive (6:14,15). So strong is the motif of reconciliation in the community of the followers of Jesus that it only reluctantly removes fellow members from this community. Rendering such a hasty verdict would be contradictory to the reconciliatory nature of the community and a denial of the message entrusted to it. The Christian judges only with hesitancy, but never assumes the solely divine prerogative of condemnation, a thought taught clearly in Luke's parallel.[2]

The pericope does not say that judgment will never take place, but rather the stress here is on the forgiving brother who shows by his act of forgiveness that he himself has received God's forgiveness. On the other hand, the brother who condemns shows that he does not know the God of mercy and hence does not believe.[3] The final judgment belongs not to this age, but to the next one. The one who judges his brother must know that he will be subjected to the same standards. No cause and effect are suggested in the promise that a person will receive the same judgment he gives to another, rather, he has already excluded himself from God's mercy. Luke's phrase "and the measure you will give will be the measure you get" is used to cover both judging and forgiving (6:37–38). Schweizer calls attention to the technical commercial idiom "with the measure by which you have measured out to me." It means the same yardstick is used in buying and selling goods, a sword which cuts two ways.[4] Thus the follower of Jesus knows that he is subject to the same standards he applies to the erring brother. The one who judges another is at the same time forced to examine himself. This is developed in the word about the speck and log in the eye.

Before its inscription in Matthew this logion seems to be used in James 4:11–12 where the one who speaks evil of his brother has judged him; with that judgment he has spoken evil against the Law and actually condemned it. The one who condemns his brother has set aside the law of love and thus he usurps the right of the lawgiver and judge. James seems to allude to this saying in the Sermon by referring to Jesus as the giver of the law, in the sense of the revealer of the message of reconciliation and as the judge.[5] This pericope in the Sermon reflects Jesus' understanding of himself as the judge and the early church's understanding of him as both judge and giver of the new revelation.

Luke includes his prohibition against judgment right after the command to be merciful as the Father is merciful (6:37–38). Though Luke's Sermon on the Plain can be regarded as his parallel to Matthew's Sermon on the Mount, he has placed other parallel material in other chapters, for example 11, 12, 13, 14, and 16, among others. With this prohibition against judgment (6:37–38), Luke's order again runs parallel to Matthew. The command to be perfect (Matthew 5:48) is interpreted by Luke to be merciful (6:36) and this requires that no brother refuse forgiveness to another (6:37). Whereas Matthew in his version of the Sermon continues with his pericopes on almsgiving, prayer, fasting, Luke's version develops with the prohibition against judging (6:36–42), which Matthew resumes in 7:1–11. Luke's message is clear and his order logical. Clement of Rome, shortly before the end of the first century, and Polycarp, closer to the middle of the second century, followed Luke and also placed the prohibition against judgment after the command to be merciful.[6] Mercy and the right to forgo judging the repentant brother are joined in Matthew's parable of the unforgiving servant, whose condemnation of his brother is interpreted by their master as a refusal to show mercy (18:33).

The command to take the beam out of one's own eye before taking the speck out of a brother's eye has two points. First, the enormity of one's own

sin in a sufficient problem for any member of the community of the followers of Jesus so that he cannot be further burdened down in searching
out the sins of others. Perfectionism is not a possibility. Secondly, the analogy of the beam not only indicates the enormity of the burden, but the
blindness of a person making such a judgment against another. Matthew
has already introduced the concept of spiritual blindness with his discussion of the evil eye and the resultant darkness of the body (6:23). Just
before his parallel account of the beam and speck in the eye, Luke introduces the parable of the impossibility of one blind man leading another
(6:39). Thus he helps us understand Matthew's material as also referring to
spiritual blindness. Blindness here does not mean a doctrinal unawareness,
but rather a special insensitivity in seeking reconciliation. Matthew
includes the parable of the blind men in a warning against the Pharisees
(15:14) and not in the Sermon. Jeremias suggests that since this pericope
addresses the hearers as hypocrites (7:5), it was addressed originally to the
Pharisees and not the disciples. "Hypocrites" is not used by Jesus to designate the disciples, and few words match its condemnatory tone, since it
precludes belief.[7] As Luke (6:42) also uses the same harsh language, it does
seem intended for the disciples and hence for all who read these gospels.

The logion on the mote and the beam, which may have been taken
over by Jesus from a Jewish proverb, has been understood in several ways.
It has been used as an excuse to avoid taking accusations from others. So
the accused can immediately demand that the accuser remove the beam in
his own eye first and thus avoid judgment. Also it could possibly suggest
that after one has put his own life in order by removing the beam, he can
go around looking for specks. Neither of these interpretations is valid. The
purpose of the pericope is for the disciple to be first concerned about one's
own life and not to act individualistically against others. Specks are virtually undetectable. Beams are not. Judgment against another cannot be
done in haste, if done at all, and if it is required, it must be done as a community action (18:15–20).

There is a certain grotesque impossibility about this entire pericope.
The accuser's eye is so damaged by the log that his efforts will have to be
directed to returning it to health. If the log is removed, the sight of the eye
may be so improved that it can now clearly see the speck in the other's eye.
However, the focus of the pericope is not the speck, but the log. The entire
Sermon revolves around the theme of making every attempt at reconciliation to avoid condemning the brother. At this point Matthew does not
introduce the words of Jesus that describe a process for bringing a judicial

procedure against a brother. That will come in 18:15–20. The pericope on the beam and the speck just points out the enormity of one's own sin and the difficulty of condemning a brother. Davies points out that 18:15–20 shows that the Sermon's prohibition against judgment cannot be taken too literally. Matthew's concern is "to avoid an indiscriminate benevolence, and, at the same time, to guard against a forgiveness governed by careful calculus of 'less and more'."[8] The community of Jesus is never without its principles, but their enforcement requires first self-examination before scrutinizing the brother.

NOTES

1   Guelich catches the correspondence here; see his *The Sermon on the Mount* (Waco: Word, 1982), 349.

2   Luke interprets "judging" as "condemning" in his parallel (6:37). For Matthew's "Judge not, that you be not judged," Luke offers "Judge not, and you will not be judged; condemn not, and you will not be condemned; forgive, and you will be forgiven." He thus intensifies Matthew's negatives so that the sense is that non-condemning Christians will absolutely never have to face the judgment, but will certainly be forgiven.

3   Guelich, *Sermon on the Mount*, 350, correctly notes that one's standing before God at the final judgment is directly related to one's relationship with others.

4   *The Good News According to Matthew* (trans. David E. Greene; Atlanta: Knox Press, 1975), 168–69.

5   David P. Scaer, *James the Apostle of Faith* (St. Louis: Concordia, 1983), 114–15.

6   *Synopsis Quattuor Evangeliorum*, 9th ed. rev. (ed. Kurt Aland; Stuttgart: Deutsch Bibelstiftung, 1976), 93. Clement has: "Have mercy, that ye may receive mercy: forgive that it may be forgiven you. As ye do, so shall it be done to you. As ye give, so shall it be forgiven you" (to the Corinthians). Polycarp has: "But remembering the words which the Lord spoke, as he taught; Judge not that ye be not judged. Forgive, and it shall be forgiven you. Have mercy that ye may receive mercy" (to the Philippians).

7   Guelich, *Sermon on the Mount*, 352–53.

8   Davies, *The Setting of the Sermon on the Mount* (Atlanta: Scholars, 1989), 392. Betz, *Essays on the Sermon on the Mount* (trans. L. L. Welborn; Philadelphia: Fortress, 1985), notes that friends are able to communicate with eye contact and that adversely a person's character flaws are often in the eyes. The speck and the beam in the eye are therefore images indicating presumed character flaws. Human nature, being what it is, tends to exaggerate the flaws of others and to overlook one's own flaws.

19

THE SACRED AND THE HOLY

MATTHEW 7:6

The prohibition against giving the holy to the dogs is without parallel in the New Testament, but used in the *Didache* as a prohibition against sharing the Eucharist with the unbaptized, who obviously must have been identified as the dogs.[1] From the similarity between the parallel sayings in Matthew and the *Didache*, Jefford concludes that they are drawing from the same tradition. Even if the origin of the *Didache*'s eucharistic interpretation is not known, it is very early, perhaps as early as 50 A.D. This does not require that Matthew and the *Didache* necessarily had the same understanding of these words.[2] The prohibitions on giving the holy things to the dogs and the casting pearls before swine are paralleled in literary form and share the same meaning. Dogs are not to receive the holy things and pigs should not get pearls. When pigs discover that they are not eating food, they will attack.[3] The latter prohibition about the pearls and the pigs was included in the Sermon, of course, for theological purposes and not as a literal prohibition. No person throws real pearls to pigs. On the other hand, giving holy things to dogs has *only* a theological meaning, though some have suggested that the original meaning is that sacrificed meat should not be given to canines.

One prominent interpreter understands this section as a warning against apostasy, that is, surrendering what is holy and precious.[4] A warning against apostasy, which involves a renunciation of a fully developed doctrinal system, would be strangely out of place at this point. Though it is tempting to understand this pericope as a prohibition against the defilement of sacred things, e.g., the Eucharist, God's Word, and church artifacts and places, the arguments are not completely convincing.[5] It would be difficult to demonstrate that Jesus had a concern for sacred things, as he is charged by his opponents with defiling the Sabbath, speaking against the temple, and breaking regulations.[6] The interpretation that mission work among the Gentiles is prohibited is, as Davies points out, also unconvincing in the light of the universal dimensions of both the Sermon and

Matthew's gospel.[7] "What is holy" was understood in the eastern church as a reference to the sacramental elements, and there is much to support this understanding, especially its antiquity in the *Didache*. The use of the early church's understanding of this passage as a prohibition against giving Communion to the unbaptized has been carried into more recent times for the use of restrictions about who may receive the Sacrament.[8] As the prohibition of giving the holy things to the dogs is grammatically joined with the previous saying, its meaning should be found within its context. It is not the beginning of the new section. Though we might conclude that Matthew's gospel and the *Didache* interpret key terms differently, taken together they provide clues to understanding this pericope.

In the gospels the word "pearl" appears only in Matthew, here and in the parable of the Pearl of Great Price (13:45–46); there is no parallel in the other gospels. The pearl has a great price, and the merchant sells all he possesses to obtain it. Interpreted, God, the subject of the parable, has not withheld anything and is acquiring the church for himself. The language of the parable suggests that the evangelist is making reference to the atonement. The church is a pearl of great value, for which God pays the ultimate price of all that he has. If we assume that Matthew is being consistent in his understanding of pearl, then we can conclude that the pearls thrown before the swine are the members of the community, the church. They are the ones redeemed by God and for this reason a disciple should not condemn a fellow disciple. Such an interpretation does fit the immediate context, which forbids rendering a verdict of condemnation against the brother; it also reflects the entire Sermon with its demands for reconciliation. Davies comes to the same conclusion: judgment within the community may be necessary, but it should be carried out with "discretion and discrimination."[9] Consider also that Luke strengthens and clarifies Matthew's "do not judge" (7:1,2) by adding "do not condemn" (6:37). The prohibition against judging forbids condemning but it does not mean the surrendering of moral standards, so that the followers of Jesus are devoid of all standards. Rather they are to be exercised with all caution and consideration.

While "holy" is often used of God, it can also be used of those upon whom God has worked. In the *Didache* the one who comes to the Eucharist is holy.[10] Here in the Sermon, "what is holy" is neuter, the *one* holy thing. The neuter permits a reference to the community, the *holy* church. Dogs and swine in 2 Peter 2:22 are used of heretics.[11] Pigs were also seen as unclean. Whatever the specific referents are for these animals, the general sense is that by searching for the speck in the brother's eye, you are treating him as one who does not belong to the community of the followers of Jesus, but in effect turning him over to the false teachers or Satan himself. Pigs can be associated with Satan. "Throwing one's brother to the dogs" expresses the thought well.[12] But in doing this a disciple is inviting the same treatment for himself. Those who destroy the judged brother will turn to destroy the brother who judges, as pigs do when they discover they have been cheated out of their food. Thus the sense here is not different from "the measure you give will be the measure you get" (7:2).

How the prohibition of giving the holy to the dogs was seen as a reference to not giving the Communion to the unbaptized is a matter of conjecture. It does mean that the Sermon even before its inclusion in Matthew was understood within the context of the Eucharist and not apart from it. Taken together with the *Didache*, it may show that Matthew and Paul with his instructions about keeping the adulterous man from Communion (1 Corinthians 5:3–5) were drawing on the same sources. As the Communion was seen as the meal of the community, it seems highly unlikely that the prohibition of giving the holy thing to the dogs could have originally been a prohibition against the unbaptized receiving the Communion. This simply was never a possibility. But here is a case where the eucharistic practice influenced a change in the original meaning.

NOTES

1   *Didache* 9:5. "But let no one eat or drink of this eucharistic thanksgiving, but they have been baptized in the name of the Lord; for concerning this also the Lord has said: *Give not that which is holy to the dogs.*" Taking the eucharistic interpretation of the *Didache* were Athanasius, Pseudo-Basil, and John of Damascus.

2   *The Sayings of Jesus in the Teaching of the Twelve Apostles* (Leiden: E. J. Brill, 1989), 138–40.

3   Eduard Schweizer, *The Good News According to Matthew* (trans. David E. Green; Atlanta: Knox Press, 1975), 170.

4   Robert A. Guelich, *The Sermon on the Mount* (Waco: Word, 1982), 356.

5   Schweizer, *Good News According to Matthew*, 170, argues with good reason that such were not the concerns of Jesus.

6   Schweizer, *Good News According to Matthew*, 170, notes that the protecting of the "holy treasure" had more to do with Hellenistic cults than with the thought of Jesus.

7   *The Setting of the Sermon on the Mount* (Atlanta: Scholars, 1989), 326.

8   For a fuller study of this matter, see Werner Elert, *Eucharist and Church Fellowship in the Early Church* (trans. Norman E. Nagel; St. Louis: Concordia, 1966).

9   Davies, *Setting of the Sermon*, 326.

10 *Didache* 10:6. "If any man is holy, let him come; if any man is not, let him repent."

11 Schweizer, *Good News According to Matthew*, 170.

12 Schweizer, *Good News According to Matthew*, 171, says that in condemning the brother we are throwing God's will to the dogs. Agreed, that such actions are hardly in accord with God's will, but it is another matter to identify it as God's will.

20

PROPER PRAYER

MATTHEW 7:7–11

It may be difficult to determine why the evangelist includes a discourse on prayer at this point. The previous pericope forbids judgment (7:1–6); the following one is an admonition to adhere to the true religion (7:13–14). The sayings on prayer do, however, fit within the overall context of the Sermon, as prayer, almsgiving, and fasting are legitimate expressions of piety for the disciples of Jesus. Their private prayers are not to be made in public or with vain babbling, and they are to pray the Lord's Prayer (6:5–13). Luke places his parallel to this pericope following his version of the Lord's Prayer, so that it serves as a minor treatise on prayer (11:1–13). The only intervening uniquely Lucan material is the parable of the importunate friend (11:5–8). By his arrangement, however, Luke shows that even though he does not place material parallel to Matthew in his version of the Sermon, he agrees with Matthew in connecting it with the Lord's Prayer.

Matthew 7:7–8 includes six references to praying, three of them in the imperative, and six assurances that the prayers will be answered. Asking, seeking, and knocking all refer to prayer. The giving, the finding, and the opening all refer to God's answering these prayers. Earlier in the Sermon Jesus sets down the required contents of the prayer, that is, the Lord's Prayer, and the manner of how it should be prayed. In contrast, this pericope (7:7–11) speaks to the inner condition of the one who is praying. Those who pray should have the complete certainty that God will answer their requests.[1] Luke makes the point even clearer by adding the parable of the importunate friend who helps the neighbor not because of friendship but because of his insistence. The argument is from the lesser to the greater: if an annoyed person will help another, how much more will God, who is not annoyed and desires to help, hear the pleas of his people?

James may also be drawing from the same material with his warning that a doubting person will not receive anything from the Lord. Only those who ask in faith will have their prayers answered (1:6). Matthew punctuates his invitation to prayer and the certainty that it will be answered with the example of human fathers responding to the requests of their children for bread and fish. Though these fathers are evil (*ponēroi*), they will fulfill these requests and not give them stones and serpents.[2] As in Luke's parable of the importunate friend, the argument is that of moral contrast. If evil fathers can do good things, how much more can we expect from the heavenly Father who is by nature good and does good to all people? What is striking here is that Jesus calls his disciples evil, individuals who still feel Satan's influence. By calling them evil he is not challenging their loyalty to him, but he is addressing this logion on prayer to those who are entrapped in the reality of sin.

Fish and bread may simply refer to basic nourishment, but these two elements appear again in the miraculous feedings of the four and five thousand, presented by Matthew with eucharistic language. It is not impossible that Jesus' illustrations were also intended by the evangelist to carry a eucharistic and christological message.[3] God the Father in heaven will in all cases feed the faithful with Christ the living Bread that never perishes. The care of earthly fathers for their sons reflects the care of the heavenly Father, who feeds his children with the living Bread.

This pericope cannot be used to demonstrate that God will fulfill the requests of *any* prayer. He obviously does not answer those of the hypocrites (since they already have their reward; 6:5), or of pagan Gentiles who do not know that in Jesus, God is their Father. The prayer centers directly on the needs of the followers of Jesus, as they are part of his community. Specifically, the promise is that the Father in heaven, to whom the Lord's Prayer is addressed (6:9; 7:11), will answer that prayer by giving the good things. These good things are not the requests of the first three petitions, but of the last four: the eucharistic bread of the Supper (Fourth Petition), the forgiving of debts (Fifth Petition), security from or safety in temptations (Sixth Petition), and deliverance from Satan (Seventh Petition). Luke's substitution of Holy Spirit (11:13) for Matthew's good things shows that the third evangelist understood that the petitions of the Lord's Prayer, which will certainly be answered by the heavenly Father, are requests to God to give the Holy Spirit.[4] The Third Evangelist has made it clear that the Lord's Prayer is for *spiritual*, not material things. Since this is the only place where Luke uses "the heavenly Father," it is difficult to escape the conclusion that his words reflect Matthew's version of the Lord's Prayer, which unlike his, begins "Our Father, who art in heaven."

Luke was clarifying some obscure language in Matthew's Lord's Prayer for a church which understood its life as a gift of the Holy Spirit.

NOTES

1   Robert A. Guelich, *The Sermon on the Mount* (Waco: Word, 1982), 356.

2   Does this saying suggest that the disciples both were married and had children? Or was Jesus just making a general reference? We know that Peter was married (8:14). This seems to be true of them all (1 Corinthians 9:5). Matthew (7:9) does not use the word "father" of the disciple, though the parallel in Luke (11:11) does: "What father among you." Also, it is most unlikely that adult Jewish males were unmarried and without children.

3   The surface meaning of bread and fish in this pericope is clear. But "bread" often refers to Jesus (e.g., in the Lord's Prayer and in Matt 15:26). In John's gospel, the identification is explicit. In addition, one of the first symbols of the faith was the fish (*ichthys*). What seems more plausible here is the bread and fish imagery anticipates the accounts of the miraculous feedings. When hearers of the gospel heard these accounts, they would recall Jesus' words about a father's gifts of fish and bread. God the Father stands behind all good gifts to the world.

4   Robert H. Gundry, *Matthew: A Commentary on His Literary and Theological Art* (Grand Rapids: Eerdmans, 1982), 124–25. "Heavenly Father" (RSV) is literally "the Father from heaven."

21

THE GOLDEN RULE

MATTHEW 7:12

The "Golden Rule" is found outside of the New Testament in a negative form.[1] Examples from Judaism are "And what thou thyself hatest, do to no man" (Tobit 4:15); "What is harmful to thee, do not do to thy neighbor" (Hill, Sabbath, 31a); and "A man should show love to his fellow by not doing to him what he dislikes when done to himself" (Targum pseudo-Jonathan ben Uzziel [Leviticus 19:18]).[2] While such sayings parallel the Sermon's version of the saying, they do not begin to approximate its full intended meaning. Outside of Christianity, the saying is intended simply to restrain a person from doing the evil to others that he himself detests.[3] In the Sermon it is a command to do the good things to and for others that you would want done for yourself. It is placing the needs of others before your own, as God himself has done.[4]

The brief pericope is marked by two characteristic Matthean features. First, Matthew uses the inclusive "all things whatsoever." The phrase depicts God's complete giving of himself (13:44) and is used to describe the disciples' obligation to preserve all of the teachings of Jesus (28:20). Second, the phrase "the law and the prophets" is also characteristic of Matthew; it is his usual designation for the Old Testament. In Matthew 5:17, Jesus' messianic obligation is the fulfillment of the law and the prophets, and in 22:37–40 the love of God and the neighbor is made the basis of the law and the prophets. Luke provides an interpretation by placing his parallel right after the commands to love the enemies with the practical command to bless the cursers, to pray for one's abusers, to offer the other cheek to the striker, to give the coat to the one who takes the cloak, and to respond to the needs of the beggar (6:27–31). The Golden Rule in the Sermon can simply be summarized as loving all people and responding with good even to those who are evil. This is not only the description of the work of Jesus (5:17) but of the community of his followers (7:12; 22:37–40). Self-giving love even to offenders is the content, fulfillment, and basis of the Law and the Prophets, the written revelation given through Moses and the prophets; it finds fulfillment in Jesus and his community.

The corruption of this commandment so that it was understood only in the negative sense, common outside of Christianity, happened very early in the church itself, as the *Didache* offers this version: "And all things whatsoever thou wouldst not have befall thyself, neither do unto another."[5] This logion in the Sermon on doing the good to others that a disciple desires for himself can serve as a summary of the Sermon. It summarizes and concludes all the previous material whose central message is that the disciples of Jesus should be like the God who does good to all men.[6]

NOTES

1   Robert A. Guelich, *The Sermon on the Mount* (Waco: Word, 1982), 360–61; Eduard Schweizer, *The Good News According to Matthew* (trans. David E. Greene; Atlanta: Knox Press, 1975), 174–75; Clayton N. Jefford, *The Sayings of Jesus in the Teaching of the Twelve Apostles* (Leiden: E. J. Brill, 1989), 33.

2   Gerald Friedlander, *The Jewish Sources of the Sermon on the Mount* (New York: KTAV, 1969), 231. See also pages 226–38 for other examples outside of the Old Testament and Judaism.

3   Friedlander, *Jewish Sources*, 231–34, disputes the claims of the scholar Johannes Weiss that the positive form of the golden rule is found only in the form which Jesus gave it. He also attempts to show how the New Testament in several places gives the negative version.

4   "Despite modern misunderstandings, the treatment of others just as one would like to be treated by them does not rest on egoism. It rests on the readiness to deny oneself in order to serve others in a way one would otherwise like to be served"; Robert H. Gundry, *Matthew: A Commentary on His Literary and Theological Art* (Grand Rapids: Eerdmans, 1982), 126.

5   *Didache* 1:2. Jefford, *Sayings of Jesus*, 33, concludes that the *Didache*'s version of the Golden Rule is not that of Matthew and Luke and could have come from any of the Jewish/Christian circles where such a phrase was in use. Similar is the parallel in the Gospel of Thomas (1:6); "And do not do what you hate." According to Friedlander, *Jewish Sources*, 234, other negative examples were given by the *Apostolic Constitutions*, Clement of Alexandria, and Tertullian. Perhaps the only conclusion is that the original words of Jesus of putting others before oneself were inverted to mean that for matters of personal safety one should avoid harming others. The change was significant.

6   So W. D. Davies, *The Setting of the Sermon on the Mount* (Atlanta: Scholars, 1989), 290. Davies sees the Golden Rule as the climax to Matthew's "treatment of the Christian interpretation of the Law, Christian worship and Christian loving-kindness" (402). William Farmer, "The Sermon on the Mount: A Form-Critical and Redactional Analysis of Matthew 5:1–7:29," *SBL Seminar Papers* 25 (Atlanta: Scholars Press, 1986), 83. "At the same time 7:12 with its conclusion '… for this is the law and the prophets' returns to Matthew 5:17, 'Do not think I came to destroy the law and the prophets.…' John Albert Bengel noted this connection and wrote: 'The conclusion corresponds with the commencement.' Heinrich Meyer takes a similar view, quoting Luther's observation: 'With these words (Matthew 7:12) he concludes the instructions contained in those three chapters (Matthew 5–7), and gathers them all into one little bundle.'"

PART 4

THE SERMON AS TEACHING AUTHORITY IN THE CHURCH

MATTHEW 7:13–8:1

Rather than setting forth further directions for the life of the disciple, Matthew 7:13–8:1 sets forth the authority of the message of Jesus for the community and how it will benefit them. It is what is called in the later dogmatic terminology of the church the *prolegomena*, that is, the introduction. Characteristic of *prolegomena* are discussions on the superiority of one theological system over against another, recognition of false alternatives and options, the absolute and true nature of the character of the doctrinal system offered, and the foundation for its claim to authority. The doctrines themselves, those things which are believed and confessed, the *corpus doctrinae*, are not included in the *prolegomena*, but are reserved for the dogmatics proper. The concluding section of the Sermon shows features later characteristic of the *prolegomena*, though it comes at the end. Jesus' words are God's own words and promise eternal life to those who do them.

22

THE TWO WAYS

MATTHEW 7:13–14

The imagery of two ways to describe different ways of life was used in the Old Testament. Some see its origin in Adam, who in Eden chose a different way. Psalm 1 contrasts the ways of the righteous and the wicked. Taken out of context in the Sermon, the "two ways" could easily be understood as contrasting an ethical and moral life with an immoral one. In Judaism this opinion was held, and it has not been uncommon in the Christian community.[1] This view, however, does not do justice to the Sermon and actually contradicts the Sermon's entire message, which finds the ethical life of the Pharisees unacceptable. The way to life must be interpreted in the light of the demand to seek the higher righteousness by which one becomes forgiving like God.

Whether Jesus has a specific gate in view, perhaps in the city of Jerusalem's wall, is uncertain, but nevertheless this idea is an attractive option.[2] Through the metaphors of the narrow gate and the hard way, though, Jesus is referring to what he has already said about the Kingdom. These sayings, like the final section (7:24–27), call attention to the importance of what Jesus has just preached in the Sermon. The command to seek the narrow way should not be taken as further imperative for the Christian to live the morally perfect life. While it might not be entirely clear in Matthew that this logion of Jesus is directed to the issue of salvation, it is made specific in Luke, where these words are used as a reply to the question, "Lord, will those who are saved be few?" (13:23). Jesus' answer is, "Strive to enter by the narrow door" (24). For Luke the gate is a reference to salvation, but he makes no use of Matthew's double metaphor of gate and way and simply has the door.[3]

Within the early church this proved to be one of the more influential parts of the Sermon. The *Didache* begins, "There are two ways, one of life and one of death, and there is a great difference between the two ways" (1:1). If the *Didache* is not dependent on Matthew's version of the Sermon, both are drawing from the same source.[4] The similarity of the Sermon to the *Didache* suggests that both were catechetical tools; each was a compendium of the teachings of Jesus for the church to which they were written. The way of life, according to the *Didache*, is the teachings of Jesus, preserved essentially in the Sermon.[5] Though the metaphors of both the gate and the way are used in the Sermon, the term "way" and not "gate" became synonymous with the religion of Jesus. The *Didache* prefers "way" for "gate." The use of the term "way" in Acts may show that the sayings from Matthew's Sermon were widely known in the early church, as it provided the word by which the followers of Jesus were called by themselves and their enemies. Paul (Saul) is sent by the authorities in Jerusalem to arrest followers of "the Way" in Damascus (Acts 9:2). If the conversion of Paul is dated c. 31 to 32 and the crucifixion-resurrection of Jesus c. 28 or 30, in a span no longer than a few years the church became known as the way—its first name, even among its enemies. Acts contains speeches of Paul in which he refers to his life before he became a Christian, in which he persecuted *the Way* (22:4; 24:14), thus indicating how widespread the use of this term was even among non-Christians, to whom these sermons were addressed. The term was used in Jerusalem, Damascus, and Corinth (Acts 19:9). It was even understood in the Gentile world as referring to Christians, since Paul used it in his speech before Felix.

Among the logia eventually included in Matthew's version of the Sermon, the one on the gate and the way made a profound impression on the early Christian community; it provided a shorthand description for the teachings of Jesus. The way was the teachings of Jesus, and those who believed them were called followers of the way. John goes one step further: Jesus calls himself the Way (14:6). The Fourth Gospel also identifies Jesus as the Door (10:9), suggesting a possible awareness of Luke 13:24, or at least these evangelists were drawing on a commonly held understanding. This is more of an elaboration than development, since the Sermon directs the attention of the disciples not to abstract teachings as in the Qur'an, but to Jesus himself. Luke, in his parallel, uses "door" and not "way" or "gate." Later, in Acts, he preserves the data that the early community was first called the Way. He may have preferred "door" because its narrowness points to the difficulty of becoming a Christian.

The Sermon (Matthew 7:13–14) and the Lucan parallel (13:24) are the only places where the word "narrow" is used. The word suggests that requirements of the Sermon with its prescribed limitations demand adherence without wavering. The word for "hard" means more literally the way marked by tribulations.[6] Thus the stress of the Christian religion is less on

its moral conduct and more on the sufferings of the community of the followers of Jesus for his sake, a back reference to the Ninth Beatitude, the
first one with a solely ecclesiological reference. They are persecuted for
the sake of Jesus. As the church began to suffer through persecutions, its
choice of "way" over "gate" to designate itself may have been influenced
by the Sermon's reference to the way that goes to life marked by tribulations. Luke slightly reassigns Matthew's meaning to different words so his
version reads more literally: "You struggle (or agonize) to go in through
the narrow door" (13:23). This may also be an allusion to persecution.[7] In
the parable of the Sower, the theme of tribulation is picked up again and
applied to those who believe and fall away (13:21).

NOTES

1 Gerald Friedlander, *The Jewish Sources of the Sermon on the Mount* (New York:
   KTAV, 1969), 240–45. This Jewish commentator provides examples from early
   Christian literature where the moral understanding of the two ways was taught,
   e.g., *Shepherd of Hermas, Apostolic Constitutions*, and *the Epistle of Barnabas*. Guelich
   understands the concept of the two ways from a christological perspective; see his
   The Sermon on the Mount (Waco: Word, 1982), 388. For the "two ways" in literature see, for example, John Milton's *Pilgrim's Progress*.

2 E. F. F. Bishop, *Jesus of Palestine* (London: Lutterworth, 1955), 83–84. Betz sees a
   possible reference to the heavenly Jerusalem, but does not pursue this line of
   thought; *Essays on the Sermon on the Mount* (trans. L. L. Welborn; Philadelphia:
   Fortress, 1985), 521. Within the context of Matthew's gospel, this interpretation
   is indeed possible and perhaps even probable. At the death of Jesus, the saints are
   raised from the dead and after his resurrection they enter the "holy city" (27:53),
   hardly a reference to the earthly Jerusalem, which has rejected the prophet and on
   that account is condemned (23:37).

3 Luke's pericope stresses how few will attain salvation; Guelich, *Sermon on the
   Mount*, 389. Matthew's "Enter the narrow gate" is paralleled in Luke with "You
   are struggling (Greek: *agōnizesthe*) into the narrow door." Outside of this one reference in Luke and another in John (18:36), the word to struggle is characteristically Pauline. Matthew's passage suggests that the Christian is already going
   through the *agony* of remaining in the faith. The choice has been made, and the
   danger of falling away is real.

4 *Didache* 1:1–2. For a complete discussion of this matter, see Clayton N. Jefford,
   The Sayings of Jesus in the Teachings of the Twelve Apostles (Leiden: E. J. Brill, 1989),
   25–29.

5 Schweizer notes the strong influence of the Sermon on the Mount on the community of the *Didache*. See his *The Good News According to Matthew* (trans. David E.
   Greene; Atlanta: Knox Press, 1975), 182–84.

6 Robert H. Gundry, *Matthew: A Commentary on His Literary and Theological Art*
   (Grand Rapids: Eerdmans, 1982), 127.

7 The long-accepted opinion that the *Didache* draws on Matthew has been challenged most recently by Jefford, *Sayings of Jesus*. Still Jefford sees Matthew and the

Didache drawing on the same source, as their similarity at points cannot be denied. The older theory that the *Didache* knew both Matthew and Luke seems less complicated, as for example with the Lord's Prayer. The *Didache* follows Matthew's version with the exception of taking over Luke's "sins" for Matthew's "trespasses." Apart from the *Didache*, the use of "the way" in Acts but not in Luke may tentatively indicate an order for the composition of the gospels. Matthew has preserved more closely the original words of Jesus with the reference to "way," the term so prominent in the first decade after the resurrection. The absence of "way" in Luke but its inclusion in Acts in the phrase "followers of the way" as to believers in Christ or his teachings in Acts seems to suggest that Luke is aware of Matthew's use. If this is true, Matthew provides a convenient and plausible explanation of why Christians were called "followers of the way." Third, John's use of Jesus as the door suggests that he might be familiar with Luke ("door") and Matthew ("way"). There is a progression here from "way" (Matthew, Acts), "door" (Luke) and again to "door" (John), though this argument is hardly conclusive. For a discussion of dependency for the two "ways" saying in the *Didache* on Matthew's source, see Jefford, *Sayings of Jesus*, 25–29.

23

THE FALSE PROPHETS

MATTHEW 7:15–20

There are many indications that the community for which Matthew was writing his gospel had a developed theology and an advanced church structure.[1] His inclusion of the warning against false prophets is one such indication. "False prophets" perhaps refer to the persons condemned in the Old Testament, but such an interpretation is not only improbable but clearly impossible. Here the term "false prophets" seems to depend for its meaning on the early church use of the word "prophet" for its preachers and clergy. In Acts 13:1, the church's leaders are called the prophets and the teachers. In Matthew 23:34, Jesus says that he is sending the prophets along with the scribes and wise men, whom Luke interprets as apostles (11:49). Jesus did warn the disciples of the teachings of the Sadducees and Pharisees (16:12); however, it is doubtful whether these words about the false prophets were intended to describe them. The false prophets came disguised as legitimate bearers of the message of Jesus. Such a description does not seem to fit Jesus' contemporaries, who clearly identified themselves as his adversaries. The warning against the false prophets is basically an anticipatory and eschatological word of Jesus projected into the community of his followers. The period of the false prophets comes when Jesus is no longer with them. It is the time between his departure from them and his appearance as the eschatological judge.

Jesus as judge is the subject of the following pericope (7:21–23). This warning necessarily presupposes that he will no longer be there and a church structure will develop where many church leaders are making a claim on the allegiance of the people. In the Sermon Jesus speaks of the judgment of the false prophets on the Last Day. The dating of the gospel will determine what specific group the evangelist may have had in mind when he recorded these words of Jesus. If a date following the apostolic council of Jerusalem places Matthew about 49 or 50, the false prophets could be a specific reference to Paul's opponents from Jerusalem who had gone to Galatia, who were superimposing certain ceremonies on the

Gentile converts there (Galatians 2:12). While they are designated as Judaizing Christians, they were called at the council of Jerusalem the sect of the Pharisees (Acts 15:5) and were typified in their requiring circumcision of the Gentiles.[2]

Of all the words used for the pastoral or clerical office in the New Testament, "prophet" was not used much beyond apostolic times. In *Didache* 11:3, it was still used of itinerant preachers. It can be taken as a general warning for any office which is entrusted with expounding the divine Word. Thus the false prophet wants to be understood as an authoritative spokesman for the message of Jesus within his community, but he has a message diametrically opposed to Jesus'.

Jesus uses two analogies in his discussion of the false prophets. The first involves animals and the second plants. In the first case the wolves appear in sheep's clothing; a better translation might be sheepskins. Old Testament prophets dressed in sheepskins.

Before the kill, the wolf gets in as close to the flock as it possibly can without being detected. The false teacher does the same thing in the community of the followers of Jesus. He remains undetected among the flock and thus causes no panic. Though the Fourth Gospel develops the understanding of Jesus and the church as the shepherd and the sheep, the imagery is already found in Matthew's gospel. After the commissioning of the twelve disciples, Jesus looks at the crowds who are described as sheep without a shepherd (9:36). Again the evangelist uses the shepherd-sheep metaphor to describe the dispersing of the disciples before the crucifixion, by incorporating Zechariah 13:7: "I will strike the shepherd, and the sheep of the flock will be scattered" (26:31). For this warning about wolves in sheep's clothing to have meaning in Matthew's church, the metaphor of the sheep for the church must already have been known.[3] W. D. Davies argues convincingly that the depiction of false teachers as lambs suggests that they are members of the community and not members of another group. The use of the flock imagery may also indicate a further influence of Isaiah 53:6, where the sheep go astray. How these wolves are to be identified is left unsaid, but the metaphor of the trees tells us something.

The pericope on the trees leads off with the statement, "You will know them by their fruits." The term "fruits" in the New Testament takes on a strictly theological meaning for the life of the Christian (Galatians 5:22).[4] In the gospel of Matthew it may refer to the church in its growth (13:8) and in its perfection at the judgment (21:34). What is not planted by the Father is rooted up (15:13). In the phrase "You will know them by their fruits," fruits refer to what *not* to expect of false teachers. The gathering of grapes from thorns and figs from thistles is an illustration to show just how impossible it is for the false teacher to have the reconciling attitude that the Sermon demands. James uses a similar metaphor by eliminating references to the thorns and thistles and substituting the question whether olives come from fig trees and figs from grapevines (3:12). While with James there is something productive about both trees and vines, nothing productive is suggested in the Sermon by the thorns and thistles, which are not only nonproductive, but destructive of the crop.[5] The community of the followers of Jesus is not to expect anything good from the false prophets who sap it of its strength. Jude takes the metaphor of the trees to a further extreme by calling them "fruitless trees in late autumn, twice dead, uprooted" (12). As one commentator has pointed out, a corrupt tree, that is a tree whose trunk is dead in parts, can still bring forth acceptable fruit.

The good tree as a reference to the Christian or the church is taken over from the Old Testament's understanding of Israel as God's vineyard and "his pleasant planting" (Isaiah 5:7). The blessed man of Psalm 1 "is like a tree planted by streams of water, that yields its fruit in its season" (3). This language was brought into the New Testament era in the preaching of John the Baptist (3:10) from whom Jesus may have heard it. The imagery of the Christian or the church as the tree not only has the advantage of suggesting that God is its planter and nourisher, but it allows for the teaching of condemnation without switching metaphors. The Baptist is more graphic in his description: "the axe is even now laid to the root of the trees" (Matthew 3:10). His preaching follows exactly the word order of the Sermon: "every tree therefore that does not bring forth good fruit is cut down and thrown into the fire" (3:10; compare 7:19). "Fire" here and in the Sermon refers specifically to hell, as it is most often understood elsewhere in the gospel. Tares and bad fish are thrown into the fire or thrown away (13:40, 42, 50). The vivid picture of hell as fire, which is the final sentence upon the false prophets, precedes the description of their trial in the next pericope (7:21–23). Matthew mixes the metaphor. Rotten trees do not bring forth rotten fruit, but evil fruit, i.e., works which Satan, the Evil One, is causing.

"Thus you will know them by their fruits" repeats v. 16 and brackets off the pericope as a recognizable unit. The meaning of "fruits" should be determined by its use in Matthew. The Baptist asks the Pharisees and Sadducees to produce fruits that show they have repented, that is, they have accepted the coming of the Kingdom. John tells us no more than that they were confessing their sins and were being baptized (3:6). Even the false teachers in Matthew's church and the Pharisees and Sadducees at the time of John and Jesus were capable of a public display of remorse, as John still demands from them fruits to show their repentant condition (3:8). In the light of the Sermon, these fruits are love of the neighbor, reconciliation with the enemy, and performing good to all people indiscriminately.[6] Limiting these fruits to mere restraint from evil and sin would only be the righteousness of the Pharisees and scribes. The false prophet may perpetrate no evil, but he refuses to be reconciled as is required by the Sermon.[7]

NOTES

1 William Farmer, "The Sermon on the Mount: A Form-Critical and Redactional Analysis of Matthew 5:1–7:29," *SBL Seminar Papers* 25 (Atlanta: Scholars Press, 1986), 85.

2 Robert A. Guelich, *Sermon on the Mount* (Waco: Word, 1982), 391, presents a list of options concerning the identity of the false prophets: Pharisees, Zealots, Essenes in Judaism; from Christian circles, Gnostics, antinomians, enthusiasts, and prophets who did not measure up to the standards set forth by Jesus.

3 Eduard Schweizer, *The Good News According to Matthew* (trans. David E. Green; Atlanta: Knox Press, 1975), 186, notes that "sheep" is a common designation for the community of the redeemed.

4 The image of crops is also used as a metaphor for the community of the redeemed; see Schweizer, *Good News According to Matthew*, 186.

5 David P. Scaer, *James the Apostle of Faith* (St. Louis: Concordia, 1983), 101–2.

6 Guelich, *Sermon on the Mount*, 396, finds that whereas Matthew stresses the evil deeds of the false prophets, Luke puts the emphasis on their words (Luke 6:46). Perhaps it can be argued the other way: Luke interprets the evil fruit of the false prophets as their teaching and thus clarifies Matthew.

7 On the connection between the "tree" and "fruit" (which is at the heart of the section), Schweizer, *Good News According to Matthew*, 186, notes that there is no parallel in Judaism. Friedlander, however, supplies evidence to the contrary; see *The Jewish Sources of the Sermon on the Mount* (New York: KTAV, 1969), 254–55. Philo, for example, writes "God judges by the fruit of the tree, not by the root"; a rabbinic saying suggests "our fruits testify against us."

24

THE FINAL JUDGMENT

MATTHEW 7:21–23

This pericope is a description of judgment day and is paralleled in the judgment scene of 25:31–46. The shorter apocalypse at the end of Matthew's first discourse anticipates the more detailed apocalypse at the end of the fifth and final discourse. Judgment will be Jesus' last word to his church. In both contexts Jesus is addressed as Lord in the honorific divine sense as applied to God.[1] In the Sermon entering the kingdom means believing on earth the message of Jesus. For the great judgment scene inheriting the kingdom refers to the final reward (Matthew 25:34). Here the Sermon calls the false prophets workers of iniquity in spite of their having prophesied, their doing great deeds, and their casting out demons in Jesus' name. In the great judgment scene the damned have failed to come to the aid of those who were in distress. At this point that scene provides a commentary on the Sermon's chief requirement of reconciliation by loving the neighbor through concrete deeds. The greater righteousness is not mere ethical life, but one which does good to all people, including one's enemies.

This pericope in the Sermon shows a high Christology. Jesus assumes that his followers will not only worship God as the Father, but himself as the Lord. This was also true of the Pauline congregations; "No one can say 'Jesus is Lord' except by the Holy Spirit" (1 Corinthians 12:3). It is hardly possible that on "that Day" Jesus would be addressed merely with a polite "Sir." This is not a mere courtesy, as Davies points out.[2] In the birth narrative, Matthew has already identified Jesus as divine. The one who is "God with us" is also Lord (1:23). The evangelist brings this together at the gospel's conclusion with "Father and Son and Holy Spirit." On the basis of Jesus being designated Lord along with other titles, Jefford concludes that "The Matthean Gospel possesses one of the more well-developed Christologies of the NT corpus." The evangelist has one Christology for the five discourses, including the Sermon, and the whole of his gospel.[3]

There can be no thought of universalism here, as if it were immaterial whether or not a person who does the will of the Father recognizes Jesus as Lord. This is impossible for three reasons. Though not everyone who calls Jesus Lord will enter the kingdom of heaven, only those who have called him Lord will indeed enter. A delimiting factor has already been introduced. Second, the ones entering do the will of Jesus' Father. It is for the performance of the Father's will on earth that the church prays in the Third Petition, "Thy will be done." Within the Sermon and indeed the entire gospel, Matthew intends that God's will should be understood as the reconciliation of all persons to himself and to each other through the preaching of the Gospel and by its actual practice. This embraces the command to love within a christological perspective.[4] Third, this is the first reference to God as "My Father." With this Jesus claims a special relationship to God as his Son. Only the Son has full knowledge of the Father and is his only revealer (Matthew 11:27). He is both the one whom God has chosen to reveal himself and whom God has designated as the final Judge of all people.[5]

Both the Sermon at this point and the great judgment scene focus on the final judgment, which seems almost limited to the church or the followers of Jesus. Judgment begins with the household of God (1 Peter 4:17). Though Matthew 25:32 speaks of all the Gentiles being gathered before Jesus, the words seem to refer only to those who confessed him as Lord. In the Sermon this perspective may be even further narrowed to those who have acted, presumably in an official way, in his name. This brief apocalypse (7:21–23) in the Sermon seems to have the judgment of the false teachers in view and thus further develops 5:19, where the one who relaxes Jesus' least commandment is least in the kingdom. The thought of a special standard of judgment for those who represent Jesus in teaching can also be found in James 3:1, with its warning that the teachers will receive a greater judgment.[6]

The prophesying, the casting out of demons, and the doing of wonderful works are not casual deeds done in the ordinary course of life by all Christians but only by those who claim to have the full authority of Jesus behind them. "In your name" is repeated three times. In Acts preaching, baptizing (2:38), healing (3:6), and removing of demons (19:13) were done in the name of Jesus. To act or speak in the name of Jesus was to do it in his stead and with his authorization. Such a phrase as "in my name" points not to the ordinary acts by members of the community of Jesus, but those performed in a formal, liturgical way. In view here is an established church, and not clusters of disciples gathered in informal ad hoc groupings. Like those who refused to perform mercy in the great judgment scene (25:45), the false prophets in the Sermon must leave the presence of Jesus. This is their condemnation.[7]

Jesus is here conscious of his unique role as the Revealer of God, since the most dreaded of all fates is to be removed from his presence. Jesus is the one through whom God works not only in this world but also in the next. The word Matthew uses for Jesus' addressing the false prophets is "confess" (*homologein*), and it is used in 10:32 for the church's creed or confession of Jesus and for his acknowledging his disciples as his own. "Confess" carries with it a high degree of certainty in which the speaker allows no doubt, or possibility for change, in what he has said. It carries with it the idea of creedal certainty. The false prophets are addressed as evil-workers (*hoi ergazomenoi tēn anomian*), those who work against the Law. This has suggested to some that the evangelist has in view antinomians, that is, unbridled people in the congregation, the kind described in Jude or 2 Peter. Such an interpretation does not fit the technical sense implied in the phrase or the tenor of the Sermon on the Mount.[8] The righteousness of the scribes and Pharisees was hardly one of unethical, immoral abandonment, and lawlessness in the sense of antinomianism. It might be better here to follow the suggestion of Davies that the lawless ones are the false prophets who fail to do the Father's will revealed in Jesus. This law is different from that of the Jews but it is the law of love to which all Christians must submit. But this is not law in the ordinary sense.[9]

Could Matthew's understanding of the law include his own gospel in written form? Since Matthew's written gospel contains the message of him by whom the world will be judged, can it be in some sense made equal or elevated to the high status given the written law among the Jews? Law (*nomos*) refers to the written message in the sense of the Torah (John 1:17). The evangelist refers to his own writing in his prologue by making the first word of his gospel *biblos*, a book with divine authority. Torah can be translated *biblos, the* book or *nomos*, the Law. The new law, the new torah (*nomos*), complementing the old law, would be Matthew's Gospel itself, with a special focus on the Sermon. Matthew has a recognizable self-consciousness about his gospel as the final expression of divine, written authority for the church. The authority of the words of Jesus is now preserved to the written page.[10] The workers of lawlessness are those who have not heeded the message of reconciliation now written down as the Sermon.

NOTES

1 The implications of deity are recognized by Eduard Schweizer, *The Good News According to Matthew* (trans. David E. Green; Atlanta: Knox Press, 1975), 188; Robert Gundry, *Matthew: A Commentary on His Literary and Theological Art* (Grand Rapids: Eerdmans, 1982), 131; and Robert A. Guelich, *The Sermon on the Mount* (Waco: Word, 1982), 398–99. Guelich notes that Matthew makes certain that the address of "Lord" to Jesus is never found on the lips of an outsider, but is said only by one who claims to be committed to him. Consider Judas, who addresses Jesus not as Lord but as Master (26:25, 49). W. D. Davies notes that the designation of Jesus as Lord "must be allowed to temper any interpretation of Matthew's conception of him as a New Moses: Jesus commands as Lord; Moses commanded as mediator," *The Setting of the Sermon on the Mount* (Atlanta: Scholars, 1989), 97.

2 Guelich, *Sermon on the Mount*, 399.

3 Clayton N. Jefford, *The Sayings of Jesus in the Teaching of the Twelve Apostles* (Leiden: E. J. Brill, 1989), 141. Graham N. Stanton, "The Origin and Purpose of Matthew's Sermon on the Mount," in *Tradition and Interpretation in the New Testament* (ed. Gerald Hawthorne and Otto Betz; Grand Rapids: Eerdmans, 1987), 181–92.

4 Guelich, *Sermon on the Mount*, 399.

5 Schweizer, *Good News According to Matthew*, 188, notes that Jesus refers to God as his Father, since the judgment is based on doing the Father's will.

6 David P. Scaer, *James the Apostle of Faith* (St. Louis: Concordia, 1983), 98–100.

7 Gundry, *Matthew: A Commentary*, 132.

8 Guelich, *Sermon on the Mount*, 402–3, offers evidence understanding this as Matthew's opposition to antinomianism. With good reason Betz suggests that groups attached to their leaders will be judged. He cites 2 Corinthians 1:14 where Paul leads his churches at the last judgment; Betz, *The Sermon on the Mount*, Hermeneia—A Critical and Historical Commentary on the Bible (ed. Adela U. Collins; Minneapolis: Fortress, 1995), 549, n. 249.

9 Davies, *The Setting of the Sermon on the Mount*, 203.

10 This would not be the only place where a New Testament writing understands itself as binding in some sense. Revelation 22:18–19 threatens those tampering with its words. Even Matthew 28:19–20 makes the words of the entire gospel authoritative for the church to whom it is addressed. Gundry, *Matthew: A Commentary*, 132, comes close to this interpretation: "The law which the false prophets disregard is the will of the heavenly Father as taught by Jesus" (5:17–7:12). In his interpretation of 28:20 Gundry sees Matthew delivering "his final, emphatic blow against the antinomians" (597).

25

Surviving the Judgment

Matthew 7:24–27

This pericope in its requirement that the words of Jesus are to be performed is not different from the previous one where failure to perform the Father's will excludes one from the presence of Jesus. It does go one step further in that the Father's will is now identified as the words of Jesus.[1] Jesus is set forth as God's revealer. Unlike the rabbis, Jesus focuses on his own words and not on those of another.[2] The words of Jesus that bring salvation if followed—and damnation if disregarded—are the words of the Sermon on the Mount. The Father's will, too, comes to expression in the Sermon.

For this reason Jesus concludes the Sermon with a warning in twin parables. Two men undertake identical plans to build houses. Upon completion they experience the identical misfortune of foul weather. The only difference is that one house is built on the rock and the other on the sand. Built on rock, one stands; built on sand, the other collapses. Its end is described with the finality of apocalyptic language: "and great was the fall of it."[3]

Luke's version (6:47–49) of the parable is simpler than Matthew's. He makes no mention of the rain or wind, but only the flooding of the river. Matthew's parable assumed that the rock is the foundation, but does not state it explicitly. The foolish man in Luke has no foundation for his house at all. In Luke's version the man who built his foundation on the rock is described as the one coming to Jesus, a kind of double reinforcement not found in Matthew. The other man in Luke has no foundation, but simply places his house on the ground and not the rock. Matthew's house is destroyed from above, so to speak, from the beating of the weather, while Luke's house is undermined by a flooding river, from below.

The subjects of the two-part parable in Matthew are the wise man and the foolish man, terminology not used by Luke. In the Sermon "foolish" suggests a person who does not understand God's will (5:22). Throughout the gospel the wise men make use of God's revelation. They are disciples (10:16), servants who know to do their master's will (24:45). They are also

the apostles sent as wise men (23:34). Luke's version makes no prior identification of the builders. Matthew's version may be suggesting that early
Christian communities should pattern themselves after the congregations
supervised by the apostles. The apostles who established those communities are the wise men who have built well. In the parables God is often
referred to as a man (*anthrōpos*), human being, not a male (*anēr*) as used
here. God is not, however, the subject of the house parable, as he is in
those parables collected by the evangelist in chapter 13. The language
resembles Matthew 16:18, "and on this *rock* I *will build* my church." Peter
may be called the rock not only because he confesses Jesus but because he
preserves his words.[4] The words for "build" and "rock" are the same in
both pericopes. In the Sermon, building a house on rock is the carrying
out of the words of Jesus. The word "house" would have suggested to
Matthew's community the house churches in which they gathered regularly for worship. The rain, the rising rivers, and the wind would suggest the
persecutions, tribulations, and temptations. The blowing of the wind in
James 1:6 is used of the temptations and trials that come to Christians.[5]
While this is a "land" pericope, it would call to the memory of the first
readers the church as a ship at the mercy of the evil forces of the universe.[6]
Both the house on the foundation and the ship survive the storms.[7]

The individual follower of Jesus who heard his words and acted upon
them survives together with the community. The final words of the parable and the Sermon, "and great was the fall of it," have a clear eschatological finality to them. In Luke 2:34, the only other New Testament use of
this word for "fall," it has a definite reference to final condemnation:
"Behold, this child is set for the fall and rising of many in Israel." In the
Sermon the words of Jesus bring either salvation or damnation.

The closing pericope is intended as an "either-or" kind of warning to
take the message of the Sermon of Jesus seriously. This is not a matter of
being a *better* Christian, but of being a follower of Jesus in whom his words
are at work. The one who fails to respond is doomed without another
chance. To catch Matthew's dramatic emphasis, the last words of Jesus
would be better translated, "and it fell and its fall was great." The closing
parable of the Sermon recognizes the words of Jesus as those of God, as
hearing and doing them mean the difference between life and destruction.
Jesus has appeared not as a prophet but as Sinai's God. The evangelist's
postscript to the Sermon picks up on that theme.

NOTES

1 Robert A. Guelich, *The Sermon on the Mount* (Waco: Word, 1982), 404.

2 W. D. Davies, *The Setting of the Sermon on the Mount* (Atlanta: Scholars, 1989), 94.
   "In the first place, the words under which the disciples stand are more emphatically presented as the words of Jesus himself: the commandments of the Sermon are
   his to be obeyed (this is the least that can be said of the phrase 'But I say unto you'
   in the antithesis), and it is as words that they constitute the standard of judgment
   on the Last Day." Davies suggests that in place of listening to "my words," the
   phrase might as just as well be translated listening to "me." Also Eduard
   Schweizer, *The Good News According to Matthew* (trans. David E. Greene; Atlanta:
   Knox Press, 1975), 190.

3 "Thus the Sermon on the Mount ends with a warning about the impending
   Judgment that demonstrates the hopelessness of the man who hears Jesus' words
   but does not do them." Schweizer, *Good News According to Matthew*, 191. At this
   point Davies notes that Jesus' ethic is related to creation; see *Setting of the
   Sermon*, 429.

4 Schweizer, *Good News According to Matthew*, 191.

5 David P. Scaer, *James the Apostle of Faith* (St. Louis: Concordia, 1983), 42–45.

6 Compare Matthew 8:23 and 14:22–27, esp. v. 24.

7 Bo Reicke sees the ship in James 3:4 as a reference to the church; *The Epistles of
   James, Peter, and Jude*, Anchor Bible, 37 (ed. W. F. Albright and D. N. Freedman;
   Garden City, N.Y.: Doubleday, 1964), 37–38. This parable also has tones of the
   Genesis flood in which Noah survives because he both heard and obeyed God
   (Gen. 7–8). This is evident *more* in Matthew where the damages are inflicted by
   floods caused by rain (7:27). Compare Gen. 7:11–12. Luke does not mention the
   rain.

26

THE SERMON'S CONCLUSION

MATTHEW 7:28–8:1

In four other places after the Sermon, the evangelist marks the end of the discourse with "and when Jesus had finished…" (11:1; 13:53; 19:1 and 26:1).[1] Thus the reader has no doubt that he has come to the end of the Sermon as Matthew's first discourse. The Sermon is further marked off as the most important discourse of the gospel, as Jesus at the beginning is described as going up into the mountain (5:3) and at the end as coming down (8:1). He has ascended into God's realm to give his message and descended from it. The crowds who surround Jesus as he comes down recall the people of Israel who gathered around Moses as he descended from Sinai (Exodus 34:29–32). They are described as amazed, but not as those who have taken on themselves the burden of Jesus' message.

Jesus' approach to authority is markedly different from the scribes whose arguments depended on their citing of various authorities. Jesus spoke from his own authority. In the postscript two points are made clear by the evangelist. First, the Sermon is called the teaching or doctrine of Jesus (*didachē autou*). The reader or hearer of the Sermon in Matthew's community has just read or heard the quintessential message of Jesus. Second, the Sermon's conclusion refers to Jesus' teaching and authority. In the Sermon the teachings impress the crowds because they recognize his authority as having a higher authenticity of a more recognizably divine origin than do the scribes. In the commission at the end of the gospel Jesus initiates his final words with "All authority in heaven and on earth has been given to me" (28:18). This authority is the basis of his disciples' teaching the Gentiles to observe all things he has commanded (28:20). While the divine authority of Jesus is explicit at the Sermon's end, it comes to a more thunderous climax at the gospel's end. Also tied together with these two pericopes is the later episode on Jesus' authority (21:23–27), in which he refuses to answer the question of from where his authority is derived until his opponents have answered whether John's authority is from God or men. The evangelist's answer is clear at the gospel's end: Jesus' authority is from God. The Sermon is the message delivered by Sinai's God, who has come to reconcile his people (1:21) and to be their judge.

NOTES

1 For a discussion on the structure of these sections see Robert A. Guelich, *The Sermon on the Mount* (Waco: Word, 1982), 414. For Old Testament comparisons see Robert H. Gundry, *Matthew: A Commentary on His Literary and Theological Art* (Grand Rapids: Eerdmans, 1982), 136.

APPENDIX I

THE BEATITUDES

The wide variety of opinion on the nature and structure of the Beatitudes challenges the hermeneutical rule that the meaning of a text is one and clear. Apart from the *unus sensus literalis est*, that there is clearly one recognizable meaning, there is no such thing as *unus sensus ecclesiasticus* about the Beatitudes, even among conservative practitioners of biblical arts. One obvious thing is that Christian theologians and leaders have used them within Matthew's Sermon as a scaffolding for their own theological programs. It is arguable this already began before Matthew gave the Sermon an established form, if James precedes Matthew. It can also be argued that the remainder of the New Testament books used and adjusted Matthew's version of the Sermon. Putting aside the question of the chronological order in which these books were written, Mark, Luke, John, and the epistles of Paul and Peter have parallels to Matthew's version of the Sermon. Of course, this argument assumes the kind of early dating offered prominently by J. A. T. Robinson in his *Redating the New Testament* (Philadelphia: Westminster, 1976), which is widely rejected or ignored by most scholars.

Our discussion of the Sermon on the Mount tries to proceed without discussing the dependency of the other biblical and early church documents on Matthew, but it will become clear that this goal is rarely achieved and that this writer's bias appears everywhere. One argument for Matthew's primacy is that his difficult sayings have no parallels or are simplified in Mark and Luke. This impetus toward simplification is carried over into the early church fathers. It is easier to explain why a secondary document would simplify material than to explain why it made it more complex, often to the point of unintelligibility. If Matthew is a later and secondary document, its complexity moves in the direction of Judaism which scholars associate with the Council of Jamnia, around 100 A.D. Such a hypothesis runs counter to the church's focus away from the Jews, which is as early as the fifth decade of the first century. For all practical purposes, the church at the dawn of the second century, where prominent Matthew scholars place this gospel, is already a Gentile community. Scholars readily acknowledge that the Jewish gospel of Matthew predominates in the second century over the much more "understandable" documents—to Gentiles—like Mark, Luke, and the Pauline epistles. How does a document like Matthew become so prominent in only a matter of years?

This issue cannot be resolved to everyone's satisfaction, but it is Matthew's Sermon on the Mount and not Luke's sermon which is incorporated and often becomes the centerpiece of later theological systems. Traditional Lutheran theology has not invested much in the discussion of the origin of the Sermon or which form is more authentic. With their Law-Gospel approach to theology, they have traditionally followed the Reformer in seeing the Sermon as Law and Paul's epistles as the major provider of the Gospel. Such an approach is possible only within a recognized canon in which a writer anticipates that his views will be complemented by another. Of course, left with only Matthew's Sermon on the Mount, the reader is faced with Law and with no explicit hope of salvation. Such a view attributes the clarification of the Gospel to Paul and not Jesus, a view which was paralleled in classical liberalism, holding that Paul substituted a doctrinal system for the simple teachings of Jesus. Confessional Lutherans find themselves in agreement with their old liberal adversaries in seeing the Sermon as a most excellent expression of the Law. They differ in that the Lutherans claim it cannot be fulfilled and the classical liberals find it can be fulfilled even by non-Christians. An historical overview of interpretation has been briefly sketched above and other resources are listed for the interested reader. The real challenge is not enumerating and critically analyzing the variety of interpretations, but providing explanation as to why some interpretations were replaced by others.

The move to simplification can be seen in that Luke substitutes "Blessed are you poor" for Matthew's mysterious "Blessed are the poor in spirit." Paul speaks of the poverty of Jesus (2 Corinthians 8:9), which also echoes Matthew's First Beatitude. Among the post-apostolic fathers, the Beatitudes are interpreted christologically. In his epistle to the Ephesians, Irenaeus says that Christ spoke of himself when he said, "Blessed are the meek, for they shall inherit the earth." So also Tertullian says when he speaks of Jesus as poor (*Adv. Haer.* III:xxxii). With the legitimization of Christianity under Constantine in the fourth century as the major religion of the empire, the Beatitudes are no longer seen as a promise of what the Christian would become in Christ, but what Christians should be in order not to fall from grace. The approach adopted in this commentary bridges the gap between the centuries to present the Beatitudes—indeed the Sermon—in the light of Christ and his gospel.

APPENDIX II

THE LAW AND THE PROPHETS

Jesus makes a distinction between the Law and the Prophets, which pass away, and his own words, which have a higher, permanent value: "Heaven and earth shall pass away, but my words will not pass away" (Matthew 5:18).[1] With its jots and tittles, the Old Testament will remain only until the passing of heaven and earth, an apocalyptic reference elaborated in the fifth and final discourse (Matthew 24) with its predictions of Jerusalem's destruction and the Son of Man coming in judgment on those who reject him (34). Jesus' words continue forever and so one tampers with them to his own peril. Faithful teachers who preserve these teachings will be called great (5:19). Crucial is determining the meaning for the passing of heaven and earth,[2] a theme taken up again in 24:34: "Truly, I say to you, this generation will not pass away till all these things take place."

Davies and Allison hold to the popular view that the disciples expected an imminent return of Jesus after his death and resurrection. Others claim that the Jewish race will survive until Christ's return, a view which is contradicted in the cursing of the fig tree. In addition, there are at least six other interpretations.[3] Davies and Allison are right in seeing that an immediate fulfillment and not a distant one is in view for Matthew, whose gospel ends with the crucifixion and resurrection. Luke opens up another future with the ascension and the angel's promise of return (Acts 1:11). Matthew builds on the theme that Jesus' life and death are a complete fulfillment of the Law and the Prophets in all their points. Jesus' own predictions about himself will also be fulfilled within the seeing and the hearing of his disciples (24:34) and those who rejected him (26:64).

Within the context of Matthew's gospel, the passing of the heavens and the earth are fulfilled by Jesus' own death and resurrection, which for Matthew comprise one apocalyptic event. Predictions of a corpse surrounded by eagles, the darkening of the sun, the failure of the moon to shine, and the shaking of the heavens (24:28–30) are apocalyptic predictions describing the passing away of the heavens and the earth. The darkening of the sun, the earthquake and the resurrection of the dead saints at the crucifixion, and their entering the holy city (27:45, 50–54) fulfill these apocalytic expectations. Perhaps there is no better description of the death of Jesus as an apocalyptic event than the Eastern Orthodox Matins for Good Friday: "When Thou wast crucified, O Christ, all creation saw and trembled. The foundations of the earth quaked in fear of Thy power. The lights of heaven hid themselves.... The whole creation was changed by fear...."[4] So Christ's promise in the Sermon to fulfill the Law and the Prophets (5:18) is his own affirmation of their authority for requiring his death (26:24, 31, 54), but by fulfilling them, he assumes them into himself and preserves them in his teachings. His words now take the place of honor (28:20). The Father's command to listen to Jesus (17:5) applies first to the Sermon on the Mount and then to the entire gospel of Matthew.

NOTES

1   Davies and Allison catch the temporal character of the Law and the Prophets; see W. D. Davies and Dale C. Allison, *A Critical and Exegetical Commentary on the Gospel According to Saint Matthew*, *The International Critical Commentary*, 3 vols (Edinburgh: T & T Clark, 1988–1997), 1:490.

2   Davies and Allison note the possibilities that the crucifixion or the destruction of Jerusalem may be in view here, but prefer to see a longer period in which the Old Testament remains in force, *Matthew*, 1:491.

3   Davies and Allison list eight possible interpretations, *Matthew*, 3:366–67.

4   Quoted from Davies and Allison, *Matthew*, 3:622.

BIBLIOGRAPHY

Aland, Kurt, ed. *Synopsis Quattuor Evangeliorum.* 11th ed. Stuttgart: Deutsche Bibelstiftung, 1976.

Betz, Hans Dieter. *Essays on the Sermon on the Mount.* Translated by L. L. Welborn. Philadelphia: Fortress Press, 1985.

Bishop, E. F. F. *Jesus of Palestine.* London: Lutterworth, 1955.

Carmignac, Jean. *Recherches sur le "Notre Pere."* Paris: Letouzey and Ane, 1969.

Carson, D. A. *Sermon on the Mount.* Grand Rapids: Baker, 1978.

Childs, Brevard S. *The New Testament As Canon: An Introduction.* Philadelphia: Fortress, 1984.

Daube, David. *The New Testament and Rabbinic Judaism.* London: Athlone, 1956.

Davies, W. D. *The Setting of the Sermon on the Mount.* Cambridge: Cambridge University Press, 1964.

Deane, Anthony Charles. *Our Father: A Study of the Lord's Prayer.* London: Hodder and Stoughton, 1926.

Derrett, J. Duncan M. *Law in the New Testament.* London: Darton, Longman, and Todd, 1970.

Farmer, William R. *Jesus and The Gospel.* Philadelphia: Fortress, 1982.

Friedlander, Gerald. *The Jewish Sources of the Sermon on the Mount.* New York: KTAV, 1969.

Grillmeier, Aloys. *Christ in Christian Tradition.* Translated by John Bowden. Atlanta: Knox Press, 1975.

Guelich, Robert A. *Sermon on the Mount.* Waco: Word, 1982.

Gundry, Robert H. *Matthew: A Commentary on His Literary and Theological Art.* Grand Rapids: Eerdmans, 1982.

Gundry, Robert H. *The Use of the Old Testament in Matthew's Gospel.* Leiden: E. J. Brill, 1967.

Jeremias, Joachim. *The Sermon on the Mount.* Translated by Norman Perrin. Philadelphia: Fortress Press, 1963.

Kissinger, Warren, S. *The Sermon on the Mount: A History of Interpretation and Bibliography.* Metuchen, N.J.: Scarecrow Press, 1975.

Lohmeyer, Ernst. *"Our Father": An Introduction to the Lord's Prayer.* New York: Harper and Row, 1965.

Lohmeyer, Ernst. *The Lord's Prayer*. Translated by John Bowden. London: Collins, 1965.

Scaer, David P. *James the Apostle of Faith*. St. Louis: Concordia, 1984.

Schweizer, Eduard. *The Good News According to Matthew*. Translated by David E. Green. Atlanta: Knox Press, 1975.

Shuler, Philip L. *A Genre for the Gospels*. Philadelphia: Fortress Press, 1982.

Stendahl, Krister. *The School of St. Matthew*. 2nd ed. Philadelphia: Fortress Press, 1968.

Wainwright, Geoffrey. *Eucharist and Eschatology*. New York: Oxford University, 1981.

Wunsch, Georg. *Die Bergpredigt bei Luther*. Tübingen: J. C. B. Mohr, 1920.